THE SCHOOLS OF ENGLAND

76650   ~~WILSON~~   Schools of
England

370·942   T 00928 501 2

THE SCHOOLS
OF ENGLAND

A STUDY IN RENAISSANCE

EDITED BY

J. DOVER WILSON, Litt.D.

PROFESSOR OF EDUCATION IN THE UNIVERSITY OF LONDON,
KING'S COLLEGE

WITH A PREFACE BY

LORD EUSTACE PERCY

PRESIDENT OF THE BOARD OF EDUCATION

LONDON
SIDGWICK & JACKSON, LTD.
44, MUSEUM STREET, W.C.1
1928

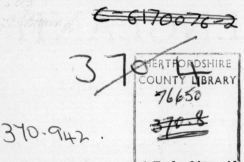
Lords and Commons of England! consider what nation it is whereof ye are, and whereof ye are the governors : a nation not slow and dull, but of a quick, ingenious and piercing spirit ; acute to invent, subtile and sinewy to discourse, not beneath the reach of any point the highest that human capacity can soar to. . . . What wants there to such a towardly and pregnant soil, but wise and faithful labourers, to make a knowing people, a nation of prophets, of sages, and of worthies ?

MILTON, *Areopagitica*, 1644.

PREFACE

By the Right Hon. Lord Eustace Percy, M.P.,
President of the Board of Education

This book is based on a course of lectures given at King's College, London, during the Michaelmas term of 1927. It appears at the right time and will, I hope, serve the purpose which Professor Dover Wilson and his collaborators have evidently had in mind.

What our national education chiefly needs just now is focus. During the last quarter of a century we have been so busy building up its various parts, criticising its defects in detail, and preparing plans for repairs here and extensions there, that we have had little time to stand back and view the structure as a whole. Moreover, we have been reminded so often of our lack of system, of our habit of developing our national institutions bit by bit to meet the needs of the moment, that we have been apt to assume that no comprehensive view of it is possible. When foreign inquirers have asked us plaintively where they can get an account of English education, we have usually been content to explain to them the futility of any such request and have expatiated rather smugly on our national genius for incoherence. Our immediate neighbours in Europe do not perhaps take our evasions very seriously, for the countrymen of de Tocqueville, Gneist and Redlich have long ago discovered that there is usually more method in the madness of our institutions than we are prepared to admit ; but we can hardly wonder if our admirers in remoter regions, such as South

America, often come regretfully to the conclusion that the English do not care about education. What matters more is that the man in the street at home, who has an instinct for order but no natural liking for uniformity—the sort of person who has the irritating but salutary habit of asking exactly where he is, but does not necessarily want to be informed that he is in the same boat with every one else— is sometimes driven to seek refuge from our vagueness in schemes for " unity of control " which he would never advocate if he did not feel that education must be tidied up somehow.

In fact, of course, our education is no more incoherent than our constitution, and its apparent shapelessness has been mainly due to our habit of leaving it surrounded with a scaffolding of statutory distinctions, administrative regula- tions, and pedagogic " terms of art," long after these have ceased to serve their original purpose. Since the war a good deal has been done to remove the administrative planks and poles in this scaffolding. The first step in that process was, perhaps, the simplification of the grant system under the Act of 1918 ; the latest has been the re-organisa- tion of the Board's inspectorate. We can now see that our division of what is known as " the public service of educa- tion " into elementary, secondary, and technical, with all the ingenious sub-divisions which we have invented to correct an originally faulty classification, cannot be regarded as part of the foundations of our system, but only as an incidental aid in the work of construction. We can see, too, that the division between " the public service of education " and other parts of our educational system is itself artificial and out of date—that, for instance, universities which are assisted but not controlled by the state can be closely associated in a common task with training colleges which are not only controlled by the state but are often actually owned by public bodies. We have still to rid ourselves of some irksome statutory distinctions, and we still tend to complicate simple issues by the invention of barbarous technicalities, such as " higher-tops," but we are becoming conscious of the unity and balance of our education as a national possession and are in the mood to give an account of it to the world. We are beginning to realise that, if our education is not popular enough, it is because it has not been popularised ; if it is not democratic enough, it is because it has not been described in language understanded by the people. For the immediate future what it needs most is not dissection but explanation, not investigation but publicity.

It has been my hope that the Board, through its re-organised inspectorate, may be able in the future to do something to meet this need, and I am the more grateful to the teachers and administrators who have shown us the way in this book. They would not claim that they have covered the whole ground, and their readers, including myself, may disagree with them on particular points ; but they have succeeded in what they set out to do, to write a popular introduction to the study of English education. For this they deserve the thanks of all who write with a heavier pen and have hitherto been condemned to speak the darker language of educational administration and debate.

EDITORIAL NOTE

THE contributors to this volume, before writing their chapters, received a copy of the Introduction together with the following brief memorandum :

"It is suggested that, in order to give unity and point to the book as a whole, each contributor, in preparing his paper, should keep before him the following questions, without necessarily feeling compelled to find an answer to them :

"(1) What place does the institution (or institutions) for which you speak hold in the English educational system ?

"(2) What is the main or the characteristic contribution which it makes to the national life ?

"(3) In what way might this contribution be made more complete or more effective ? "

Since ten of the chapters were first delivered as lectures some of the contributors were able to listen to their predecessors in the original course, and one or two of them made use of this opportunity. Otherwise the chapters were written independently of each other, the writers being left entirely free to express what opinions they chose.

The editor, who is deeply indebted to all those whose names occur in the Table of Contents, cannot allow the volume to appear without including that of Professor Ernest Barker, who, while Principal of King's College,

not only took from the beginning a lively interest in the
enterprise of which this book is the outcome, but rendered
the editor the greatest possible assistance in the all-
important preliminary arrangements—an interest and
assistance continued by his succesor, Principal Halliday,
who lent support equally indispensable to the book in
its final stage of preparation. Lastly, the editor desires
to acknowledge his obligation to Mr. R. S. Wood, of the
Board of Education, for useful criticisms and suggestions,
and to his colleague, Mr. B. C. L. James, not only for the
valuable appendices appearing under his name, but also
for the index and for help in seeing the book through
the press.

J. D. W.

CONTENTS

PREFACE

PAGE

INTRODUCTION

CHAPTER

PRIMARY EDUCATION

SECONDARY EDUCATION

SUMMARY

THE TRAINING COLLEGE

UNIVERSITY AND ADULT EDUCATION

EDUCATION IN THE FIGHTING SERVICES

APPENDICES

INTRODUCTION

B

Change wide, and deep, and silently performed,
This Land shall witness ; and as days roll on,
Earth's universal frame shall feel the effect ;
Even till the smallest habitable rock,
Beaten by lonely billows, hear the songs
Of humanised society ; and bloom
With civil arts, that shall breathe forth their fragrance,
A grateful tribute to all-ruling Heaven.
From culture, unexclusively bestowed
On Albion's noble Race in freedom born,
Expect these mighty issues : from the pains
And faithful care of unambitious schools
Instructing simple childhood's ready ear.

WORDSWORTH, *The Excursion* (Bk. ix), 1814.

THE
SCHOOLS OF ENGLAND

CHAPTER I

THE SCHOOLS AND THE NATION

By J. DOVER WILSON

ENGLISH education is no mushroom growth. It did not begin with the Act of 1902, or even with that of 1870. Still less is it a tender sapling transplanted from Germany or Switzerland or the United States of America. It is sometimes well to remind ourselves of these things, since the journalists of education, who are ever with us, are prone to disable the antiquity as well as the other benefits of their country and to write as if the only names in educational history that matter are foreign ones, and the only ideas those of yesterday or the day before. We can honour the work and personality of Pestalozzi, this side of idolatry, without hailing him as the founder of our system of primary education. We can reverence the august name of Froebel without supposing that he was the first to give thought to the teaching of infants.[1] Or, to be more topical still, we can feel grateful to Miss Parkhurst of Dalton, U.S.A., for providing us all with much to ponder, while still

[1] Impious indeed would such a supposition be on the part of the present writer, seeing that his own great-grandfather was establishing a large infant-school at Walthamstow in 1824, two years before the publication of Froebel's *Education of Human Nature*.

3

suspecting that something like her " plan " has been long in vogue at a school called Eton College.

Other lands can show institutions of greater antiquity than ours, but none can rival English education in its combination of age with continuity. Our universities, for instance, are the children of the University of Paris, but whereas the University of Paris to-day is so different from its counterpart of the middle ages as to be virtually another institution, modern Cambridge and modern Oxford can look back to the thirteenth century without a break in the historical vista. In a sense, indeed, Cambridge and Oxford are older than the state itself, the state which they have often of recent years called in to assist them in self-reform, but which they have seldom allowed directly to mould their internal economy. The exact date of the establishment of the oldest of English universities is unknown, but it was almost a century before Edward I. began to lay the foundations of our parliamentary structure that a group of scholars, misliking either the climate or the inhabitants of Oxford —or both—left the Isis to set up a second university on the pleasant banks of the Cam.

And if the universities are older than the state, the schools are older than the nation. Whitby and Canterbury, Jarrow and York, became the homes of scholarship before the English had realised their common nationality. Moreover, when Charlemagne established at Aachen that court which was to become the parent of all the courts of Europe and looked around for some one to supply the necessary culture, he was fain to turn to England and English Alcuin. The centres of monastic learning in our island were destroyed by the viking raids : but these same vikings welded the English into a nation on the anvil of their wrath, and it is no accident that Alfred of Wessex, the man in whom England first found national expression, should have been our first real minister of education. Like Charlemagne, he knew that a state cannot exist without educated administrators nor a nation survive without a common culture. Thus, when he had beaten back the Danes, christened Guthrum, and rebuilt London, he became both organising master and educational publisher for his people, importing foreign scholars to assist him, founding schools for the sons of noblemen and thegns, translating and editing text-books in history, geography, philosophy, and theology, and dreaming all the time of a day when the child of every freeborn Englishman would have an opportunity of plying his studies until he could at least read English with ease. It is doubtful whether any one again, until the days of Kay-Shuttleworth and Matthew Arnold, envisaged national education as a whole and set himself to tackle its problems in detail as Alfred did.

Certainly, centuries were to elapse before the nation attained a condition even favourable to the realisation of his dream. Dane was to be followed by Norman, and Norman was himself to be conquered in spirit by the population he had conquered in arms, before a truly English culture became possible for a once more united English people. By the fifteenth century, however, everything seemed ripe for a great step forward. The educational institutions available were numerous, and they embraced all the three grades—university, secondary, primary. It was not a national system in the full sense of the word, but given normal development it might have become so in the course of a few generations. Moreover, such as it was, it still exists in main outline. It still exists, but it stands to-day surrounded and augmented by what, because of its modernity, looks at first sight like another and different system. I refer, of course, to those institutions, based upon compulsory state elementary education and directed by state administrative machinery, which have sprung up during the last fifty years in response to the needs of a modern nation. In perspective the total effect is that of some ancient city, like Durham or York, in which the scene

is dominated by venerable buildings, still " whispering from
their towers the last enchantments of the middle ages,"
though now serving a purpose rather different from that
which inspired their mediæval founders, while there
stretches out on all sides the less imposing, as yet far less
beautiful, but infinitely more extensive and serviceable
structure of the modern township, with its shops, its factories,
its municipal offices, and its protean villadom. Yet, if there
be two styles, there is but one city, pursuing however dimly
and erringly some common purpose, and continuing a
tradition which can be traced back to the day when cathedral
and castle were themselves newfangled and modern—to
that day and beyond. So it is with our national system of
education. We are one people, and despite all signs to the
contrary, becoming one people more and more every year.
The schools, too, are ours. Endowed or state-aided they
belong to the nation for which they were founded and built,
whether in the fourteenth, the sixteenth, the nineteenth,
or the twentieth century. An unbroken tradition links
Alfred's preface to the *Cura Pastoralis* with the recently
issued *Handbook of Suggestions for Teachers*, while Wykeham's
" Manners makyth man " finds its echo in the opening words
of the Board's Code : " The purpose of the public elementary school is to form and strengthen the character
and to develop the intelligence of the children entrusted to
it." It is hoped that this volume may serve, in however
small a degree, to promote that unity, to emphasise that
continuity.

Nevertheless there have been times when the unity was
merely nominal, and the thread of tradition worn so thin as
to come near breaking-point. While your cathedral town
will contain many a substantial red-brick house dating from
the days of Queen Elizabeth, Queen Anne, or the royal
Georges, the striking thing about the city of English education is the almost complete absence from it of buildings
belonging to the eighteenth century, while even many of

those bearing a sixteenth century date over their portals turn out on examination to be adaptations, often for the worse, of structures erected in a previous age. Something clearly happened to education in the Tudor and Stuart period, and as that something did much to determine the proportions of the present-day structure, and still influences its spirit, a word must here be said upon it.

The main function of school and university in the middle ages had been to furnish a supply of professional men and administrators for the service of church and state. With few exceptions the children neither of the nobleman nor the villein found their way into scholastic institutions, most students coming from what we should now call middle-class homes, and being clever sons of yeomen, retainers, and tradesmen, who wished to make their way in the world. In other words, side by side with the aristocracy of birth which crowned the feudal system was an aristocracy of intellect, reached by the ladder of education. It was this professional caste which ran the mediæval state, since it controlled learning, including all clerkly accomplishments such as penmanship, a knowledge of Latin (the international language), medicine, law, and so on. Then came the Reformation, with its mighty sequel the Puritan Revolution, and dealt blows at the mediæval polity from which our national system of education has never completely recovered to this day. In the first place it destroyed the spiritual unity of the nation by drawing a sharp line, a line marked in red by the blood of persecution, between those who adhered to the Church of England and those who, desirous of carrying further the principles of the Reformation, had founded Protestant sects of their own. Among the spiritualities to which the reformed Church of England succeeded was education. This meant that education ceased to be national, since the schools and universities were closed against the children of those who refused to conform to the established religion, so that they were compelled in the long run to set up " academies " of their own. Thus the nation made no use of persons of ability born of dissenting parents, since it shut the door of all professions upon them save that to the ministry of their own persuasion, and by forcing them to be educated in a sectarian atmosphere still further embittered them against the privileged denomination. Yet until the eighteenth century the nonconformists made up so small a percentage of the population that the state could afford to ignore the poison in its system. With the rise of Wesleyan Methodism, however, nonconformists became as numerous as Anglicans, and they were able successfully to oppose all attempts during the first half of the nineteenth century to establish a state system of popular education, knowing, as they did, that so long as they themselves remained outside the pale of the constitution a state system would inevitably have meant an Anglican system.[1]

The religious changes of the sixteenth century affected education in the financial as well as the spiritual sphere. Mediæval education, as we have seen, possessed wealthy endowments. These the schools were not allowed to inherit intact. On the contrary, as Leach has revealed to us, they were confiscated wholesale by the greedy hangers-on of the court, many of the schools which were suffered to remain being renamed, with a cynicism hard to parallel in the pages of history, King Edward VI.'s Grammar Schools.[2] Finally, and perhaps most disastrous of all, the Reformation and the consequent political changes which culminated in the settlement of 1688 not only robbed the schools of their funds and closed their doors against a minority which with the accession of Wesleyanism became half the nation, it also cut at their roots by depriving them of what had hitherto been their principal national function. For the upshot of these changes was the substitution of a

[1] The Church of England was almost equally distrustful of proposals for state education, since it tended to regard education, at this time, as its special and exclusive domain.

[2] A. F. Leach, *English Schools at the Reformation*, pp. 1-7.

hereditary aristocracy, composed partly of the old feudal nobility, partly of the Tudor and Stuart new rich, for the clerical aristocracy of intellect, as the controlling force in the nation's affairs. For a time this did not seem to impair education, the quality of which certainly improved under the inspiration of the Renaissance, while Elizabethan and Stuart foundations compensated to some extent for the Edwardian spoliation. Indeed, the abolition of the monasteries, and with them of that clerical celibacy which had meant the sterilisation of the best brains in the country, must have incalculably promoted the richness and continuity of English intellectual life. And it has been well said that " the expansion of Elizabethan England, which took the world by surprise, not only in navigation, in commerce, in colonisation, but in poetry and the drama, in philosophy and science, was due to the immense extension of lay initiative and effort in every department of national life ; and not least in the sphere of education and the schools." [1] But in the long run, as the English social structure settled down after the upheavals of the sixteenth and seventeenth centuries into the hierarchy of the Augustan age, institutional education was found to be sick unto death.

The condition of schools and universities in the latter half of the eighteenth century and the early years of the nineteenth was scandalous. In 1751 there were only eight commoners at Winchester, while the number of annual admissions at Oxford " often fell below 200 " at the same period.[2] Yet Oxford frightened no one from her doors by the burden of scholarship she laid upon her sons. It is recorded [3] that Lord Eldon, the famous Lord Chancellor, who took his degree in 1770, earned that distinction by answering two questions, which constituted his whole examination. The questions were : " What is

[1] Leach, *Schools of Medieval England*, p. 332.
[2] J. W. Adamson, *Short History of Education*, p. 219.
[3] Campbell, *Lives of the Lord Chancellors* (1847), vol. vii, pp. 14–15.

the Hebrew for the place of a skull ? " to which he replied
" Golgotha," and so passed in Hebrew ; and " Who founded
University College ? " to which he replied " King Alfred,"
and so passed in History.   Since the time of the Renaissance,
indeed, the universities had been increasingly filled by the
sons of noblemen and gentlemen, to the exclusion of the
classes which had previously studied there, and in the end
they became little more than residential clubs at which the
gilded youth of the land sowed its wild oats.   It would, of
course, be absurd to seek a single cause to account for this
general decay of English educational establishments.   But
when we remember that the decay was simply part of a
still more wide-spread degeneration, which affected the
institutional life of the country as a whole, we shall be wise
to attribute it to a morbidity of the body politic rather than
to any particular defect, such as the tyranny of the classical
tradition, which may be alleged against the schools.   In
a word, I suggest that the principal cause of the disgraceful
condition of English education between 1750 and 1840 was
the fact that the government of the country, once the province
of a skilled bureaucracy, had become the private property
of the landed class.   Birth and bribery, not brain, now gave
the entry to political, official, and professional life.   Why
then bother too much about education ?   For where there
was no climbing to be done, what was the use of a ladder ?
Say what we will about Liberal Education, contemn as we
may vocational aims, secondary and university education
has and will always have a definite function to perform in
the national economy, viz. to discover and train those minds
best able to direct the ship of the state.   Deny it this
function, you check the flow of blood in the organism, you
decree first decline and ultimately death.

As for the children of " the labouring poor " at this
period, if a charity school or a dame school happened to
be found in their neighbourhood they might consider
themselves fortunate.   Whether they also considered them-

selves happy is another question.   William Blake apparently
thought not.   His *Songs of Experience*, published in 1794,
contains a poem entitled *The Schoolboy*, one stanza of which
gives us a glimpse of a dame school from the inside.   Thus
it runs :

> But to go to school in a summer morn,
> O ! it drives all joy away ;
> Under a cruel eye outworn,
> The little ones spend the day
> In sighing and dismay.

No poet writing to-day with a knowledge of the elementary
school could speak like that.   But indeed, the greater the
educational destitution of our great-grandfathers, the more
are we to be congratulated upon our present wealth.   The
modern English educational system is defective enough,
Heaven knows ; but how magnificent it is when compared
with the provision a century and a half, a century, even half
a century ago ! If there be any reader of this volume who
suffers from pessimism about the future of the schools,
let him cure himself by glancing at their immediate past.
With nothing at the end of the eighteenth century but a
handful of moribund institutions to go on, the nation has
built up its educational structure afresh, without in any way
sacrificing those native traditions which go back to Colet,
to William of Wykeham, and to Alfred.

And yet the task was taken in hand and carried through
without aim or plan, and as part of a far larger sphere of
operations.   It has been said that the British Empire was
founded in a fit of absence of mind.   The rebuilding of our
educational system in the nineteenth century was equally
unpremeditated.   Institutions were established or ideals
realised as the occasion required, and their originator was
now some great headmaster or headmistress, now a religious
community,[1] now a city guild, now an examining body,

---

[1] Of these, of course, the chief was the Church of England, which,
working through its voluntary association, the National Society, made
some amends, by the elementary schools and training colleges it founded

now a public authority, whether central or local, but most
often a small group of public-spirited men and women
—like the founders of the great university of London—
who saw a crying need, hoisted a banner, set up an
association, collected the funds, and if they succeeded, as
they generally did, bequeathed to the nation one more wing
in our haphazard scholastic structure. It is an untidy way
of doing things, a way leading to much waste of energy,
a good deal of overlapping, and not a little friction and
inefficiency—a way very irksome to precise and autocratic
minds, and very different from that in which the systems of
France and Germany took shape. The untidiness reaches
its maximum naturally enough in a matter like the training
of teachers, in which all other parts of the system are in
some measure concerned.   Listen to Lord Esher's impatient
comment upon a recent book dealing with this subject.
" This volume," he writes, " is brimful of industry and
research, but through no fault of its author the English
system of training teachers remains in great part un-
intelligible to the ordinary reader. After reading it twice
through I understand the method of training teachers in
France, I realise the system in vogue in the United States of
America, but I have not the foggiest idea how the majority
of teachers under our English system are selected and
trained." [1]   It is not difficult, especially if one is head of
a university department for the training of teachers, to
sympathise with this exasperation. And yet have we not
treated education in exactly the same way as we have treated
the constitution, the common law, the imperial structure,
and all the rest of our political and social apparatus ?

Consider, for example, from what humble beginnings
is sprung that imposing edifice now called the Board of
Education, and how its control stole as it were upon the

in the nineteenth century, for the wrong which the state had done, in
the name of religious uniformity, to the cause of national education in
previous times.

[1] Lance Jones, *The Training of Teachers*, pp. 465-466.

schools gradually, almost imperceptibly and through the will of no man, as some odour may steal upon the senses through an open window. At the beginning of the nineteenth century there was considerable agitation in certain circles on the subject of the education of the poor. It was a trivial and tiresome business in the eyes of statesmen who were busy fighting Napoleon or foiling Metternich, quelling Peterloo riots or organising Reform Bill demonstrations. But Parliament was at last induced to do something about it, and in 1833 voted a paltry £20,000 " in aid of private subscriptions for the erection of school-houses for the education of the poorer classes in Great Britain." To its surprise " the erection of school-houses " proceeded so rapidly under this stimulus that the grant had almost immediately to be converted into an annual one and later began to increase in amount. Supervision of the grants became necessary, but supervision if it got talked about would seem like that dangerous and highly debatable business, the state provision of education. Supervision was therefore instituted more or less *sub rosa* by establishing a special committee of the Privy Council, not through parliamentary action but by order in Council, to see to the proper distribution of these grants. But this supervision could not be carried on without an office possessed of a clerical staff and inspectors, which office in course of time, with the increased funds passing through its hands and the growing weight of business, attained to such a pitch of importance that it was created a department of State, known as the Education Department. This was in 1856, and in 1861 the new department proceeded to tidy up the regulations and minutes, under which the Committee of Privy Council had worked, by issuing the first Education Code. " Thus," as a foreign student admiringly observes, " the English nation had governmental inspection of schools and a public code of education before a single school was established at the public expense and before any form of

local organisation had been instituted for educational purposes. . . . This growth of a large administrative department with rules and principles of its own creation, without
any assistance from the legislature, is the most remarkable
instance of the experimental and empirical fashion in which
some of the great English institutions have developed." [1]

And the growth continues and will continue, however
the prophets of political individualism may shudder at the
prospect. Since 1861, of course, the Board, as we now call
it, has buttressed its position and extended its influence by
a wealth of legislative enactments. Yet education acts have
seldom done more than register the various stages of an
inevitable and involuntary development, a development
which without a doubt will only end when every form of
English educational activity is subject to the surveillance—
please note that I do not say control—of the central authority.
If any one hesitates to accept this prognostication, let him
ponder the implications of one only, and that far from the
most conspicuous, of the recent actions of the Board. In
1908 it began to publish, for its own purposes, a list of
secondary schools which it recognised as efficient. In other
words, it instituted an educational hall-mark, which all
schools soon began to discover it advantageous to acquire.
One after another of the great endowed schools showed
themselves anxious to get on to this list, which now twenty
years after its inauguration includes also a large proportion
of the reputable private schools of the country. The coveted
title " recognised as efficient " is purchased not by any loss
of autonomy but in return for a visit of the Board's inspectors
followed by a favourable report. And the ever-lengthening
list implies two facts of great significance for the future of
education. It means first of all that every year the eyes of
the Board, which are its inspectors, come to survey a larger
and larger area of the total field of English education, whereby
not only is information of ever-increasing value placed at

[1] Redlich and Hirst, *English Local Government*, I, p. 185.

the disposal of the state, but the best features of one type of institution are made available, through the missionary zeal of the inspectorate, for imitation by other types. It means in the second place that the experience of state inspection, so greatly dreaded in prospect and generally so harmless and helpful when it comes to the point, tends to break down the instinctive dislike of central supervision on the part of the schools outside the state-aided system.

There are, I say, persons who view such tendencies as this with horror and affect to see in them the beginnings of the " servile state." Professor Archer, whose admirable and stimulating history of English *Secondary Education in the Nineteenth Century* is marred, I think, by over-much distrust of state action, has well said " The true function of the government in education is like the irrigation work of British rule in Egypt and in Mesopotamia ; it can control a huge system which is beyond the power of any smaller organisation." To speak thus and yet, as he does elsewhere, to deny the possibility of any originality to a government department, appears to me inconsistent. Surely the conversion of a swamp into a system of clear and flowing canals, vitalising a whole country-side and bringing prosperity to its inhabitants, must be described, if words mean anything, as both original and creative ? And that is what in effect the Board of Education has done for secondary education during the last quarter of a century. Yet the word " control," which Professor Archer uses, is inappropriate. There was a time when the department actually " controlled " schools, when it examined indeed through its inspectors every child in attendance. That day is long past, and of recent years the Board has given up its rights of control even over the curriculum of schools and training colleges.[1] As the central

[1] This was effected by the drastic simplification of the Regulations in 1926. It is one more example of the fashion in which the development of our educational system keeps step with the development of our constitution as a whole that this abdication by the Board synchronises with the Imperial Conference of 1926, at which the Dominions were given the

department comes to overlook a wider and wider field of the nation's education, it would seem that its control of any particular area grows less and less. As for " tyranny at Whitehall," the phrase may mean something to excitable readers of educational journals ; to one who has been a servant of the Board it is merely ludicrous. The mistakes made at Whitehall arise not from lust of power but from timidity, or simply from that passion for tidiness which is at once the virtue and the temptation of the bureaucrat. No doubt " payment by results," usually regarded as the greatest crime in the annals of the education department, was originally introduced as a measure of economy.[1] But it commended itself especially to the heads of the department as an administrative convenience ; it lasted for over thirty years, in the face of the weightiest opposition, because of its convenience ; and it finally disappeared only because it has ceased to be convenient. When all is said, the real and abiding safeguard of the institutions for higher education against undue interference by the central authority is the fact that the Board of Education is historically a parvenu beside the natural leaders of higher education, Cambridge, Oxford, and the great public schools, and still more by the fact that the Board is staffed and will always be staffed to some extent by the loyal sons of these ancient bodies. The ethos of Eton and King's, of Winchester and New College, is never likely to be wittingly tampered with by those who profess to owe the best of themselves to it.[2]

status of Sovereign Powers. In the one case as in the other " authority " was found incompatible with modern conceptions. *Cf.* what Mr. Ward says about the Board's control of training colleges, pp. 208-209.

[1] *Cf.* pp. 49-52.

[2] A striking recent example of this was Mr. Fisher's refusal to allow the universities to participate in the salary and pension schemes for teachers which made his ministry so memorable, because he feared that to do so would have opened the university door to state control. It is worth noting here that relations between the universities and the state are carried on not through the Board of Education but through a special Committee of Privy Council known as the University Grants Committee. In other words, the universities to-day are, in this respect, very much where the elementary schools were in 1839.

Trouble is obviously more likely to arise when the task of providing and supervising higher education is placed in the hands of those who have themselves never experienced it ; with the best will in the world such men are bound to make mistakes through sheer misunderstanding. Yet this is just what the Act of 1902 has done in most administrative counties and county boroughs. The local control of education, like that from the centre, has grown up piecemeal and in experimental fashion, and the history of educational administration is as typical and as illustrative of English constitutional development during the nineteenth century in the one sphere as in the other. The problem peculiar to local government was to decide whether its various functions were best carried on by means of separate bodies specially elected for a particular purpose, *ad hoc* bodies as they are called, or by some general body representative of a whole locality and elected to carry out all its functions. The one would tend to be a body of specialists or at least of persons with a special interest ; the other represents the good old English principle, one of the corner-stones of political democracy, the principle of government by the average or ordinary citizen, assisted by specialists in the form of paid officials who are his servants. Jeremy Bentham, who was as much the creator of modern England as Napoleon was of modern France, in his projected scheme of local government naturally favoured the former alternative, since he lived in the days when the corrupt corporations were a stink in the nose of all decent citizens. His disciple Edwin Chadwick, founder of Poor Law administration and of Public Health, likewise favoured it, partly for the same reason and partly because, as an expert in a hurry, he was impatient of the tedious pace of non-specialist committees. Thus our first experiments in the sphere of modern local government were mainly by means of *ad hoc* bodies, of which the Boards of Guardians and the School Boards were the most conspicuous examples.

C

Indeed, in rural areas there was no choice because, though the Municipal Corporations Act of 1835 provided the towns with popularly elected councils of the modern type, the country-side had to wait until 1888 before it got the county councils which might take over the functions of the various *ad hoc* bodies. Moreover, of all public services education would seem to be particularly adapted to specialist supervision. Learning has always appeared a high mystery to the unlettered ; and the learned, especially the little-learned, have naturally always done their best to encourage this belief—dare I call it superstition ? However we look at it, to place the control of education, and not merely elementary education, in the hands of farmers and shopkeepers, the manufacturer and the industrial worker, and to decree that schooling should be provided and administered in the same way and by the same body as gas, tramways, highways, cemeteries, and the rest, was a most amazing experiment, and one that implies an extraordinary faith in the democratic principle. And yet, as I have said, that step was taken in 1902. We can hardly call it an " act of faith," because the country, stunned and bemused by the factions raging furiously together over the question of putting the Church schools on the rates, was hardly aware of what it was doing. Nevertheless the faith was there, even if we were unconscious of it. Once more a great corner in the history of English civilisation was turned, as a matter of course, and in a fit of absence of mind.

It is a quarter of a century since that day, and the municipal and county secondary schools, which were taken in hand as the result of the Act and were some years in building, are now celebrating their coming-of-age all over the land. How has the experiment answered ? As far as elementary education is concerned the unhesitating reply is " admirably," which does not mean, of course, that either local education authorities or their elementary schools are perfect institutions. And on the material side, few who know anything of the splendid buildings and equipment of the council secondary schools and training colleges, would refuse to give the same reply as regards higher education. Yet the public is uneasily aware that all is not well. There is some smouldering trouble which occasionally blazes up into a reverberating crisis involving resignations and recriminations, but which more often takes the form of a grim strife behind closed doors. I do not say these things are common ; but we all know they happen and that they are not confined to any one part of the country. Do they mean that local democratic control, while suitable for elementary education, breaks down when it comes to deal with the more difficult and delicate problems of the secondary school and training college ?

Let me say at once, as one who has at close quarters seen something of the troubles referred to, that I do not believe it. I am confident that the disease is but the infantile complaint of a sturdy youngster, which probably in another decade, certainly in another twenty-five years, it will have entirely outgrown. And the reason for my confidence is not that in course of time members of local education committees and governing bodies will become learned men or scholastically minded. God forbid ! For I regard the lay control of education, in all its grades, as the surest possible guarantee of the liberty of the teaching profession, the sanity of its practitioners, and the security of our children against intellectual malnutrition by cranks, doctrinaires, and charlatans. Much will be gained, no doubt, in the way of sympathy and understanding, when, as must inevitably come to pass, every member of a higher education committee and governing body will himself be a product of secondary education. But the real crux of the problem is the official who is paid to advise the lay committee, and who is or ought to be an educational expert. Taken as a whole the education officials of English local government form a body of men as far-sighted, disinterested, patriotic, intelligent, and

skilful as that to be found in any other country in the world.
I am proud to think that I number some of them among my
best friends ; and readers of later chapters in this volume
will be privileged to taste of their quality. Let me only
instance here, as typical of their spirit, a certain veteran
director of education in an industrial centre, a true shepherd
of his flock and withal the wittiest and best educated man in
the place, who, when his second son died fighting for his
country, replied to my pitiably inadequate letter of sympathy
and respect, " Don't worry about me !   I'm one of the lucky
ones ; I still have all the children of the borough."

Yet there are also spirits of another sort. When the
borough council was made the local authority for education
by the Act of 1902, the secretaryship to the education committee in some of the smaller boroughs inevitably devolved
upon one of the clerical staff in the town clerk's office, often
a man with no previous experience of educational administration and sometimes with very little education of his own.
Many of these, gifted with native ability and powers of
sympathy, have been promoted from one locality to another
and have deservedly risen to the top of their profession.
Others endowed with equal ability have also risen, but devoid
of sympathetic imagination, and prompted unconsciously
at every turn by the love of power, are constitutionally
incapable of handling the delicate situations that arise from
time to time in the public administration of higher education.
It is men of " push and go " like these who are generally
to be found at the back of the troubles in the sphere of
state-aided secondary education.   And my optimism on that
head springs from the fact that they are a vanishing race,
that the service of local education is every year being recruited
more and more, like the rest of the civil service, from among
men who, whatever their origin, have passed through the
universities, who having themselves experienced the benefits
of *Lehrfreiheit* will know how to value it for others.

Educational administration is a fascinating theme, and,

though some of my readers may think I have dwelt too long upon it, they cannot at least accuse me of wandering from the main thread of my discourse, which is the relation between education and the national life. Turning now to the schools themselves, do they not express the nation in all its moods, from all its aspects, and with all its classes and sects ? Our system is not like others, a house made with hands. It has grown like a living thing, like a tree the sap of which is English blood. No other educational system in the world is so native, so national, so flexible, so perfectly adapted to the sum total of its country's purposes and ideals as our own. Nor, as we stand back and contemplate it as a whole before we examine its component parts, as we shall be doing in the remaining chapters of this volume, does its outline seem so ragged or its style so patchy as its heterogeneous and fortuitous origins would lead us to expect. There are gaps here and there, and some ugly ones ; there are parts in which the planning is inconvenient or the materials cheap ; there are others which are quite obviously of a temporary character, to be rebuilt at a later date. But taking it all in all, the vision is granted to us which was denied to our fathers, the vision of a unity, of a balance and a poise that would have seemed impossible even thirty years ago. Our schools and the administrative structure concerned with them are not only growing but growing to a point, and beginning to display a proportion which is none the less beautiful because it is the creation of a nation and not of an individual artist.

The building, I have said, was carried through as part of a far larger sphere of operations. The nation remade its educational system by remaking itself. It is impossible to disentangle the story of the renaissance of English education from the general history of the English people in the nineteenth century. And what an epic that history is ! Is there anything more inspiring in the annals of civilisation than the spectacle of this nation dragging itself out of the

slough of ignorance and brutality which was the normal life
of the eighteenth century, and hampered at every step by
the ever-rising tide of population, which, as we are only
now coming to realise, was due almost entirely to a decline
in the death-rate, so that every measure of health and sanitation really increased the burden the nation was required to
carry ? Other peoples have remade themselves during the
nineteenth century, and perhaps done so more scientifically.
But if the Germans, for instance, were able to avoid some
of our mistakes, that was because they had the benefit of
watching us make them. We were the vanguard, the
pioneers, in the great trek towards industrial democracy.
We had no plan, no compass, no previous experience to
guide us in the adventure. It is easy to blame our great-
grandfathers, and to do so is an easy way of writing history.
But, though their standards were not ours—how could they
be ?—they defaulted, as our great-grandchildren will see
us to-day defaulting, as much through ignorance as from
lack of good-will. The appalling conditions of the industrial
areas, for example, in the thirties and forties of last century,
which gave rise both to cholera and to chartism, were in the
main due to the simple fact that the engineers had not yet
discovered how to furnish these mushroom cities with
sewerage or clean water. Furthermore, while France
specialised in democratic institutions and Germany in
industrial efficiency, we took the double burden upon our
shoulders, and though often stumbling and always groaning
beneath the weight, have never sought to lighten it, knowing
that to do so would be to purchase the ease of the moment
by losing sight of that delectable city, towards which, call
it the Co-operative Commonwealth or the Kingdom of
Heaven as you will, our steps have set with ever steadier
purpose every succeeding decade of the past 150 years.

And each new stage of the pilgrimage has brought with
it fresh developments in education. It is no accident that
1832 and 1867, the dates of the two great Acts of political

enfranchisement, coincide with dates equally important in the history of education. A year after the first Reform Act, parliament made that first public grant towards the instruction of the poor which marks the beginning of state education in this country ; and four years earlier Thomas Arnold had gone to Rugby to set on foot reforms which, as a discerning prophet declared before he got there, would " change the face of education all through the public schools of England," and which, as no one could have foreseen, changed the face of domestic and imperial administration by feeding it with a new type of Englishman, the Englishman who, learning to govern as prefects or præpostors, subscribed to that ideal of the Liberal Christian Gentleman which Arnold first formulated and which became incarnate in a thousand builders of civilisation in India, at home and abroad. Even more striking are the cluster of events of first-class importance in education which follow hard upon the Reform Act of 1867. In 1869 was passed the Endowed Schools Act, which immensely stimulated secondary education for girls and prepared the way for public secondary education by freeing the ancient endowments from obsolete conditions and so placing them at the disposal of the nation at large. And in 1870, of course, came the great Elementary Education Act, a piece of legislation which would have been impossible but for the extension of the franchise three years before. It was not merely that, as Robert Lowe said, " we must educate our masters." The Reform Act of 1867 had done more than give the vote to the urban working man ; it had for the first time since the Puritan Revolution tilted the balance of political power in favour of nonconformity. This meant not only that " the people " no longer continued to dread state action in general as an interference by the " upper classes," but also that state education ceased to present itself to Baptists, Wesleyans, Independents, and the rest, as Church of England education.

Two other events of the same date, each closely con-

nected with education, contributed to the same end. By
the substitution of open competition for patronage as the
gateway into the Civil Service, Gladstone in 1870 at once
acknowledged that, the state being now the property of the
nation as a whole, its administration could no longer remain
the perquisite of a class, and restored to higher education
what we have seen to be its natural function, viz. the training
of brains for the administration of the state. The other
change was equally significant, viz. the University Tests
Act of 1871, whereby fellowships, lectureships, and pro-
fessorial chairs at Oxford and Cambridge were thrown open
to men of all creeds and denominations. It was a declara-
tion that the older universities no less than the elementary
schools were national institutions. And it went far to deepen
the unity it proclaimed ; for, as we have already noted, the
sectarian strife during the first half of the nineteenth century
had been much exasperated by the exclusion of the abler
dissenters from all higher professional and political posts.
" It is only since Oxford and Cambridge have been thrown
open to all creeds," observes Professor George Trevelyan,
" that men who would formerly have been leaders of a
militant Nonconformity have been absorbed in the general
stream of national life." [1] After 1870 the English people
became more united than at any period since the Reformation. Religious differences continued to exist, but since
they no longer carried with them political or educational
disability they ceased to divide England into two camps.
The nation opened a new volume of its history, a volume
which is not yet closed, though the Education Acts of 1902
and 1918 begin fresh chapters of it, while between them
lies an interlude of intense social liquefaction and national
consolidation, the European war. This volume may be
called The Great Unification.

A preface to the volume was written by Thomas Arnold's
son, Matthew, and published in 1869 under the title of

[1] *British History in the Nineteenth Century*, p. 284.

Culture and Anarchy. England at that date seemed to Matthew Arnold

> a darkling plain,
> Swept with confused alarms of struggle and flight,
> Where ignorant armies clash by night

—an anarchy for which the only cure was education, or rather the ripe fruit of education, which is culture. To the politicians and sectaries of his age, unable to conceive of progress save in terms of party strife, the prescription appeared a piece of sheer cynicism, the superior gesture of an " elegant Jeremiah." Yet he has been completely justified as regards one section of the national arena. The spirit of peace—of " sweetness and light " he would have called it—which since his day has descended upon the field of religious controversy may, I think, be almost entirely ascribed to the measures just referred to, together with that new-found sense of a common culture and common aspirations which fifty-five years of universal elementary education and twenty-five years of municipal secondary education have engendered in the most self-willed and pugnacious people in the world. Within two years of the General Strike is it idle to suggest that Arnold's remedy will prove as sovereign in the economic and social sphere as it has in the sectarian ? Our industrial troubles arise, I am convinced, from the same cause as produced the denominational strife of previous generations : a whole section of the people feels itself to be disinherited, to be living and working outside the pale of privilege and opportunity. This is a big subject to open up at the end of an introductory chapter, and I will say but one thing about it. The next great step in the development of the English educational system, which is the provision of schooling, whether whole-time or part-time, for young persons who do not now find their way into secondary schools, that is to say who are destined for industrial and commercial rather than professional life, will, I believe, prove an even greater step towards the solution of the social problem. For it must inevitably bring with it some kind of alliance between culture and industry, to the great advantage of both, since what is wrong with our industry is not so much low wages or long hours as its lack of social meaning in the eyes of those performing its operations, and what is wrong with our culture is its divorce from the crafts of common life. Certainly, Arnold himself believed in education as the only panacea for the ills of English society, and words which he wrote in 1869 may well stand as the text for a volume which purports to survey the educational field in 1927.

" Again and again I have insisted," he writes, " how those are the happy moments of humanity, how those are the marking epochs of a people's life, how those are the flowering times for literature and art and all the creative power of genius, when there is a *national* glow of life and thought, when the whole of society is in the fullest measure permeated by thought, sensible to beauty, intelligent and alive. Only it must be *real* thought and *real* beauty ; *real* sweetness and *real* light. Plenty of people will try to give the masses, as they call them, an intellectual food prepared and adapted in the way they think proper for the actual condition of the masses. The ordinary popular literature is an example of this way of working on the masses. Plenty of people will try to indoctrinate the masses with the set of ideas and judgments constituting the creed of their own profession or party. Our religious and political organisations give an example of this way of working on the masses. I condemn neither way ; but culture works differently. It does not try to teach down to the level of inferior classes ; it does not try to win them for this or that sect of its own, with ready-made judgments and watchwords. It seeks to do away with classes ; to make the best that has been thought and known in the world current everywhere ; to make all men live in an atmosphere of sweetness and light, where they may use ideas, as it uses them itself, freely—nourished, and not bound by them.

" This is the *social idea* ; and the men of culture are the true apostles of equality."

REFERENCES

ADAMSON, J. W.   A Short History of Education.   Camb. Univ. Press, 1919.

ARCHER, R. L.   Secondary Education in the XIXth Century.   Camb. Univ. Press, 1921.

BARKER, ERNEST.   National Character (esp. ch. ix).   Methuen, 1927.

CARR-SAUNDERS and JONES.   The Social Structure of England and Wales.   Oxford, 1927.

LEACH, A. F.   English Schools at the Reformation.   Constable, 1894.

——.   The Schools of Medieval England.   Methuen, 1915.

REDLICH AND HIRST.   Local Government in England.   2 vols.   Macmillan, 1903.

SADLER, M. E.   Outlines of Education Courses in Manchester University.   Manchester Univ. Press, 1911.

SELBY-BIGGE, L. A.   The Board of Education.   Putman, 1927.

SMITH, BOMPAS.   The Nation's Schools.   Longmans, 1927.

TREVELYAN, G. M.   British History in the XIXth Century.   Longmans, 1923.

——.   History of England.   Longmans, 1926.

Board of Education Annual Reports.   (The introductions to these contain valuable historical material.)

PRIMARY EDUCATION

CHAPTER II

By LILLIAN DE LISSA

THE education of infants has passed through many phases since Robert Owen opened a school in 1816 " where children from two to six years of age were to dance and sing, to be out of doors as much as possible, to learn when their curiosity induced them to ask questions, and not to be annoyed with books." In his school, children " were to be trained to mutual kindness and a sincere desire to contribute all in their power to benefit each other. They were to be trained and educated without punishment or the fear of it ; a child who acted improperly was not to be considered an object of blame but of pity, and no unnecessary restraint was to be imposed on the children." [1] This ideal set forth by Owen was not maintained, and until 1870 the education given to infants in the elementary schools was very meagre. After that date some slight improvement came about, largely as a result of the beginning of the Froebel movement and the opening of kindergartens. The children of the poor attending the infant school did not immediately benefit by this movement, as the private kindergartens were for the children of the well-to-do classes, but in time the ideals spread by the Froebel Society began to take root in elementary schools, and were reinforced by the special training of infants' teachers which was beginning in various centres

[1] *Life of Robert Owen, written by himself,* 1857.

31

about the same time.   Progress, however, was slow, and it
was not till 1905 that the Board of Education published a
" Report on children under five," in which there was a
prefatory memorandum stating that " a new form of school
was necessary for poor children, and that parents who must
send their little ones to school should send them to nursery
schools rather than to schools of instruction, where there
should be more play, more sleep, more free conversation,
story-telling, and observation." But the nation did not
provide such schools : the few free kindergartens that
existed were all the result of voluntary effort, and though
many elementary infant schools had kindergarten periods
on their time-table, there was very little either of the method
or of the spirit of Froebel to be found in them.   Gradually,
however, infant schools here and there began to take forward
steps, and since then method, equipment, organisation,
and the training of infants' teachers have all undergone many
revolutionary changes.

Educationalists of twenty years ago, having either forgotten or never understood Froebel's teaching, or his plea
for self-activity, self-directed growth, based their educational
methods not on a belief in the power of the human organism
to open " from within outwards," governed by natural laws
which the educator must follow, " in order to lead," but upon
theoretical considerations, expressed in methods of compulsion and external control.   To theorise about the nature
of man, and to decide on a system of education to fit that
nature is a pleasant occupation. But as Professor Whitehead has pointed out, " the delightful thing about man is
his ability to react on your decisions and prove himself to
be the exact opposite of what you had expected.   Man can
change his nature while you talk about it ! " A system
of education based on abstract considerations would be
suitable for a Robot without man's ability to create himself,
for in it nothing is left to chance, but all is prescribed and
planned.   Yet this was the type of education in general

practice in infant schools until comparatively recent times. Children were classified according to age, and all those in one group were practically chained together and made to travel in lock step, the pace being set by the slowest child. None could deviate from the path that all must follow ; all were expected to act as a unit, reaching a uniform standard, and everything was controlled by that most deadening of educational devices—a fixed time-table. Teachers and children alike were driven along in the machine without any opportunity for the exercise of will, judgment, initiative, or imagination. Added to this was that absurd worship of knowledge to which everything else was sacrificed. Education (if such a method can be so called) was like the packing of a trunk, and all the chidren of one age-group were expected to have the same capacity for the reception of knowledge. Such methods had no place for the development of the individual, whose existence was never considered. The most artificial type of discipline was employed, for it was necessary constantly to repress the whole stream of the child's natural energy and interests, and his physiological need of movement. The assumption that nature was wrong forced the teacher to act in the dual capacity of policeman and creator. She had to correct the blunders of nature and to make the child something different from what these mysterious forces within intended him to be ; to hold him in silent passivity and to endeavour to mould him according to a given plan.

As teachers became better trained and more thoughtful they began to revolt against this soul-destroying organisation. Life is more important than knowledge, and the conviction gained ground that infant education should be less like the packing of a trunk and more like the providing of a meal, the giving, in an atmosphere of freedom, of something that would stimulate, enrich, and strengthen. Two powerful influences encouraged and strengthened the conviction and gave definite stimulus to experiment in infant

D

departments. The first was the research and writing of Dr. Montessori, and the second the growth of the Nursery School Movement. Montessori's teaching re-affirmed all Froebel had dreamed of and tried to express in the word " child-garden," all his pleading for an environment in which little children could grow according to nature's plan, in beauty and harmony, with the teacher as a gardener, giving right conditions, aiding and co-operating with natural laws, " following the child in order to lead him." And it went much further. Dr. Montessori " followed the child with scientific skill and insight, keeping records, testing, experimenting with the effects on his growth of differing environment, playthings, and adult conduct, and finding out after some twenty years of research what in her experience was the best environment for all-round development." It is not the English way to accept, uncritically, and apply unmodified, any methods, however excellent they may appear, but the stimulus and inspiration of Montessori's work gave fresh impetus to English teachers, many of whom were already trying to find a better way. Experimental methods, begun tentatively here and there, spread rapidly to a large number of infants' departments. Teachers became indefatigable in making fresh types of apparatus, and were generous with their money in buying necessary equipment, for though many found their local authorities willing to give them freedom for their experiments, few were so fortunate as to receive any financial help ! The value of these experiments has naturally varied according to the understanding and the skill of those conducting them, but on the whole sound and valuable work has been done during the past ten years, and there has been a complete revolution in the methods employed in many infants' departments. The influence of these developments, though wide-spread, is not found everywhere. There are still backward authorities, jealous of power, unwilling to give the teacher the necessary freedom ; still conservative inspectors who dislike the

"busy workshop" appearance of class-rooms, so bewildering
to those who prefer what has been called the " sit-stillery "
type of education ; there are still unprogressive teachers.
But their number is steadily dwindling.

The second influence was the growth of the Nursery
School Movement. The Education Act of 1918 gave a thrill
of hope to all interested in the welfare of children, for it
suggested that the importance of education in the early years
of life was to receive official notice and encouragement.
Infant-school teachers, especially those in crowded and poor
areas, rejoiced to think that some of their gravest problems
and most persistent obstacles were to be removed ; for the
devitalised bodies, dulled and twisted minds, the perverted
habits of the large majority of entrants present very serious
problems, difficult to deal with in the large classes of an
infant school. Nursery education has been developed both
in nursery schools and in nursery classes. The first, which
are self-contained schools under the medical branch of the
Board of Education, are in receipt of grants from the Board
and Local Authorities.[1] There are at the present time
twenty-seven nursery schools in England, varying in size, with
accommodation for from forty to two hundred and sixty
children, who are divided into groups of twenty-five to thirty-
five. The schools are mostly of the open-air type. They
are equipped with baths, beds, and isolation rooms, and all
provide a mid-day meal, which is paid for by the parents.
The children spend the whole day in the school ; some
keeping to the usual school hours ; others, in districts where
both parents go early to work, attend from 7.30 or 8 a.m.,
and remain late into the evening, having all meals at school.
There is regular medical supervision, and charts showing
height, weight, and general health conditions are kept. In

[1] Nursery schools are, strictly speaking, of two kinds: some are
conducted by the local authority and are aided by a 50 per cent. grant
on net expenditure from the Board ; others are voluntary schools which
get 50 per cent. from the Board on their net expenditure, and also, in
some cases, grants of varying amounts from their local authority.

many of the schools there are, in addition, similar records of all-round growth, *i.e.* conduct, intelligence, skill, and the relationship and interaction of physical, mental, and spiritual growth. The nursery school in which children are natural, free, and happy is providing an excellent centre for conducting observation or research in that practically unknown field, the mental and emotional life of a young child.

Nursery classes, unlike the nursery schools, are in and part of the existing infants' schools. They have increased more rapidly, and in Manchester alone there are about fifty. It is not possible to state the actual number of such classes in England, as many " baby rooms," though referred to as nursery classes, are as far removed from all that such a nursery should be, as was the drill in " Froebel material " removed from all that is implied by " kindergarten." The introduction of milk, a few toys, and " beds," in the form of canvas sheets slung from the legs of upturned tables, into a room inhabited by three-year-olds, though undoubtedly meeting a certain need, does not constitute a nursery class ! Few, if any, of the nursery classes have any provision for a mid-day meal, which is essential for infants, not only because of the health value of a well-balanced diet and food properly cooked and eaten, but also because of the accompanying training in hygienic and social habits, and the elimination of the tiring journey to and from home at mid-day. Few nursery classes have open-air buildings, or buildings suitable in any way, gardens, or playgrounds equipped for the needs of little children. But a beginning has been made, and progress is already noticeable. The Manchester Education Committee has made a step forward in these matters by building a special nursery wing in its latest infant schools. The wing faces south, is " open-air " in type and self-contained, having its own entrance, playground, and garden, its bathrooms, kitchen, and rooms for play, rest, and meals.

In neither nursery schools nor classes is there any formal

instruction, but rather that education by living, in which every act has its educative importance. The care of pets and the garden ; the dusting, arranging, and tidying of the playrooms ; the setting and serving of meals, the learning to wash and clean the teeth ; the play with educative toys, listening to stories, singing and playing games, fill all of the day that is left over from bath-time, sleep, and meals. The nursery school teacher, aware of the importance of subconscious influences, gives much thought and care to the appearance and arrangement of the rooms and shelters, and to the daily routine. Beauty, to which all children are sensitive, and of which most are robbed, orderliness, cleanliness are no less important than her own appearance, clothes, tone of voice, attitude, and ideals. These features of nursery education and the general organisation for, and insistence on, all-round nurture, have had a marked influence on both the methods and atmosphere of the infants' schools, and in many of them the lower " standards " have been converted into modified nursery classes.

In the largest number of infant schools to-day class teaching has given place to this " education by life " in a carefully prepared environment. Children move about freely as their work demands, taking and replacing material from shelves and cupboards, working alone or in groups, teaching themselves by means of the apparatus provided, and organising and arranging their own education. Just as a well-nourished child brought up in sunshine and fresh air is eager for meals and full of activity, so do children in a wisely equipped schoolroom and garden find themselves mentally hungry, and begin to work with interest and intensity. Interest in work brings the only real discipline, and it is remarkable to note how severely these children discipline themselves, concentrating on a puzzle till they have found its solution. These lessons in self-control and self-discipline are the foundation of any real freedom— for no man is free who is not master of himself—and freedom is not a birthright, but a prize each may win. The infants' departments are giving a training for free men, and the national significance of this needs no stressing.

The contribution that nursery and infant education make to the national life, then, seems too obvious to require mention. It is its special function to quicken into life, and to nurture all those qualities and powers and tendencies that the school seeks to bring to fruitful issue. The growth of a strong body and the development of language, muscular co-ordination, and refined sense perceptions are of fundamental importance in the early years. Added to those the children in the nursery and infant schools are helped to develop self-reliance, self-control, intellectual curiosity, honesty, and fearlessness, coupled with the desire and the ability to plan, to judge, and to make independent decisions. They acquire habits of fellowship, co-operation, and consideration for others, and have their feet set upon the road that leads to self-realisation, through learning to forget themselves in work and in the service of others.

The contribution made to the national system of education by these schools might be increased considerably in two ways. There must be more specially trained infants' teachers. Far too many of the teachers at present employed in infants' departments have neither the desire nor the training for infant work. Nursery and infant teaching is as different from that of the upper grades as is the teaching in the preparatory schools from that in the university. A different type of teacher and of training is necessary. It is not enough that the intending infants' teacher should take special " subjects " in the training college ; the whole nature of her training must be different and have a different bias. Her interest and attention must be less on subjects and more on human nature ; less on children's standards of attainment in certain directions only and more on all-round growth ; less on her own academic attainments and more on the development of her personality in ways that make her sensitive to children's needs and enable her to get quickly into sympathetic touch with other human beings. Her study of hygiene must be wider than that required by the average training-college course and her practical experience with children infinitely greater than is usual in colleges. This does not mean that a lower standard in training and culture is sufficient for the infant and nursery school teacher. It is an accepted truth that only the wisest and most cultured teacher is capable of dealing adequately with a child's bewildering questions and setting him on the way to discover the answer for himself, and that it is only the most sensitive and spiritually-minded woman who is good enough to nurture the tender early growth of the highest and most easily damaged human quality—man's spiritual endowment.

The other way is by a wise and general extension of the Nursery School Movement. There are to-day approximately two million children under five receiving no systematic educational or medical care, and the positive harm that results from the neglect is detrimental and hampering both to the educational system and to national life. An extension of this care to all children in need of it should be controlled by the Board of Education, and kept within the national system of education of which it is clearly the first step. There should be unbroken continuity in the nurture and training of children from babyhood onwards. Education, as understood to-day, includes bodily nurture as definitely as mental and spiritual nurture, and educators are aware of the close relationship between healthy-mindedness and good health. But the most complete and perfect hygienic conditions are in themselves insufficient for the health of a human being, who cannot be in good health save through the full and satisfying use of all his human powers. It is the duty of a teacher to see the child as a living unity and to help him to develop as such, and conditions for all-round health are more easily provided by an education authority assisted by its medical branch than in any other way.

Is it too Utopian to look forward to the time when, as a result of the new organisation into junior and senior schools with the break at eleven years, the junior school will contain a department of children from two to seven, under the headship of a specially trained nursery teacher wise in matters of health and education, and housed not in the barrack-like buildings, which hold the infants' departments to-day, with their rooms of uniform shape, their appallingly high ceilings (so frightening to a child), their out-of-reach windows, and their general unattractiveness, but in beautiful and simple buildings or sheds, more suggestive of a home or of a children's land, open to sun and air, with a garden full of the beauty of growing plants and insects and birds, and where the little ones could live and play, growing strong in body, alert in mind, and full of that wondering attitude that is the beginning of religion ?

With such organisations as these, providing the first step in the national system of education, leading naturally without break into the junior school, the whole population of England could be transformed, mentally, spiritually, and bodily in a single generation.

REFERENCES

CAMERON, H. C. The Nervous Child. Frowde and Hodder & Stoughton.

DRUMMOND, MARGARET. Five Years Old or Thereabouts. Arnold.

——. The Dawn of Mind. Arnold.

GESELL. The Mental Growth of the Pre-School Child. Macmillan.

HOLMES, EDMOND. What Is and What Might Be. Constable.

McMILLAN, MARGARET, C.B.E. The Nursery School. Dent.

MURRAY AND BROWN SMITH. The Child Under Eight. Arnold.

OWEN, GRACE. Education in Nursery Schools. George Philip.

—— (editor). Nursery School Education. Methuen.

RUSSELL, BERTRAND. On Education. Geo. Allen & Unwin, Ltd.

STERN, WILLIAM. Psychology of Early Childhood. Allen, Unwin.

CHAPTER III

By F. H. SPENCER [1]

IN England and Wales, according to the last available statistics, there are, in round figures, 21,000 public elementary schools, and 5,600,000 children on the registers of these schools, with an average attendance of 4,900,000. In London alone there are about 960 schools, which are organised, however, in about 2,350 departments, each having a responsible head teacher, and there are some 665,000 pupils. In England and Wales there are employed in the elementary schools about 162,000 adult teachers, of whom about 74 per cent. in England and about 85 per cent. in Wales are certificated teachers, usually having been members of a training college for two years or more. In London no uncertificated teachers are employed, and a very great majority are college-trained certificated teachers. The elementary schools, as is well known, are either provided schools or non-provided schools. The provided schools are those which are both owned and maintained by the local education authority. The non-provided schools, as their name indicates, are those which are not provided by the local education authority, but are maintained by that authority. The number of council or provided schools

[1] As an official of the L.C.C. I wish to make it clear at the outset that any opinions which I may express are personal to myself, have not the sanction of the Authority I serve, and are not to be taken as necessarily indicating their policy.

in England and Wales, in 1926, was 9,101, and non-provided or voluntary schools, about 11,626. It follows from these figures that the elementary school is the great training ground of the nation at large. It is, in effect, probably the most important single means of affecting, for good or ill, the intellectual and moral quality of the population.

If we remember that of all those millions of young people, some enter the schools at three years of age, and practically all remain at least from the age of five until the end of the first term after they reach the age of fourteen ; that they attend the school usually for about five and a half hours on each of five days a week, and for about forty-four weeks in the year, it must be obvious that what is taking place in the schools is a most momentous matter. What is taught, by whom, and how, are questions of first-rate importance.

From time to time persons, and perhaps even chiefly persons who have enjoyed considerable social and intellectual advantages, but whose acquaintance with the people's schools is of the slightest, utter the wildest suggestions as to the actual curriculum of those schools. Not long ago a doctor in a first-rate practice said to me : " What you had better do is to stop teaching trigonometry to these girls in the council schools and begin to teach them cookery." The truth is, of course, that the cookery is taught and the trigonometry is not. Not all criticism is so ill informed as this ; but, nevertheless, the ignorance of middle-class people about what goes on in elementary schools is astonishing.

The characteristic feature of the contemporary English elementary school is its freedom. Except as to certain essentials and a few leading principles, the head teacher of the school has the greatest liberty in determining what shall be taught in his school and how it shall be taught. For this, among other reasons, we may dismiss ignominiously the notion that there is " an ironbound elementary school system." I do not think that it is an exaggeration to say that there is at least as much variety among elementary schools as there is among any other types of school. They differ from one another in every imaginable way. But, when people in large numbers attack a given problem such as the curriculum of the elementary school, some fairly general solution usually works itself out. As a result of tradition, of the various experiments of the teachers, the working of the rules and regulations of central and local authorities, and the influence of the various species of inspectors and organisers who circulate in the schools, a normal curriculum results ; and it is possible to give a general notion of what goes on, always remembering that the curriculum of each school will vary in detail, in the methods upon which it is treated, and in the spirit and personality of the teachers who deal with it.

CURRICULUM

In the first place, religious or scriptural instruction of one kind or another is given in every school ; and in this connection it is worth remarking, perhaps, that the population which has passed through the elementary school has probably for at least seven or eight years for two hours a week, and more often than not by means of a daily lesson, been kept in touch with the English Bible. This in itself is an important moral influence, and is not without its effect on the taste and on the literary content of the pupils' minds. I incline to believe that in the matter of religious instruction, at all events biblical instruction, the elementary school child has more adequate attention than any other part of the population. Doctrinal teaching is, of course, confined to the non-provided schools.

Next are our old friends, " the three R's." Reading, writing, and arithmetic are a necessary constituent of the school programme. Arithmetic is made more of in the elementary school than in preparatory schools, and, whatever else may happen, every child is taught to read and to write.

In one form or another, English literature, history, geography, and some science, which, in the case of young children, takes the form of nature study, are taught in every school. Drawing or some form of pictorial art is also universal, and practical instruction in some craft—woodwork, metal-work, leather-work, and so forth—is, if not universal, almost ubiquitous.[1] In girls' schools, with possibly some isolated exceptions, the economy of the household is an essential feature of the instruction, and in almost every case this takes the form of the teaching of cookery, housewifery, or laundrywork.[1]

Music, chiefly in the form of singing, the tonic sol-fa method being predominant, is also universal, and there are now very few schools where physical education, on recently revised methods which are at once interesting and scientific, is not carried on. It is also the rule rather than the exception that the playing of games forms part of the curriculum, which, in most instances and in urban schools, also includes swimming during the summer months.

In addition to this, a characteristic school will, for the majority of its elder pupils, have arranged during the school year educational visits under the guidance of the teacher to places of interest from the historical, geographical, artistic, or civic point of view ; and it is becoming increasingly common for schools, with or without public assistance, to undertake also, for their elder pupils, a school journey, which offers opportunity for practical teaching and for widening the outlook of pupils in ways which would not otherwise be possible.

This anatomy of the school curriculum really constitutes the reply to those critics who allege that subjects

[1] Dr. Spencer speaks for London here. A great deal of provision has yet to be made in other parts of the country before every child will be certain of getting practical instruction in handicraft or domestic subjects during his or her elementary school course. [Ed.]

are too many or that the curriculum is too advanced or too elaborated. Bearing in mind that the curriculum varies in detail, we may summarise the time-table in the upper classes of the urban school somewhat in the following fashion :

	Hours per Week.
Bible instruction, prayers, and hymns	$2\frac{1}{2}$
English (including reading and writing) and arithmetic	10 or more
History, geography, singing, and drawing	5
Science and practical work (including needlework and domestic economy for girls and woodwork and metalwork for boys)	$5\frac{1}{2}$ or somewhat less
Physical education	$1\frac{1}{2}$
Play intervals, registration, etc. ...	3 or less

The intelligent citizen who regards this programme will have the greatest difficulty in suggesting what, if anything, should be omitted. As a matter of fact, if he has strong individual interests, it is highly probable that he will suggest the insertion of some pet subject of his own. It may be a language such as French or Esperanto ; if he is an ancient politician, it may be economics, or what he is pleased to call civics ; while if he is an enthusiast and really up to date, he will ask that some time shall be expended in listening to the wireless or in watching the cinematograph. As a matter of fact, it is the teachers and the educational administrators who are constantly having to resist new claims upon the time of the elementary school. The truth is that the present normal programme has been arrived at by a process of trial and error lasting over sixty years, and in so far as a school curriculum can be separated into subjects or brought under some other form of classification, we may take it that it is a tried and tested, and, on the whole, an excellent programme, though, of course, variations upon it will, it is to be hoped, continue to be always in process. Substantially, it forms a programme of study at once utilitarian (since in order to live under modern conditions we must be able to read, write, and reckon), and an attempt to hand on to the children of to-day as much of the accumulated experience and culture of our civilisation as is possible in the conditions under which the work is done.

Organisation

On the organisation of the elementary school we need not dwell very long. In our own country, at all events in urban centres, the usual organisation is that providing for an infants' school which terminates approximately at the age of seven, taking infants of both sexes, of course, and then bifurcating into two separate schools, one for boys and one for girls. The mixed school for boys and girls is the exception rather than the rule in large towns. It is much more common in the smaller towns—in many it is characteristic, and is the rule in rural parts. My own experience is mainly of separate departments for the sexes : on the whole, this plan seems to work well and is in accord with the general trend of public and expert opinion. It is noticeable, however, that those teachers who work in mixed schools generally acquire a belief in and an affection for them ; but as it would be administratively futile to think of any radical change of the present organisation, and as there is strong reason for belief that at all events the elder boys should be taught by men and the elder girls by women, I will refrain from entering at length into the thorny question involved by a consideration of the question of co-education.

The characteristic modification of recent years from the point of organisation has been the emergence of what is called the " central school," which the Consultative Committee of the Board of Education would wish to rename the " modern school." Of these there are two main types : (a) as in London and other large cities, the selective school ; or (b) the non-selective school. In the first case, children, usually in their eleventh year, are selected by some form of examination or test for transference to a school which is carried on under the regulations for elementary schools, but where the duration of school life normally, but voluntarily, extends to at least fifteen years of age. There is a selected staff and a more advanced curriculum which often, and in London always, has some general vocational aim. In the second case, as carried out in one or two provincial towns, the whole elementary school provision is divided into junior schools and senior schools, a definite break for everybody being arranged at about the age of eleven. There is no process of selection, nor is there any necessary general advance of the leaving age.

In London a beginning has been made in the process of supplementing the selective central school by organising certain groups of schools into junior schools and senior schools. The selective and non-selective systems are, therefore, at work side by side. It also seems pretty certain that in London and probably in some other of the largest towns of the country, some schools will remain in which a break at eleven is impossible owing to the topographical or other conditions.

The oldest examples of the selective central school are to be found in London, where they were first organised as early as 1911. They now number about seventy. There is not the slightest doubt that they have been a very great success. What happens is that in a given group of schools, after the very best pupils, so far as can be judged by examination, have been drafted to the secondary school, the more intelligent of the remaining pupils are drafted to a school which is, in fact, central to the group, and is, therefore, appropriately so named. The selective basis makes a more advanced curriculum and a more thorough treatment of it possible ; and the greater length of elementary school life to which in many districts it is not difficult to get parents to agree, all make possible a far more generous and effective educational provision. For the abler boys and girls who alone are admitted to these schools, the selective central school is appropriate and is a great boon, and from the social standpoint, the schools constitute a genuinely economical organisation, inasmuch as they maximise the efficiency of the teaching and learning processes.

The justification for the non-selective schools is to be found in the fact that it is easier to classify, say, 400 children between the ages of eleven and fourteen according to their ability than to classify the same number between the ages of about seven and fourteen. The opportunities for fine grading are doubled and the opportunity for an appropriate curriculum increased. I have little acquaintance with this system outside London, but in the few cases in London where this form of organisation has been adopted it promises to be very successful. The case for supplementing the selective central school by junior and senior schools seems to be a strong one, specially suited to large towns. In smaller towns the non-selective system by itself has many advantages.

Finally, it must be remembered that within the category of elementary schools come such institutions as open-air schools intended for those not positively ill, but in danger of becoming so, and the special schools for mentally defective and physically defective children. Moreover, in London and to a less degree elsewhere, in addition to the ordinary schools for those completely blind or completely deaf, there are separate schools or classes for myopic and partially deaf children, while we must not forget institutions lying outside the jurisdiction of the Board of Education, such as the industrial and reformatory schools which in diminishing numbers cater for those children whose good or ill fortune it has been to appear before the police magistrate.

CHANGES IN THE ELEMENTARY SCHOOL DURING A GENERATION

A criticism of the present condition of elementary schools must necessarily have an historical basis. We cannot judge by any absolute standard whether at present they are good or bad, effective or ineffective, for no such standard exists. We can only say whether, looking back for fairly extended periods of time, they are better or worse than they were and in what directions. It is not my purpose to scarify my readers by detailing to them the condition of the child population of this country in the days when there was no universal provision of elementary education. It is sufficient to say compendiously that it was almost incredibly bad, and that the most potent single factor in the improvement which has undoubtedly taken place has been the elementary school. I will confine myself, therefore, to a very brief consideration of the actual changes in internal school conditions.

The greatest and most sweeping change in the schools has been brought about by the abolition of " payment by results " based upon the old annual examination of every pupil. The change took place in the middle nineties of last century. The generation of teachers and others familiar with the interesting, rather cruel, but not unamusing process is passing away ; but there are many still in the schools who can remember when that great potentate, His Majesty's Inspector, accompanied, or rather, in the case of large schools, preceded by one or two of his assistants, came down and solemnly examined the whole school in reading, writing, and arithmetic, and also examined each class in two class subjects, usually grammar and geography, and possibly some of the elder children in two " specific subjects " such as, to give instances from my personal recollection, algebra and mechanics. The grant paid in the case of the school depended upon the percentage of individual

E

passes in the three basic subjects, together with the prescribed rate of grant for the class subjects, and specific
payment per head for the specific subjects. Under a good
many School Boards or bodies of managers the salary of
the head teacher, and at least a part of the salary of the
assistants, was dependent upon the financial results of this
examination. It was an amusing sight to see, as I have seen,
a white-headed old clergyman, once a fellow of his college,
examining sixty children in Standard I, ranged on a gallery,
in reading *The Royal Reader* No. 1.

I have not time to describe the process at greater length;
but what were its consequences? Obviously, if schools
are to be examined, there must be prescribed syllabuses,
and one consequence of the system was that the school
programme, within very narrow limits, was prescribed by
the central government. No teacher, therefore, had the
burden and privilege of arranging his curriculum and
preparing his syllabus. The stimulus to thought and to
enterprise in the matter of the school programme was almost
completely absent. Another consequence was that the
teaching was never really inspected, the persons who were
actually seen to teach by these great emissaries being the
pupil-teachers alone. These were lads or girls usually
between the ages of fourteen and eighteen, who in the later
years and in the bigger towns taught for half their time at
least and were instructed for half their time or less at a
pupil-teachers' centre; though right down to the end of
the system, a pupil-teacher in nearly all the smaller towns
and villages of England, and in many of the large ones, was
in charge of a class which might number anything from
thirty to fifty or sixty or more, for the whole day, and was
educated out of school hours for an hour a day before
breakfast or in the evening. Naturally the quality of their
education depended on the accident of their head master,
and there are known cases where the instruction was, within
its limits, on the one hand excellent and on the other farcical.

These pupil-teachers had to be examined in the art of teaching, and were therefore seen to teach, not infrequently, by a learned, and sometimes tolerant, gentleman who had never taught himself.

The annual examination disappeared and was replaced by inspection. As a consequence, the teachers were thrown upon their own resources, and the inspectorate, which even then numbered many able and liberal-minded men, were free to act, not as mere assessors of results on a prescribed plan, but as friendly critics and advisers. This has brought about a complete change in the relations between the inspectorate and the teachers. A good inspector is now an important constructive force.

Another consequence was the, at all events theoretical, freedom of the teachers to classify their pupils according to their abilities and their attainments. It was no longer the case that he who passed in two fundamental subjects out of three must be promoted, nor that he who happened to fail on the day of the examination must spend a whole year in labouring painfully through work that he had already done. As a consequence, children are now promoted more rapidly and the freedom of classification is both theoretically, and I think practically, as great in the elementary school as it is at the most aristocratic of our public endowed schools. I say " theoretically," because in practice, as our schools are built with the class-rooms approximately equal in size, and as attendance is compulsory, the liberty of the teacher to classify as he thinks wise is subject to the limitation imposed upon him by the size of the separate rooms at his disposal. This, of course, is not peculiar to elementary schools. But there can be little doubt that the liberty of classification, consequent upon the abolition of the old examination, has been a great progressive force. Under the old examination system there was, of course, much good teaching, and I think it at least possible, that as a craftsman in the actual technique of exposition, in questioning and recapitulation, the teacher brought up under the old conditions has never been excelled. I think it very doubtful whether, in point of craftsmanship, teachers produced to-day are the equals of their forebears ; but it is certain that their training is now more intelligent and humane and that their better education and greater opportunities of culture outweigh any initial technical losses that may have accrued. After all, if the great task of the elementary school is, as I have already said, to hand on as much as possible of our great inheritance of culture to the mass of the people, the primary qualification must be that the teacher himself shall be well educated, reasonable, and cultured.

The freedom from restrictions has been accompanied, as will be seen from the outline of the curriculum which I have already given, not by the insertion of unsuitable subjects or, on any large scale, by the rule of cranky notions, but by a steady liberalising and humanising of the curriculum. The framework of the curriculum, with some differences which we will presently mention, is what it then was, but there is a great difference in the point of view from which subjects are approached and the emphasis has been placed rather upon what is being learnt and upon the mode of teaching and of learning it, than upon examinable results.

Once the art of reading has been fairly mastered, mechanical reading aloud round the class has been largely replaced by the study of literature. The mere dictation of passages from a well-worn reading book, an exercise actually prescribed formerly in every standard up to the highest but one, has been very largely replaced by English composition upon interesting themes, often gathered, in the best schools, from other subjects of the curriculum, such as history, geography, science, or art. History is no longer merely the learning of dates, though I think that dates have got to be memorised ; and geography has become an interesting and well-illustrated branch of science and not the recital of the capes which jut out into the British seas from our own island or a list of the rivers of Asia. We may, indeed, have cause to regret that the disappearance of " learning by heart " has been too complete.

In fact, enterprise and reasonableness in the framing of the curriculum and its treatment have been very greatly encouraged.

There have been very notable advances in the teaching of art and the teaching of elementary science, and, above all, in practical handwork of one kind or another, for not only is nearly every girl taught cookery and probably some other branch of housekeeping, and nearly every boy wood-work or metal-work, but an amazing variety of design and of craftwork is carried on in a great many elementary schools. If readers of this volume will visit the local exhibitions of handwork of all kinds which are held by the local handwork guilds in the various districts of London, they will find something to criticise and, possibly, something to deprecate, but they will, on the balance, be amazed at the variety of well-finished and tasteful work in all sorts of materials which the elementary schools can now produce.

Time has also been found, under these conditions of liberty, for the introduction of a sane and enjoyable system of physical education, and, allowing for the limitations inevitable in great urban centres, the achievements of the teachers in the matter of organised games, not only in school hours but out of them, are beyond all praise.

In one other matter progress is noticeable. When I came back to regular touch with elementary schools in London about four and a half years ago, after a long interval, I was struck, in visiting the schools, not merely by the changes in teaching methods and curriculum to which I have alluded, but, more than all, by the greater ease of discipline ; by the fact that the relation between teacher and taught, once almost a condition of enmity, was now, in the normal case, one of a friendly co-operation ; and further, by the almost uniform courtesy of the boys and girls. Discipline is as good as ever it was, but is achieved by vastly better methods. The improvement in the manners of the children, at all events inside the school, has been very great indeed. I venture to think that there has been a corresponding improvement in out-of-school manners, and could produce evidence to that effect. If there is still deterioration after the elementary school age, we must remember not merely that boys and girls have to be made fit for industry and social life, but that industry and social life have to be made fit for them.

The question arises how far this grant of liberty, with the resultant liberalising process that I have briefly described, has affected the elementary attainments of the pupils. On this point we have much uninstructed criticism. Nobody contends that every elementary school is perfect. This is very far from being the case. If we are to have 120,000 teachers, not all of them can be paragons of wisdom and industry. My view is that, on the whole, the change has worked very well indeed. People forget that, under the old examination conditions, relatively few children reached the top of the school; that most children never passed even Standard VI, let alone Standard VII, for the simple reason that they never reached it. And to those who say that the results now are poor, there is only one real answer, namely, that they always were, and that there is good reason for supposing that, if all children in elementary schools were to-day examined, the results would be better and not worse than they were a generation ago. We have some evidence on that point. In 1924 the inspectors of the London County Council selected forty-eight school departments, chosen deliberately as a fair sample of the whole from the point of view of social conditions, the quality of the children, staffing, and so forth. Every boy and every girl in those schools who were in their last school year, whatever the classes in which they were working, were given a paper in arithmetic, English composition, history, and geography. It is the composition, spelling, and arithmetic which are sometimes criticised, but the test proved beyond question that in English the results were incomparably better than they were in the old days, and there is a sound statistical basis for asserting that the arithmetic proved to be good. The results in history and geography were not what we should have wished, but these are difficult subjects for a written examination of young children. One is not prepared to say that the more liberal spirit which now pervades the schools has not had any concomitant disadvantages. Of course it has. But also, of course, the cramming after school hours, the punishment of boys and girls, actual corporal punishment for not getting sums right, and so forth, which were the inevitable accompaniments of the old system, have disappeared. Results in the narrow sense are not forced as they were. This, however, is scarcely a disadvantage. On the balance, I have no hesitation whatever in stating my personal belief that elementary education is not only a pleasanter and a more humane, but a far more effective process than it was a generation ago.

The editor of this volume has asked me to say what is the place of the group of schools I am dealing with in the general educational system, and how those schools can be made more effective. As to the first question, the answer is simple, and I have already given it. The elementary school is practically the cultural foundation of our English social life. Compared with the $5\frac{1}{2}$ millions of children in the elementary schools, there are about 376,000 in grant-aided secondary schools, and a few odd thousands in trade schools of one kind or another. Practically, therefore, the elementary school provides all the education that the mass of the population will get, especially as only a minority of the pupils, taking the country over, ever attend even a continuation school. In London, the number of pupils who at one time or another proceed to some form of continued education has reached 40 per cent. But the number who effectively persevere is much smaller than this.

A moment's reflection will show that none of our great services could be carried on were the elementary school system to be wiped out. The railways could not run, the post office and the telegram and telephone could not function ; and practically all the work of the world to-day is carried out on a basis which would be impossible, except to a literate people. The problem of the elementary school is to produce a literate people, and in England it does so— and, moreover, a well-mannered, a reasonable and a good-humoured people, compared with their forebears. On the whole, I think it can be said to have succeeded. On purely practical grounds alone we want people trained to read and reckon with fair accuracy, and, as far as possible, to consider and to reason. In this last respect we probably have not yet succeeded, and, as only a minority of human beings have the necessary gifts, we probably never shall succeed. But I believe that the standard is gradually and very slowly rising, within the limits prescribed by natural gifts, even in this direction. And in the standard of general culture and taste there is undoubtedly, I think, a perceptible general rise. Some day, no doubt, our scientific friends will measure it.

To the editor's second question, namely, how the system can be made more effective, I am not able to supply a complete answer. Changes in the methods of teaching will be very fruitful and are in constant process. The influence of Madame Montessori and of the so-called Dalton plan has on the whole undoubtedly been for the good, and it has led, in all sorts of ways, to more individual work, to more learning and less teaching. The chief weakness of the teacher in the elementary school has been to teach too much by way of oral exposition. He should be added to an old-fashioned grammar-school master and the sum divided by two. Again, leavers' classes have been organised, in which boys and girls are polished up before being thrown on to the world. Specialisation by teachers in elementary schools is rapidly becoming the rule rather than the exception. One teacher takes several classes other than his own in history, or geography, or science, or undertakes the whole music of the school. We no longer ask a man without a voice or ear to teach music, or a person whose experiments never come off to teach elementary science. This process, if not carried to excess, is a powerful factor for good.

In the education of teachers, we now proceed upon the principle that they should all have a complete and uninterrupted school career until eighteen. In the training colleges many, if not most, of the men are getting something which, if not a complete university training, approximates to it, and this process will, no doubt, develop further. Whether the present training is really adequate upon the side of technique is open to doubt ; but, as I have already said, my belief is that the first qualification of a teacher is that he himself shall be an educated person, and the training colleges at least provide a beginning on the practical side. Probably it will become increasingly evident that the probationary first year of teaching must be painful to the teacher and not entirely profitable to the taught.

As to the duration of primary education, it appears to be agreed in principle that the school age will, sooner or later, have to be raised to fifteen. The practical side of this question is a political, and particularly a financial, one, and the question when or how this should be done is one which cannot be entered upon here. Undoubtedly, however, the re-organisation of elementary education into junior education, terminating at about eleven, and followed by a separate senior course, is the chief line of development for the moment. While this form of organisation may not prove to be the solution in all cases, it is certainly a move in the right direction. It offers, as I have said, a greater prospect of reasonable classification of pupils according to their ability than any other organising device I know. And it involves no considerable new expenditure.

The size of classes has diminished, but in principle no one outside Bedlam would agree indefinitely to classes even of forty-eight in infants' schools and forty in boys' and girls' schools, which is now, at any rate, the elementary standard towards which we are working. The well-to-do would not send their own children to schools where classes were as large as that. But the present standard is at least a great advance upon the old classes of fifty, sixty, seventy, or more. In fact, the attainment of a reasonable ideal in the size of the classes is now a financial problem, and therefore a very difficult one.

Another very desirable improvement is the replacement, especially in the provinces, but in London also, of old, ill-lighted, ill-arranged, and imperfectly sanitary buildings by new school premises. These should be airy, light, where the price of land permits on one floor only, and should be built for time and not for eternity. The replacement of unsuitable buildings can only proceed slowly ; and it will be long after my time before it is completed up to any reasonable twentieth-century standard. Such buildings should be as little costly as possible, but should be externally pleasant to look at and should be internally simple and beautiful, and furnished with pleasing and congruous pictures. The subconscious effect of decent, orderly, and beautiful environment is very great. Wherever conditions are suitable, I should also like to see much more of the school education carried on in the open air, or in surroundings approximating to it. We want young people to be fully vital, not semi-vital, and they should not be submitted more than is necessary to the vicious indoor life in which most of us, as adults, have to spend our days. Open air seems almost if not quite as important as good and suitable food for the attainment of full vigour. Children are now better nourished than they were. The next move is properly to ventilate them.

There is one other condition which occurs to me as necessary if the best is to be made of elementary education. It is useless to educate children up to a statutory limit of school age, be it fourteen or fifteen, and to stop at that. Some system of keeping not a small minority, but all adolescents, in touch with educational influences up to (say) eighteen years of age is not only reasonable but economical. To fail to do this is largely to waste the work of the elementary school. Probably we shall not see this reform for some years to come, as times are not financially propitious ; a partial or local scheme is almost bound to fail, and ministers and administrators with sufficient faith and courage do not seem to be abundant. But it is right, and some day it will come.

Finally, it would be easy to write pages on the shortcomings and the partial failures, not of the elementary school system as a whole, but of units and individuals. As a whole it is no failure, but a great success—a success, for instance, far beyond the dreams of Mr. Forster and beyond the beliefs of Robert Lowe. One might, of course, speak of weak schools, of ineffective, or foolish, or even lazy teachers, of inferior school-books, bad buildings, and backward local authorities, of second-rate officials, and even of failure and defeat, lack of vision or lack of courage on the part of the Board of Education, progressive and enlightened as it often, or perhaps usually, is. But if the expression of indiscriminate satisfaction with the system would be disingenuous and foolish, to belittle the splendid industry, the self-sacrifice and the enterprise of teachers (perhaps especially of women teachers), of local authorities, and central and local administrators, including even inspectors, would be an unpardonable stupidity, and, at least in my case, despicably ungrateful. For they have produced a system as good as, probably better than, any other in the world.

REFERENCES

ASHBY AND BYLES. Rural Education. Oxford, 1919.

BIRCHENOUGH, C. A History of Elementary Education in England and Wales from 1800 to the present day (2nd edn.). Univ. Tutorial Press, 1925.

NEWTON, A. W. The English Elementary School. Longmans, 1919.

PATERSON, A. Across the Bridges. Edward Arnold, 1921.

Board of Education. Annual Report, 1925–26.

——. Annual Report, 1913–14 (" Elementary Education in the N.W. Division ").

——. Annual Report of the Chief Medical Officer.

Reports (annual or triennial) of any local authority.

London County Council. The London Education Service, 1927.

CHAPTER IV

THE PREPARATORY SCHOOL

By ALAN RANNIE

I

IT is the task of this chapter to explain and defend what must appear to many to be an excrescence on the national scheme of education. Preparatory schools are now indeed a most important institution. They are widespread and numerous, they have customs, atmosphere, almost a literature, of their own, and they are, as I shall hope to show, an indispensable part of our " public school " system (using the term in its more exclusive sense) as it exists at present. But they have no exact parallel in other than Anglo-Saxon communities, and even there they are of comparatively recent growth. It cannot be claimed that they were directly provided for by Alfred the Great, to whose genius as the founder of our educational system Professor Dover Wilson pays a tribute in the introductory chapter. Yet, if it comes to an examination of ancient origins, I will not be outdone by the mention of Alfred, or even of Bede—I will claim that the first preparatory schools were those of Sparta. Let any who doubt consider these words of Kenneth Freeman in his *Schools of Hellas* :

> At seven the boys were taken away from home and organised in a most systematic way into packs and divisions. . . . These packs fed together, slept together, on bundles of reeds, and played together. They were under the con-

trol of a Superintendent of the Boys, a citizen of rank, repute and position, who might at any moment call them together and punish them severely if they had been idle : he had attendants who bore the ominous name of Floggers.[1]

All this sounds very like a preparatory school. But as the author goes on to remind us that the education was almost entirely physical, and that the curriculum included organised stealing, we are perhaps glad to remind ourselves that a considerable gulf, both spiritual and temporal, separates the great days of Sparta from the nineteenth century in which our English preparatory schools began.

It will be well at the outset to enumerate some of the main features of preparatory schools. I will mention four, which taken together provide a reasonably satisfactory definition.

1. They are private ventures, without endowments, and free of government control.

2. They have consequently to charge substantial fees.

3. As their name implies, they deal only with young boys who will be going on, not later than the age of fourteen, to other and larger schools.

4. In their most characteristic form they are boarding schools, though exceptions are numerous, and the day school fulfils a most useful function, particularly in the large towns.

Though frequently, and correctly, referred to as private schools, they form but a small proportion of the almost innumerable educational establishments to which this name could be applied ; yet there are over seven hundred schools which may with some justice claim the title " preparatory." Five hundred of these are within an Association, now incorporated, which safeguards their interests, whilst affording some guarantee of efficiency, and these five hundred form between them the chief recruiting ground for the " public schools." It is in fact true (and this is the key

[1] Pp. 17–18.

to the whole position) that they are practically the only gateway by which boys may enter Eton, Westminster, Marlborough, Sherborne, and the other public schools of which these may be regarded as types. The same statement is true of admission to the Royal Naval College, Dartmouth. It follows that most of our activities are conducted with the public schools or the Navy in view, and since, amongst other things, they tell us what to teach, they form a convenient buffer between us and a critical outside world. In one aspect, indeed, we may be described as the junior forms of the public schools.

Preparatory schools, however, can show a good deal of variety. Some have a century of tradition behind them, a hundred or more pupils, and palatial buildings. Others are of exceedingly recent origin, number perhaps twenty boys, and are housed in villas of moderate size. Between these extremes there are many intermediate positions, and in mixed schools the proportion of day boys to boarders knows no fixed laws. The scale of fees varies within narrower limits, and, what is of more importance, the individuality of the headmaster has considerable scope. It is, however, common ground that the development of character and leadership is an aim as important as excellence in the actual classroom work.

It is impossible that I should range, within the space at my disposal, over the whole of a field which presents so much variety, and my remarks will frankly apply chiefly to those schools which have sent, and are sending, numbers of acceptable boys to the greater public schools, and which have therefore proved themselves to be efficient and reliable institutions. Their headmasters are nearly always graduates of one of the older universities, and many of their staffs possess the same qualification. It is, moreover, with boarding schools that I shall chiefly deal.

Let us now transport ourselves in imagination to the beginning of the nineteenth century. A hundred years ago public schools were few in number. Winchester had been in existence since 1382, but had only recently begun to extend its narrow limits by admitting commoners in greater numbers : Eton and Harrow had almost a monopoly for the training of statesmen and the upper classes in general, though it should be remembered that great day schools also existed, such as St. Paul's (1510) and Westminster (1560). Boys often went to all these at an earlier age than is now common. Palmerston and Gladstone, for instance, both entered Eton at eleven, and there is evidence that boys of eight or nine were sometimes to be found there, who might therefore spend as much as ten years at their public school. But it was not unusual for boys to attend some form of school before going on to the larger ones. These might take the form of a small day school kept by a " Dame," or they might be of a character well known to readers of *The Mill on the Floss ;* that is to say, some country rector would take a few boys into his home and educate them there. But there was also a large private school at Cheam in Surrey, which was frequently in use as a stepping-stone to Eton, and this can claim a seventeenth-century origin. It is doubtful, however, if it could be rightly called preparatory until a much later date, as there seems to have been no age limit upwards. Again, in 1809, a rectory school at Twyford in Hampshire had become so important that it required premises of its own, and it seems to have rapidly become a genuine preparatory school, chiefly for Winchester. But that the Twyford of the early 'thirties differed considerably from the Twyford, or other first-rate preparatory school, of to-day can be gathered from the pages of *Tom Brown's School Days* where it is described in one of the early chapters. To the description given by Hughes it may be added that the boys washed at an open tap, yet thought themselves extremely comfortable, and that the curriculum was severely classical, the boys being required to learn hundreds of lines of Greek and Latin poets by heart.

Mention of *Tom Brown* leads one on irresistibly to Thomas Arnold, whose name can with difficulty be omitted from any educational discussion. Arnold exercised a profound influence on preparatory schools, partly by insisting on the moral side of his work, partly by definitely discouraging boys from coming to Rugby before the age of twelve. It was with his sympathy and approval that a retired naval officer started at Windlesham House, Brighton, in 1832, the first preparatory school of a more modern type, in which the usher—an unsatisfactory, because underpaid and imperfectly-educated, official—disappears, and the contact between masters and boys becomes closer, with a consequent improvement in the tone of the school. Preparatory schools of this type, however, remained exceptional for some time longer. Before the 'seventies there were probably only a dozen. But then public schools also were few, and it was the founding of Marlborough, Wellington, etc., and the improvement of such old schools as Uppingham or Sherborne, that produced the remarkable increase in the number of preparatory schools during the last quarter of the nineteenth century. A wider diffusion of wealth and the increase of travelling facilities had produced a greater demand for education, on the lines laid down by Arnold ; hence new public schools had arisen, and new preparatory ones were needed as a direct consequence. At the opening of the present century there were four hundred of them, and they were considered sufficiently important to be the subject of a special report of the Board of Education.

Thus the small boy with a brightly coloured cap who almost monopolises Victoria Station for some days at the beginnings and ends of terms, and is to Eastbourne what a herring is to Grimsby, or a bishop to the Athenæum, is not only a peculiarly English institution, but a modern one as well. He is indeed part of the great Victorian revival of education, which is the main theme of the introductory chapter.

F

It is notorious that the disturbance caused by the Great War has brought us all to the verge of bankruptcy, yet, paradoxically enough, the demand for education of the type which we are considering has been stimulated rather than diminished. The founding of Stowe and other kindred developments has been paralleled by a further increase in the number of preparatory schools, of which, as I have said, there are now over seven hundred.[1]

This brief historical outline has perhaps been sufficient to establish the facts :

1. That our schools are an integral part of the " public school " system.

2. That they attempt to supply what the public schools have, generally speaking, ceased, since the days of Arnold, to supply : namely, a training, in full sympathy with public-school ideals, for boys under the age of thirteen.

3. That they have developed contemporaneously with the numerical increase in the public schools.

4. That their position will remain a strong one, so long as the public-school ideal retains its present hold over the nation.

II

We have now to enquire into the nature of the education provided in preparatory schools—physical, intellectual, moral.

Physically, we try to develop sturdy boys by giving them plenty of sleep and wholesome food, whilst regulating the incessant supply of chocolate and sweets which mothers, aunts, cousins, and well-wishers would fain shower upon them in inverse proportion to the degree of relationship ; by breaking up the hours of study into periods of suitable length and interlarding them with breaks in the fresh air ; by daily games ; by Swedish (but not generally by military) drill ; often by gymnasium ; in many cases by Scouting ;

[1] King, H. C., article in *Journal of Education*, 1925.

by measuring and noting physical development ; by implicit trust in the carefully-chosen school doctor—in these and in many other ways we try to live up to our heavy responsibility in this matter. No school can hope to succeed if it does not make health a main consideration.

When I turn to the question of the curriculum, I find myself on the edge of a vast and stormy ocean. The problem of what boys should be taught, and still more of what they should be expected to know, is one upon which I have thought much, but I do not propose to enlarge upon the matter here. Fortunately, it is unnecessary to justify or condemn the retention of Latin and mathematics as the basis of training for all our boys, for, as has been said, these matters are decided for us by the public schools who set us a double standard—scholarships for our better boys, and a Common Entrance Examination for our ordinary product. I will content myself with a few observations on recent tendencies, some complimentary, others of a critical nature.

The education which we provide is partly elementary but largely secondary. The majority of our boys come to us able to read and write, and with an elementary knowledge of arithmetic and the Bible. Some schools are fortunately able to insist on these minimum requirements, but it is alas all too easy to find the boy who has been allowed to " run wild " in his early years, on the theory that subsequent development of the brain will be more rapid and satisfactory. Personally, I have no sympathy with these unconscious disciples of Rousseau, even if they are bolstered up by a certain amount of medical support, and I hold that the home training from the very earliest years is all important. According to whether boys have or have not been taught at home to regard work—definite and accurate work—as one of the conditions of life from their earliest years, so will not only their mind but also their character develop, except in rare cases.

Now the elementary stage of education is scarcely controversial. All are agreed that reading, writing, arithmetic are essential. The real question open to discussion is whether the transition to the secondary stage is too early or too universal, and there is an occasional complaint that boys come from preparatory (as also from elementary) schools, unable to write and spell. But the moment that we pass beyond, we find ourselves in a most bewildering atmosphere. Great diversity of opinion exists as to what boys should be taught and at what ages. I have read, as who has not, an infinite number of theories and pronouncements, from the celebrated remark of Dr. Johnson that whilst you are arguing which of two things you ought to teach a boy first, another boy will have learned them both, to the doctrine that everything depends upon the exact method and sequence by which each subject is presented to the pupil's mind.

Out of the welter of conflicting opinion the following conclusions seem to me at length to emerge.

1. That what boys actually know when they leave preparatory schools matters comparatively little. It can never satisfy all, and must in any case be trifling in comparison with the knowledge which will be quickly acquired in ordinary life by an alert mind. This is accentuated by the short hours we work and our reluctance to give to the classroom that predominant place which it holds in France and Germany, almost to the exclusion of the other aspects of school life.[1]

2. That what matters intensely is—first, the creation of a right attitude to work by inculcating a high standard of duty, of accurate thought, of self-discipline; secondly, that our boys should have a broadminded conception of the universe as a whole, that they should leave us with open and receptive minds. I would add that a spirit of reverence

---

[1] This is probably one reason why the average Englishman does not readily master foreign languages.

seems to me to be one of the chief needs of the present time. Accurate and dutiful concentration, intelligent and reverent interest, these are twin aims and neither is complete without the other. Much of our after-life must necessarily consist in doing uncongenial tasks at times not of our own choosing, and only a habit of mental discipline will carry us through. Mere interest is a dangerous guide, and leads to dissipation of energy ; this seems to be a weakness of some of the most attractive schemes of educational reform. On the other hand, work without interest makes at best a dull boy, and at worst creates a reaction against intellectual effort of all kinds, and this may have been one of the faults of the past.

Whether classics or geometry are necessary in order to promote the first of the educational aims which I have indicated, I will not here put forward an opinion. I am a great believer in the classical training for those who are able to carry it through, and I am prepared to believe that what is sauce for the goose is also sauce for the gosling.

There can, however, be little doubt that the teaching of Latin and Greek was overdone in the past, and even as recently as thirty years ago. There were, in 1899, schools in which the higher forms spent over sixty per cent. of their working hours in classics, with the result that a single weekly period each for history and geography, together with three-quarters of an hour for writing and dictation, constituted the only time devoted to English, at an age when the study of one's own language is surely of great importance. There are, I think, few who would not agree that however valuable the disciplinary training involved, there is, from the intellectual point of view, a grave lack of proportion in a scheme such as the above.

Now all this has changed, and changed I think for the better. The subject and standard of both the entrance examination and scholarships are subject to periodical review by a joint committee, which represents both the Head-masters' Conference (Public Schools) and the Incorporated

Association of Preparatory Schools. As the result of reports of this committee, published in 1916 and 1927, the classical burden of the preparatory school-boy has been very considerably lightened. Thus, while less on the whole is expected of the average boy in Latin, he is able to dispense altogether with Greek, and such boys as do take it either for scholarship purposes or because they seem capable of reaching a standard which will repay their study, need not begin it until they are eleven. This reform has created time-table problems of its own, but that it is a reform, I for one cannot doubt. For whilst I am sufficient of a Hellenist to desire that every boy of literary bent should learn Greek, I am convinced that for the majority to know something of Greek history, mythology and art is far more valuable than to grind for a year or two at the paradigms of the verbs in $\mu\iota$, only to drop the whole subject in disgust at the first opportunity which occurs. I have found it most profitable to keep one period a week for various aspects of Greek and Roman civilisation without reference to the language, just as one studies the life of the Jews without embarking on Hebrew.

But Latin remains the dominant feature of our curriculum, and the standard to be reached by the age of thirteen is still comparatively high. This becomes apparent when one examines the syllabus of such outside institutions as the P.N.E.U. school, where an advanced standard of English subjects keeps company with a standard of Latin which requires at the age of sixteen what is often achieved in preparatory schools by boys who are not more than eleven.

There is a general and growing opinon that the study of English still receives too little attention. Two tendencies may be observed amongst those who feel dissatisfied with the present position :

(*a*) There are those who wish to see our own language substituted for Latin and mathematics, as the general basis of preparatory school training.

(*b*) Others, whilst retaining the more exact subjects as a training in accuracy and concentration, would like to see English freed from the more hampering type of examinations.

I confess to a leaning towards the latter school of thought, though I would not go so far as to justify the retention of any subject for its disciplinary value alone.

I am sure that the preparatory schools which are not in the happy position of being able to exclude all but the best boys, are at present too much under the spell of the Common Entrance Examination. It serves no doubt as a good test of at least one kind of efficiency, and it is only fair to say that nobody is entirely satisfied with it. To most educationists, however, viewing the system from outside, the idea of all boys, of whatever temperament or tastes, being submitted to a written examination, as a crucial test, at the age of thirteen is abhorrent.

I am thinking not only of the few who fail, though I cannot help doubting the wisdom of branding any boy as a failure at the age of thirteen, but also of those who pass as the result of a " cram." I am not unaware that the examination is supplemented and even dispensed with in the case of particular schools and particular boys, nor do I suggest that the standard is at all too high, for the public schools can obtain more than enough boys who pass it without difficulty. But I do say that it has up to now occupied too large a place in the mentality of the average preparatory schoolmaster and of our duller boys. For one thing, there are at present too many papers, as the late headmaster of Sherborne recently pointed out. English, fortunately as I think, is confined to one, but there are also separate papers in history, geography, and scripture. Now, if these papers are to be taken seriously, there is a strong temptation to cram the boys' minds with facts, whether about " cities of refuge " or Scottish counties or the deaths of kings, and to scan the back papers too anxiously, in order to guess what will be set next time. Many of us, whilst not undervaluing accurate knowledge, feel that this is not the way in which these subjects should be taught. In geography, for instance, the boy who has grasped the importance of a pass or knows the elementary principles of climate and natural vegetation, is surely better educated than one who can distinguish Cardiff from Swansea on an outline map, or name correctly Great Orme's Head or The Calf of Man.

And my sense of the fitness of things is somewhat disturbed when I receive the prospectus of a book dedicated to preparatory schoolmasters, which includes, as a specimen page, a table of the sovereigns of England " in the order of their Common Entrance importance." The industrious author has worked out the number of times that each monarch has figured in the history papers for the last eleven years. One is reminded perforce of a cricket match. Edward V. fails to score, and Richard III. can contribute only a single. But at this disastrous stage in the innings, the Tudors make a useful stand, and towards the close of play Queen Victoria has the misfortune to be bowled when within three runs of completing her century.

But the welcome news has now got abroad that the examination is to be shortened and simplified in the near future, and as a further sign of reform, great efforts are being made to modify the French papers so as to permit of this subject being taught as a living language, rather than as a kind of secondary Latin.

If, therefore, I have followed the custom of " heaving half-a-brick " at the Common Entrance, it is with a full sense that much has been already accomplished, and much is still being done towards remedying its principal defects.

I have little but praise for the Scholarship Examinations, which absorb the energies of our best boys. These also have lately been much improved, and though the papers are often hard, they are set less to demand a rigid standard than to detect signs of ability, and the candidates generally come from intellectual homes, and are boys of resource and initiative for whom advanced classics and mathematics are suitable studies. For the better public schools it is becoming less and less possible to cram, and though strenuous work is required, this is a stimulating experience for the boy. Many parents comfort themselves with the theory that geniuses were all dunces at school, and that boys who win scholarships are invariably unsuccessful in after-life, but this is far from being the case. Many of the scholarship papers are extremely enlightened. The English papers set recently by Wellington, Winchester, Stowe, to take a few random examples, have been beyond all praise from the general educational point of view.

The standard reached by the boy who wins a public school scholarship at the age of thirteen is certainly a high one, and is something of which the preparatory schools ought to be proud. It is doubtless partly due to an important feature hitherto unmentioned : namely, the smallness of the classes, which seldom exceed twelve, and are sometimes less than half that number.

There is a movement towards including in the curriculum of every boy a number of subjects such as English literature, picture-study, singing, science, nature-study, drawing, which are calculated to produce a wider type of culture rather than to lend themselves to examinable results. The mind cannot be opened too early to beauty in all its forms, and some of us are turning with interest towards the philosophy and teaching methods of the late Miss Charlotte Mason. There are many things which ought to be, but are not always, part of the home training. In a boarding school much can be and is done out of school hours, by acting Shakespeare and other plays, by concerts or the gramophone, by expeditions of various sorts. The object of all this is not so much the acquirement of a smattering of knowledge, as an opening of the windows of the mind. Some of it

perhaps will come to nothing, but much of it will bear fruit
as the years proceed.

III

In one sense the life of a preparatory boarding school
begins when the classroom is left behind.   It is a community
with an *esprit de corps* of its own.   It is a public school
in miniature : there are " colours," a motto, a school song,
perhaps an old boys' tie ; there are desperate encounters
with other schools at football and cricket.   Within its walls
boys learn to bear the separation from home and find their
feet with other boys of the same age and older.   Here they
learn to sink their individual interests in those of the community as a whole, and perhaps at the end of their time are
entrusted with their first responsibility in the leadership
and management of others.   It is sometimes a hard struggle
at first, for boys between the ages of nine and eleven often
combine manners and winning ways with an extremely
refined cruelty towards each other.   They are passing
through a barbaric stage and are as unaware as any other
savages of the inconsistencies of their conduct.   They are,
in fact, experimental beings who have not yet adjusted themselves to civilisation, and there is a reverse side to Wordsworth's great words that " Heaven lies about us in our
infancy."   For it is my firm belief that some of the " clouds
of glory," which we trail behind us in our childhood, are
due to absence of realisation of the needs and sorrows of
others.   School has, in fact, many social and political lessons
to teach, and it seems to be the considered opinion of our
race that they are best learned in boarding schools of the
type we are considering.   I find that boys of twelve have
usually surmounted the first difficulties of adjustment, and
are, within obvious limits, most rational and companionable
beings.   I think, moreover, that these qualities survive into
their public school days, and it is gratifying to notice that

Canon Lyttelton, the late headmaster of Eton, is inclined to attribute the undoubted decline of bullying there chiefly to the civilising influence of preparatory schools. He remarked also that a great change for the better came over the relationship between masters and boys towards the close of the nineteenth century. It would appear that the process of social adjustment which used to take place at public school time is now put forward to an age when it can be more easily controlled, whilst at the same time the close and early contact of master with boys has led to a new theory of their relationship, which has changed the atmosphere of public schools.

This closer contact has added new weight to the responsibilities which preparatory schoolmasters feel, for most schools tend to become a very faithful reflector of the headmaster's own character and outlook on life. The result is usually good, and sometimes magnificent, for some of the finest men of modern times have chosen this as their profession. It is only necessary to mention the names of Lionel Helbert of West Downs, or S. S. Harris of St. Ronan's, both of whom died prematurely within recent years, to illustrate this contention. Such men live lives of complete self-sacrifice, and exert an incalculable influence for good over hundreds of young lives, for it is certain that however immature the recipients may be, and however unconscious the process, the impress received during these early years will be one of the decisive factors in determining the whole life. The work of a teacher has been compared, on Divine authority, to that of a sower, and this is conspicuously true of the spiritual side of a schoolmaster's work. He sows on ground peculiarly well adapted to receive seed. He sows plentifully, but he cannot tell how much of his seed will ever see the light. Much, perhaps, is doomed to disappear completely; some certainly (and possibly that which is least expected) will begin to come up at once; other again will lie dormant for years, and ultimately emerge when the play of maturer thought has acted on an early impression.

The majority of preparatory schools have a definite religious outlook on life. They may be confined to one particular church or sect, or not. In many of them there is a chapel where services are conducted either by a clerical master on the staff, or by the headmaster, who, in spite of being a layman, often assumes the rôle of " priest in his own household," and, with the help of the boys, conducts the services himself. The school will contain boys from homes where many different shades of religious, and irreligious, opinion prevail, but it should not be difficult, at preparatory school age, to provide a simple and wholesome religious teaching for all. Happy is the school of which the chapel is the central point and a manly religion the foundation.

The system of discipline is also largely an individual matter, but there is an almost universal tendency to trust the boys as far as possible. Some schools claim to be able to dispense with punishments altogether—here one suspects the presence of a personality of more than normal proportion —almost all would aim at reducing their number as far as possible. But I should like to protest against the idea that punishments, and particularly corporal punishments, are unnatural or undignified for the small boy. To entertain this notion is to read into the boy feelings which belong entirely to adult life. The stick is only one of many weapons. It should be used occasionally and decisively, and in some cases only when higher appeals have failed; but a child who has been brought up to believe that it is degrading to be beaten under any circumstances is as much a hothouse product as those six young Communists who desired to fraternise with their school comrades of Moscow. At the same time punishment should not be the normal order of the day. Everything that can be done to secure self-discipline from within, as opposed to external restraint, is a step in the right direction ; therefore the principles underlying rules should be explained simultaneously with the rules themselves, and experimental legislation by the boys themselves may be, and is, tried with good results. It seems to me, too, that the punishment should not be repeated. There is a *primâ facie* case against the punishment itself, or the way in which it was administered, if the need for repetition occurs. The minimising of punishment is, however, so much a commonplace of writers on education nowadays, that the need of the moment seems to be to emphasise the fact that an entirely reasonable creature cannot be produced, at any rate between the ages of nine and thirteen (if he could be he would be intolerable and unrecognisable as an English boy), and that a complete abolition of what diplomatists call " sanctions " may easily be interpreted as a sign of weakness, and produce bad and slovenly results.

A kindred question is the extent to which boys of twelve or thirteen may be wisely entrusted with a measure of authority and responsibility. The prefect system introduced into public schools by Arnold, and so scathingly described by Mr. Lytton Strachey, has been widely adopted in preparatory schools also. Objections are often raised on the grounds that the boys are not mature enough to use their powers of discretion, and that they arrive at their public schools with an exaggerated idea of their own importance, which leads to trouble later on. The first of these is a point which calls for careful reply. It is true that boys of thirteen are not men, and are not qualified to judge of the relative seriousness of offences or of the appropriateness of punishments, but they do not, at this age, have the same objections to being advised or over-ruled as grown men, and there is no difficulty about reserving a right to veto or modify their decisions. Boys are shrewd judges of each other's motives, and are refreshingly outspoken on the simple moral issues. Whilst they should emphatically not be given the right to punish without reference to higher authority, they can be of real help in keeping the school up

to scratch, and to invite their co-operation helps to get rid
of that atmosphere in which so-called school-boy honour
protects the undesirable individual to the damage of the
community as a whole, which can be one of the worst features
of the small boys' school. There is a right balance which can
be struck between an atmosphere in which tale-bearing is
encouraged and one in which the dread of sneaking becomes
a cover for all kinds of abominations. It is, after all, the
maintenance of a supply of leaders for our nation and Empire
which affords the only justification for the segregation, under
the particularly favoured conditions which I have been
endeavouring to describe, of perhaps ten per cent. of the total
number of boys in England who are receiving secondary
education. Surely then the opportunities, the sacrifices,
the joys of leadership cannot be presented to the boys too
early ? Within wise limits I can see nothing but good in
giving a measure of authority to the older boys in preparatory
schools, and if the system became general the second
difficulty (which seems to me exaggerated in any case),
that of starting again at the foot of the ladder in a public
school, would automatically cease to exist.

The value of games from a physical point of view has
already been mentioned ; their importance as a means of
inculcating public spirit, unselfishness, and co-operation has
often been stated by English writers, but can scarcely be
exaggerated. It is a right instinct that gives them such an
important place in the life of our boarding schools. Dean
Inge (whom one would certainly not accuse of under-
estimating the importance of the intellectual side of life)
quotes an American Rhodes Scholar, who said of Oxford
University, " What impresses me most is that here are
3,000 young men, every one of whom would rather lose a
game than play it unfairly " ; and the Dean goes on to say,
' The maxim ' play the game ' may seem to the German
childish,[1] to the French foolishness : but rightly applied,

[1] The English view is making great headway in Germany at present.

it is the foundation of all that is best in the English character, and it is the real reason why we have been successful in foreign politics and in governing backward races." We in preparatory schools are usually well off in facilities for games : for the reasons just given, it is the team games that we value most, and our boys have an opportunity of playing football, cricket or hockey practically every day. In placing a high educational value on games, we are building on the sure foundation of the best Greek traditions. The errors of over-athleticism would seem to me to lie not so much in compelling all boys to play, as in attaching too much import- ance to the result of matches, or in over-estimating the boy who plays well without much effort, and, per contra, in despising the boy who cannot play well though he tries hard. There is usually something which needs correction in the character of a boy who takes no interest in games.

I will end my description of preparatory school life by mentioning that it is important that there should be female influence in the school. The headmaster should probably be married, though for personal reasons I do not press this point. The female element is in any case necessary, both because of the care of the boys' health, and because of the close intellectual sympathy of women with the smallest boys. Our junior forms are commonly taught by governesses, and most schools owe a great deal to the ladies on their staff.

The character and aspirations of the preparatory school ought by this time to be fairly clear. I have claimed for it that :

1. It supplies a well-balanced education, largely secondary in type, to boys who will afterwards go on to public schools or enter the Navy.

2. It improves the situation at the public schools (a) by relieving them of boys under thirteen, thus enabling them to deal with larger numbers or to keep their boys later ; (b) by fitting the boys for public school life—breaking them in, so to speak—and doing this in an atmosphere which permits

of more friendly and satisfactory relationship between masters and boys than was formerly usual.

Our faith is well summed up in the following quotation from the late Mr. S. S. Harris :

" I am sure that the preparatory school with its wonderful opportunities in every direction should not only be able to preserve its unique position in the educational world, but should be able to produce a boy equal or superior in all-round power to that of any other product by any other system in the world. It is true we are fettered to a slight extent by the shackles of an educational scheme on which we are dependent, but it really is only to a slight extent. We have plenty of opportunities to spread ourselves, and in the production of our specimen, as typified by spiritual outlook, intellect, character, physique, self-reliance, and leadership, we ought, with the opportunities at our disposal, to be able to produce the finest youth in the world." [1]

IV

It was laid down, in the introductory chapter of this book, that the original purpose of education in England was to foster an intelligent governing class. As will have been gathered from the foregoing remarks, it is precisely this that the public schools, and we in our humbler way, claim to do. We are quite definite in our belief that we are providing the best all-round education in existence, and we point with pride to the way in which our boys have become the admiration, and the administrators, of half the world.

There are, however, many who will say that our system is not democratic, inasmuch as financial and social considerations play their part in determining whether a boy shall or shall not receive this highest form of training.

It is attractive to outline a different scheme, a system of general day schools, in which a beneficent state would provide a first-rate education, suitably graded no doubt to

[1] *The Master and his Boys*, p. 81.

suit varying degrees of intelligence, but equally available for all sorts and conditions of men. Such a scheme exists, and works tolerably well, in France, Germany, and other European countries. But the judgment of Anglo-Saxon communities, and they have proved in practice to be not the least truly democratic, has been given definitely against it. How else can be interpreted the facts that in Scotland, where the municipal day school attracted, until quite recently, the sons of the cultured classes, the English system is now being introduced ; that in the United States, and in all parts of the Empire, private boarding schools are fast growing up ? Professor Findlay indeed has written that the working of this instinct can be traced in all the countries of Europe, and " in the New World, as soon as a pioneer district loses the homogeneity of social condition by reason of the influx of wealth and culture, all sorts of private and endowed schools are created, which express the failure of the public system to meet a complex situation." And again, " it is folly to attempt to rule out this instinct as inimical to progress." [1]

Admitting then that it is desirable to have a proportion of boys receiving a special education, the question arises : Are the right boys being selected for this purpose ? In the main I think the answer must be " Yes," inasmuch as the children of those who appreciate the value of our type of education, because they have themselves received it, and are prepared to make the necessary financial sacrifice in order to hand it on, are on the whole the most likely to profit by it. It is not necessary, or indeed wise, to assume that the majority of those who have achieved culture and sufficient means have done so otherwise than as the result of a mixture of ability and character, which will tend to be transmitted to their sons. But this is a rough and ready statement which needs qualification in several directions ; for outside the main block of boys who both deserve and get this training, there are perhaps three groups in respect of which the situation is

[1] *The School*, Home University Library, p. 147.

G

unsatisfactory. They are : (1) those who do not deserve it but get it; (2) those who deserve and get it, but whose parents cannot really afford it ; and (3) those who deserve it but do not get it. The first are the children of either the merely wealthy or the merely genteel, whose intelligence is mediocre, and who cumber the ground at public schools if they get there. Preparatory schools, being more numerous and less well-endowed than public schools, are perhaps specially tempted to take these boys and tinker them up, without much profound thought as to their future. Putting it quite crudely, our job is to get all our boys into public schools, chiefly by means of the Common Entrance Examination, but I feel sure that there ought to be an alternative which would sufficiently commend itself to parents, would cast no stigma on the preparatory school, and would at the same time reserve the present public schools for those who can be confidently recommended on every ground. It is, after all, only quite lately that a public school education has become such a fetish with the upper classes.

Take next the question of the "New Poor." Preparatory school education, in so far as it concerns boarders, is expensive. Headmasters may help in necessitous cases by reducing fees, to an extent which it is impossible and undesirable to estimate, but the standard fees of boarding schools vary roughly between £100 and £200 a year. If we take £150 as being a very fair average, it is obvious that a large sum is required to cover the eight or nine years which precede the university stage. Nor is it easy to see that the fees can be lowered, if the present standard of teaching and housing is to be maintained. A school equipped with playing-fields, sanatorium, and perhaps gymnasium, swimming-bath, and chapel, requires a heavy expenditure of capital, and the comparatively small numbers at many of the schools is probably uneconomic, for it is notorious that a large number of small units are a bigger problem financially than a few big ones. Profiteering by the proprietors of the school was always rare, and must now be almost impossible. Competition is so keen that few schools are able to secure more than a very narrow margin of profit, in relation to the risks involved. And, be it observed, public schools, in spite of endowments of which we know nothing, and in spite of the larger classes and other economies which should be possible with larger numbers, are obliged to charge fees slightly higher than those of preparatory schools. It is indeed doubtful whether our fees are high enough, for the question of remuneration of assistant masters is one that causes us anxiety. For the moment let us consider the case of the parent who has to spend from £1,200 to £1,500 on the education of each boy who does not rise to scholarship standard. Enormous sacrifices are being made in this cause, and the outer world knows little of what the professional classes in particular are prepared to deny themselves, in order to give their children the best start in life. One is reluctant to accept unreservedly the well-reasoned pessimism of Dean Inge, but however much one believes that Providence has compensations and fresh triumphs in store for the English race, it is impossible to avoid the conclusion that we are now living largely on capital amassed during a century-and-a-half before the Great War, and that the country is destined to grow poorer, at least for a time. The problem of finding the large sums necessary for education is likely to become more, rather than less, acute, and it is bound to increase the tendency, so regrettable from every point of view, towards smaller and ever smaller families in the classes from which the nation most needs recruits. For the father of many children, who is not within reach of a first-rate day school, has either to find a large sum for each boy (and it may cost hardly less nowadays to educate each girl), or else to condemn his children to what is regarded as an inferior form of education in an ordinary secondary school.

Here again there would seem to be room for the establishment of some alternative scheme which involved no loss of social prestige, and also for the simplification of preparatory school life in ways which would tend to keep down expense.

From another point of view I think it is possible to argue that we do too much for the boys. Their time is so fully occupied with a variety of occupations and entertainments, mostly of an agreeable nature, which are provided by the school authorities, that one wonders whether there is not some loss of initiative in seeking out occupations of their own. Certainly one hears parents remark that boys get bored with the holidays, and though the old joy of going home still persists, there is often as much enthusiasm for going back to school. It is certainly right that boys should be happy at school ; it is certainly wrong that they should be bored and unresourceful at home. This is a point worth remembering, when considering the addition of extras to the school programme.

One is also tempted to think that it is unnatural and therefore wrong to remove boys from their home surroundings during two-thirds of the year, from the early age of eight or nine, and it is a phenomenon which causes foreign observers a good deal of surprise. But surely it depends entirely on the home. Conditions of modern life are such that one may say of the majority of homes, that a boy is either likely to be neglected or spoilt if always there. Another point which should not be lost sight of is the large number of English parents who are forced by the exigencies of Empire to live abroad. And there is no doubt that the average boy benefits by the association with others and the enlargement of his horizon—spiritual, intellectual, physical— which comes with his entry into school life. It is difficult to assess rightly the relative merits of day and boarding schools. Theoretically perhaps the day school which has managed to establish a real spiritual hold over its sons, backed up by a home in which the parents have the wisdom, leisure, and enthusiasm to co-operate in the work of education, is the ideal ; in practice the boarding school has been found to give the best result.

But it is time to turn to the third group in respect of which the present system is open to criticism. This, it will be remembered, contained those who deserve a public school education but do not get it. It is possible to regard us as a barrier standing between the elementary and the public school, since by imparting secondary education from about the age of ten, we have placed the public school scholarships far beyond the reach of elementary boys. To throw open the public schools to their ablest representatives is undoubtedly an honourable ideal, and may be conceived to be in accordance with the plans of those men, such as William of Wykeham and Colet, who originally founded public schools. How far the demand exists, or could be stimulated, I am unable to say, but I feel certain that the preparatory schools would be ready to play their part in any scheme which was likely to promote better class understanding or the national well-being in any way.

But what part should they play ? It would undoubtedly be possible, as has I believe been suggested, for public schools to resume taking boys at eleven, contenting themselves with a purely elementary entrance examination, or to provide their own preparatory departments as is already done at Christ's Hospital and elsewhere, but it is important to realise what this would entail. Preparatory schools, as we know them, would disappear (for it would be absurd to maintain them for the elementary education of boys under eleven only), and with them one of the most characteristic achievements of the Victorian Educational Renaissance. When one considers the deadening effect of eight or more years in the same school, the physical changes that come at about the age of fourteen, and the difficulty of providing rules and routine equally suitable for boys of eleven and eighteen, it must be admitted that much wisdom underlay the decision of Arnold that there ought to be a division between the parts of school life. It is not for me to estimate the difficulties which would confront the already congested public schools, but I may be permitted to doubt whether they would continue to hold the majority of their pupils to the age of eighteen, as they do at present. The loss of capital involved in the use of so many well-equipped preparatory school buildings, would perhaps be less serious than the dispersal of devoted staffs, and of fine traditions laboriously built up through many decades. I can hardly feel that the number of elementary school candidates would be sufficient to justify so wholesale a piece of destruction as this. I would suggest that, if there is to be experiment in this direction, it would be far more truly progressive to admit a proportion of elementary boys to preparatory schools first. The age of eleven is usually taken as the point of classification for admission to central or secondary schools, and the beginnings of such subjects as Latin could advantageously be postponed to this age, if the public schools made it possible by lowering their entrance requirements. Though I am quite aware of the difficulties, which the differences of home environment would create, I believe them to be not insuperable. The boys themselves would be far less self-conscious, and far more likely to receive a favourable reception at the public schools if they came to us first at eleven. The chief obstacle, of course, is finance, but there is already in existence an arrangement by which the boys accepted for the Foundation of at least one public school are maintained in selected preparatory schools at the former's expense, until the time arrives for them to go on. This plan would seem to be capable of extension.

Meanwhile there are many ways in which we can mitigate the charge (which we cannot hope altogether to escape) of helping to stereotype class distinctions. Not more than one per cent. of the two million English boys between the ages of eight and thirteen are in preparatory schools. The 20,000 who are, are certainly a privileged few. One of the first duties of those that teach them should be to imbue them with a sense of the responsibilities which their privileges ought to carry, to instil the spirit of self-sacrifice, of that Divine compassion which leads to energetic action for the betterment of those less well off than themselves.

I have had the experience during my student days of teaching in an elementary school, and over a number of years since then, I have had the privilege of approximately equal intimacy with some scores of boys of widely different positions in the social scale. I have taken them to camp together and I am proud to call them equally my friends. I say emphatically that great as are the differences which varying social conditions produce, there is a common quality of British boyhood which far transcends them all, and the different classes have a great deal to learn from one another. Many schoolmasters and parents already realise the need for a campaign against snobbishness, but I am not sure that the national importance of the question is sufficiently studied, and there is room for an advance all along the line.

An excellent weapon lies to our hand by which the danger of class misunderstanding may be combated ; it is the Boy Scout movement. I am glad to say this is gaining more and more recognition in public and preparatory schools. I wish it might receive universal recognition, for I believe it to be a force for good of tremendous value. It is not so much that our boys need scout training, for our whole system is intended to teach the principles which underlie scouting, and though it will certainly do them good, the school programme may be overfull without it. It is rather that here is a great common ideal and a meeting ground for boys of all classes and conditions of life. It may be desirable for the school to have its own troop, but a real link can and should be established between it and the local scouts, for boys who wear the same uniform, pass the same tests, enter for the same competitions, and meet perhaps in holiday camps, can never feel that they are other than the same flesh and blood. Of the international value of the Scout movement it is not necessary here to speak.

There are other ways—by playing football and cricket matches, for instance, with elementary teams, or by lending ground and instructor's time to help with games—in which we can assist. Universities have given a splendid lead in this direction.

No one can fail to notice the beneficial effect on the life of a whole town, of the existence within it of a public school. The preparatory schools ought, in their smaller way, to be centres of light of a similar kind. I think it is possible that we withdraw the boys too much from the outer world. This is chiefly due to a fear of infectious disease. It is of course one of the defects of a boarding school that infection has a good run, if it once gets in, and some terms are quite overshadowed by an epidemic of some trifling kind. We are in the hands of the doctors in this matter, but one sometimes wonders whether we should be really worse off if we mixed a little more freely with the outer world. We may be inflicting an injury both on the community and on the boys themselves, if we hold ourselves too rigidly aloof.

V

Preparatory schools are typical of English institutions in having grown up almost imperceptibly, as the result of individual initiative. The aroma of the Board of Education has as yet been borne but faintly on the air in our direction. I do not know that we are particularly anxious for bureaucratic intervention, and it would be a great loss if that intense individuality which at present characterises preparatory schools were to disappear. Yet many schools have already applied for government inspection and have found the inspectors helpful and sympathetic. And have not more august institutions—the University of Oxford, for instance —found that the state after all possesses tactful qualities ?

For many years the insufficient prospects of our assistant masters has been a point of anxiety, and long efforts to establish a pension scheme under government guarantee, though without the use of any public money, have at last met with a certain measure of success. To participation in this scheme, government recognition of the efficiency of the school is a necessary preliminary, and closer co-operation with the Board of Education would also be essential, if we were to take our share in the broadening of the basis on which boys are admitted to public schools. If there is a certain loss of freedom to be regretted in these tendencies, there are also compensating advantages. Any lingering doubts as to our efficiency would be brought to a clear issue, the possibly excessive numbers of small preparatory schools would be held in check, the profession would become more attractive to able and ambitious men, and we should have the satisfaction of feeling ourselves more firmly welded into the national educational system.

I have tried faithfully to lay bare the weaknesses, as well as the strength, of the preparatory school, and to suggest remedies for some of the shortcomings. We shall do well to recognise that the latter exist, but given courage and good-will, there is no reason why they should not all be overcome.

It is particularly easy to attack any educational system, for the subject is one which lies partly within the experience and interest of all, whilst the results must always remain to a great extent incalculable and intangible. It is easy also to construct a Utopian system in which constraint or boredom, extravagance or class privilege, superfluous or unpractical knowledge, are completely done away with, and the ideal type of human being is produced. But men will not readily agree as to what is the ideal type, or what knowledge is superfluous or unpractical. Dreams and theories have their value, but in the infinite complexity of human nature it is, alas, easy to lose sight of one aspect of our problem, while pursuing another to its logical conclusion.

It is unwise to set aside the accumulated wisdom and experience of mankind, and, for the sake of what might be, to undervalue what is.

And in connection with preparatory schools we have certain facts which cannot lightly be dismissed by any true patriot, or by any wise reformer. First, they have won for themselves a firm position as a portion of the " public school " system. Secondly, they are the creation of a band of enthusiasts who have risked, and are risking, both health and wealth in a single-minded desire to give of their best to the training of the youth of the nation. Thirdly, a high degree of efficiency is, in fact, maintained. Fourthly, they have commended themselves increasingly to British parents, and the demand for them is at any rate not diminishing yet. Lastly, wherever amongst Anglo-Saxon communities the other system (which may be characterised as one of class-unconscious day schools) has been tried, whether in Scotland, in the U.S.A., or in the Dominions, it has been found wanting, and boarding schools of the English type have begun to spring up.

And whether we judge him by the crucial test of the years 1914–1918, or by his record in the administration of the modern world, we can scarcely say that the boy who spent four of the awakening years of his life, fought his first battles, and learned the first lessons of manhood in his preparatory school, has not made good.

REFERENCES

BENSON, E. F. David Blaize.
HARRIS, S. S. The Master and his Boys. Warren & Son, Winchester.
HUGHES, TOM. Tom Brown's Schooldays.
KING, H. C. Article in " The Journal of Education," April, 1926.
NORWOOD AND HOPE. Higher Education of Boys in England. Murray, 1908.
SADLER, M. E. Preparatory Schools. Board of Education (Special Reports), 1900.
WAUGH, ALEC. Public School Life. Collins.
Memorials of Lionel Helbert. Oxford Univ. Press.
The Preparatory Schools' Review (Quarterly).
The Story of Twyford School (privately printed). Warren & Son, Winchester.

SECONDARY EDUCATION

CHART SHOWING

I. The small transfer to Secondary or Central Schools about the age of 11

II. The transfer to Evening Classes and Day Continuation Schools about the age of 14

III. The comparative neglect of children after the age of 14

the various types of Education

University of London Press, Ltd.

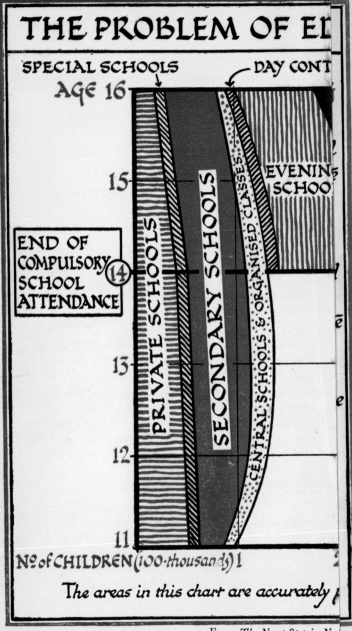

SPECIAL SCHOOLS   DAY CONT

AGE 16

15

END OF
COMPULSORY
SCHOOL
ATTENDANCE ⑭

13

12

11

PRIVATE SCHOOLS

SECONDARY SCHOOLS

CENTRAL SCHOOLS & ORGANISED CLASSES

EVENING
SCHOO

Nº of CHILDREN (100-thousands) 1

The areas in this chart are accurately

From *The Next Step in Nat*

CHAPTER V

THE BOYS' DAY SCHOOL

By R. F. CHOLMELEY

I PREFACE this chapter with a diagram for three reasons. First of all it is a pictorial representation of the facts, so far as they can be so represented, which form the subject-matter of what I have to say. In the second place, " secondary education " is one of those expressions which are difficult because of their apparent simplicity : it stands, or has at different times stood, for three things, a stage, a type, and a standard ; as a stage it stands for what comes next to primary education ; as a type it stands for something which, though related to a certain intelligible classification of things to be learnt, is constantly being modified and enlarged, but the fundamental idea of which can only be expressed by a still more elusive name, humanism, or a liberal education ; as a standard it aims at that measure of erudition of which universities can take cognisance. The part that secondary schools will play in the future as an element in the national system will depend largely upon the manner in which these three meanings can be brought into a harmonious relation.

My third reason is this. After remarking in his introductory chapter upon the unifying effect of the measures which threw open universities and schools to the Nonconformists, Professor Dover Wilson goes on to say, " Our industrial troubles arise, I am convinced, from the same

cause as produced the denominational strife of previous
generations ; a whole section of the people feels itself to be
disinherited, to be living and working outside the pale of
privilege and opportunity." The two spaces on my picture
that are wholly white and wholly black respectively show how
much has yet to be done before that feeling of disinheritance
can be said to be an illusion. What the boys' day schools
are doing and may go on to do towards the extinction
of that feeling constitutes the chief justification for what
follows.

The story of an educational system is not generally
thought of as a subject for romance. Yet every educational
system must be judged by the quality of the institutions
that it creates and cherishes : and of all institutions none are
more essentially romantic than universities and schools.
They are romantic in two directions ; whether we look back
at their history or forward to their future possibilities, they
are, in the widest sense of the words, poetically exciting.
This has its disadvantages. Poetry may be a criticism of
life ; but the charm of poetry is sometimes due to the fact
that in casting upon the facts of life a " light that never was
on land or sea " it lures us away from the contemplation of
the facts as they are ; we are amused, and we are satisfied
to be amused. Whether there is any human activity about
which we should be satisfied to be merely amused is a large
question ; at any rate, just as the virtuous person, knowing
nothing about crime, and regarding it as something with
which he has nothing to do, reads the most preposterous
stories about crime for his amusement, so elderly people in
general, knowing nothing, or having forgotten everything,
about schools, read *Stalky and Co.* and *The Hill*, with the
result that not only the facts but the essential romance, the
real and fruitful poetical excitement belonging to the
adventure of education, passes them by and they never
understand it at all.

Yet the position, the quality, the possibilities of our

schools—and perhaps above all of our secondary day schools—have never been more exciting than they are to-day, never more worthy of imaginative interest. Noble as were the aims of the great founders of the sixteenth and seventeenth centuries, great as was the advance from the Idea of Wykeham to the Idea of Colet—which is nothing less than the advance from the idea of professional education to the idea of education in general—their outlook was inevitably narrower than ours. They did not, they could not, contemplate, as we must contemplate to-day, the education of a people. They laid the foundations : Wykeham saw that the Church must be learned or the Church would perish ; Colet saw that for England to hold her own among the nations nothing could be more effective than the provision in England of the highest type of education then conceivable " for children of all nations and countries indifferently." Cranmer, anticipating the Departmental Committee on Scholarships and Free Places, said : " If the gentleman's son be apt to learning, let him be admitted ; if not, let the poor man's child, that is apt, enter his room."

I have said that the story of the day schools is a romantic story ; and so it is : and there is no reason for demanding that a story should be long in order that it may be recognised as romantic. It is only a certain incurable shyness that prevents us from making the foundation of a free secondary school by a municipality as stimulating an achievement as the foundation of Harrow by John Lyon or of Rugby by Lawrence Sheriff. It is odd, when you come to think of it, that so many of those who are most interested in the old foundations, who have owed their own education to them, are still inclined to be horrified at the idea of free secondary education, which is just what most of the old founders desired within the limits of their own vision to establish. In any case, this shyness is a fault ; it leads to putting up imperfectly equipped schools in odd corners on exiguous plots of ground, taking no trouble to provide them with a governing body or a cheerful name or any of the things great or small that help a school to develop a tradition of personality and self-respect, as if they were of no more spiritual importance than an incinerator. And with this vice of shyness goes another, which is in some ways a contrary characteristic, that sort of secretive individualism which, being fast bound in misery and iron to the competitive spirit, regards every school as a rival to every other school and every new type of school as a rival to the old, with the result that no school either contributes to or gets from the common stock of educational experience anything like what it might either get or contribute. I believe that there is much less of this spirit than there was ; but it is a growth whose roots are intertwined with the fibres of our national character, and it is not likely that it will ever be quite eradicated ; and it is one of the things that prevent us from making the most of our heritage.

What is the heritage of the Boys' Day School in England ? It is in part what it shares with all other schools, the story, the whole collection of stories that go back, as Professor Dover Wilson tells us in his introductory chapter, at least to Alfred the Great. There are schools that go back further : Canterbury, York, and Carlisle, for example, existed in the seventh century ; King's School, Rochester, boldly gives its date as 604 ; there was a tradition, commemorated in one of the few really good school songs of modern origin, that Alfred went to school at Sherborne, though the school authorities do not countenance the tradition except in song.[1] But all down the centuries, sometimes rarely, sometimes in remarkable numbers, schools were being founded, by churchmen, by nobles, by merchants, by yeomen ; Dr. Leach says that by the end of the Middle Ages there was one grammar school to every 5,625 people, and it has been estimated that at the time of the Reformation there were three hundred in existence. What proportion of these were

---

[1] The words are by the Rev. J. H. F. Peile.

day schools it is not easy to determine ; nor is it important, for the distinction between day schools and boarding schools as representing types of education is a distinction of recent growth.   I think it can be said that at any rate the lay founders in general, and many of the clerical founders, were chiefly concerned with providing for the children of some particular place in which they were interested.   The question whether it was better for children to be educated away from home or not was never in their minds.   I doubt if even the point of view of the younger Pliny occurred to any of them, as he put it to his fellow townsmen of Como when, after urging them to put up a school at Como instead of sending their sons to Milan, he added that if the school at Como got a good name they would find the Milanese sending their sons to it.   If Pliny had been making the same kind of appeal to-day he might have gone on to say something like this : " Establish at Como a school that shall not only meet the needs of the present inhabitants of Como, and allow for the natural expansion of the town, but shall by the excellence and cheapness of the education provided attract the attention and extort the admiration of the whole of Italy and ultimately even of the whole Empire.   One of two things will follow—perhaps both : half-pay officers, retired administrators, all kinds of people who want their sons educated and who are not tied to living in a particular place, will come and settle at Como, to the great benefit not only of the school but of the trade and general prosperity of the town.   Or, again, parents who desire the kind of education that your school will provide, but who are unfortunately unable to come and settle in this desirable spot, will urge you to make provision for taking their sons as boarders ; in which case your assistant masters will make money—even your headmaster, if you are foolish enough to allow him to take boarders—and you will not have to pay such large salaries."   Examples of both these processes are numerous in England ; perhaps the most conspicuous

H

—particularly interesting because it is an example of both—
is Bedford, where the two great schools of the Bedford
Charity educate between them some 1,500 boys, of whom
about 350 are boarders.

The story of the endowed schools may be read in the
works of Dr. Leach and in the Reports of the Royal Commissions of 1858 (the Newcastle Commission), of 1861
(the Clarendon or Public Schools Commission), and of
1864 (the Taunton or Endowed Schools Commission).
The Clarendon Commission dealt with the nine great school
endowments—Eton, Winchester, Westminster, Charterhouse, St. Paul's, Merchant Taylors', Harrow, Rugby, and
Shrewsbury. Three of these, Westminster, St. Paul's, and
Merchant Taylors', were and are wholly or predominantly
day schools, though at St. Paul's about 10 per cent. and at
Westminster about 35 per cent. of the boys are boarders.
The Taunton Commission dealt with 782 schools, containing at that time 36,874 pupils, about one-fourth of whom
were boarders. The Newcastle Commission had dealt
with such of the old grammar schools as had been reduced
to providing elementary teaching only. It is clearly impossible within the limits of a single chapter to do justice even
to those aspects of the history of the endowed schools as are
strictly relevant to my subject ; but two observations may
be made, because they bear directly upon the relation of
that history to the state of day-school education to-day.
The first is this, that in the Report of the Taunton Commission it is stated that " in at least two-thirds of the places
in England named as towns in the census there is no public
school at all above the primary schools, and in the remaining
third the school is often insufficient in size or in quality "
(Report, Vol. I, p. 102). I do not know how many places
in England are now named as towns in the census ; but
according to the Report of the Board of Education for
1925–1926 there were, in October, 1926, 1,453 secondary
schools in England recognised as efficient by the Board.

My second observation concerns what had been happening to most of the old endowed schools since their foundation. Some had quickly gained and never entirely lost a high reputation. Some had passed through strange experiences, especially during the eighteenth century, when in some cases the post of headmaster became a comfortable sinecure in that age of sinecures. To a large number nothing at all happened; like a stream which, before it has had time to become anything particular, goes underground and trickles along invisible till the moment comes for it to emerge and collect rain and affluents and become a noticeable piece of water, these schools just continued to exist. That they did continue to exist—some, of course, did not—was largely due to the tenacity with which English people stick to a trust involving the administration of property, even when they have no very clear notion of what might be done with it. Of the school with which I am best acquainted nothing is known for about 250 years after its foundation except what can be gathered from the minutes of the governing body about their relations with its headmasters —how one petitioned for an usher to help him and was told that he might have an usher provided that he paid the usher's salary; how one was imprisoned under the Commonwealth and was allowed to have his salary paid to his wife till he got out; and how another was more than once dismissed but could not be persuaded to go until he was given the equivalent of a month's salary—amounting to £6 13s. 4d. These are but indications of a history, some of it no doubt serious history, but they are scarcely more. The point I want to make is that the revival of the interest in public education, and in particular of the aim to make public education accessible everywhere and to all who needed it, owed very much to the mere existence of these earlier foundations. The fact that they had money was something; some of them even had much money, more than they had ever expected, more than they knew what to do with ; and that eased the financial side of the new developments. But more important even than their money was the appeal that they made to the historical sense—and the historical sentiment. If all of them had been as imperfect, considered as places of education, as many of them were, it would still be worth while to remember that they furnished not merely the tradition of a particular type of education, but a dignity and a romantic inspiration to every kind of new development such as no country but our own has enjoyed. And it is because, from the very nature of the case, the day school has gained most and has most to gain from this sort of inspiration, that we must not forget the old grammar schools.

I turn now to statistics. I do so with reluctance, because I distrust them. They are like miracles, valuable so long as you do not use them to prove anything, but are content to display them as illustrations. My statistics will not be of that precise and comprehensive kind by which Ministers are enabled to answer or to evade questions in Parliament, and which when they are published tell you everything except the one or two things you happen to want to know. But I have to answer the question : What is a boys' secondary day school ? and I cannot answer it in terms of ideas without first trying to answer it in terms of facts. Let us, therefore, observe which are the boys' secondary day schools, and, generally speaking, where they are, in accordance with the Aristotelian principle that we must attend to the " which " before we can discover the " what." It would, of course, be possible to begin with the definition and to sort the facts accordingly ; indeed, nobody can sort the facts without having at least the elements of a definition in his mind. But whether the Idea is prior to the facts or the facts are prior to the Idea, I think that in this particular case the facts should come first. The difficulty of taking any other course was felt, you will remember, by the White Knight when, in answer to Alice's intelligent questions, he tried to make it clear to her in advance what he was going to sing about. The same difficulty occurred to Professor Ker when he desired to explain exactly what he meant by a ballad ; and Professor Ker got out of his difficulty as I propose to get out of mine. The White Knight's method may fall to be considered later : Professor Ker said : " A ballad is *The Milldams of Binnorie* and *Sir Patrick Spens* and *The Douglas Tragedy* and *Lord Randal* and *Childe Maurice*, and things of that sort." Very well : the boys' secondary day school is St. Paul's and Merchant Taylors' and George Green's School, Poplar and—dare I say it ?— King Edward VII. School and all the other boys' secondary schools in Sheffield, and schools of that sort.

The figures that I submit, inaccurate as they probably are, are compiled on the assumption that it is important to know roughly how many schools of that sort there are in England now, and what they are doing. They come from the Board of Education's list of Efficient Secondary Schools, commonly known as List 60 (1925–26) ; and anybody can work them out for himself. But although, as I have said, they are probably inaccurate, I am quite certain that they are accurate enough to illustrate the Idea, which is all that figures are good for. List 60 contains the names of 1,473 schools, not counting preparatory schools (which in my opinion ought not to be there at all). This is 20 more than the Board's figure which I quoted before, since List 60 belongs to a slightly later date. Of these schools 295 are not in receipt of grants either from the state or from local education authorities ; and all the 295 except 7 (Westminster, the City of London School, Highgate, Rochester Cathedral School, Truro Cathedral School, Liverpool College, and Birkenhead) and a few proprietary schools, are essentially boarding schools. Add to these 7 St. Paul's, Merchant Taylors', and Mercers' School, the only day schools of any importance, so far as I know, which are still shy of inspection by the Board, and you will observe that there are only 10 public secondary day schools for boys which do not definitely form part of the educational system supported by the aid of public funds. Day-school education is the form of education for which the state and the local education authorities are almost entirely responsible, responsible both as guaranteeing, so far as they can guarantee, its efficiency, and as providing for its financial stability.

Now, as to the number of the schools so guaranteed and so supported, the figures are as follows : 324 are boys' day schools in the strictest sense, 285 are day schools for boys and girls—generally speaking, in fairly equal numbers. These 609, then, may be considered as day schools without qualification ; the number of boarders educated in them is quite inconsiderable ; they educate, or were educating in 1926, 150,640 boys. Besides these there are a considerable number of schools educating both boarders and day boys, and the question naturally arises, which of them should be considered as day schools admitting boarders and which as boarding schools admitting day boys ? This question cannot be properly answered by figures, except in so far as the character of the whole society of which a school consists can be thought to depend on the relative numbers of the day boys and boarders in that school. I have assumed that where the boarders are more than half the school, the boarding school characteristics will be found to predominate, and to influence the day boys and their homes to such an extent that the Idea of a day school will not have much of a chance. Where the proportion of day boys is much under 50 per cent. it has no chance at all ; there is, I think, no kind of school life more generally unsatisfactory than that of the day boy attending a large boarding school. Whatever the authorities may try to do for him, the spirit of the herd—I use the term technically and in no offensive sense—is sure to be too much for t hem : the day boy is, so far as the rest of the boys are concerned, there on sufferance, and sufferance is the badge of his tribe. There are, however, 129 schools in which the

proportion of boarders varies from 5 to 50 per cent. ; in
110 of these it is 30 per cent. or less, in the other 19 it is
between 30 and 50 ; the 110 include 21,515 day boys,
the 19 include 2,010. If we take all these together with my
earlier figures, the total number of schools will be found to
be 738, and the total number of boys 174,165.

As I may as well give all the statistics together by which
I want to illustrate the subject, I add that 64,849 of these
boys pay no fees, and that about 400 of the schools are
foundation schools, most of them of considerable antiquity.
There are 30 schools entirely free : 14 (out of a total of 15)
in the administrative county of Durham, 5 in Bradford,
3 each in Manchester and Sheffield, 1 each in Halifax,
Oldham, Plymouth, Salford, and Wallasey. The fees
payable in the rest vary from £1 17s. 6d. at Warrington to
£60 at Westminster ; but the Warrington fee is quite
exceptional, fees being generally anything from £9 to £20.
An appreciable number of schools charge between £20 and
£30, and anything over £30 is rare, at any rate among
grant-earning schools ; there must be very few schools in
which the fee-payer contributes more than half the cost of
his education. At St. Paul's some thirty years ago, when
about 450 boys out of 600 or more paid £24 9s., the total
just about covered the salaries of the staff—and in those days
salaries were low. " The average cost per pupil in grant-
earning secondary schools has risen from about £16 before
the War to about £27 at the present time." [1] The L. C. C.
estimates the cost of tuition in London at £42, but when some
years ago the fees were revised, the main if not the only
principle upon which the revision was based was that in
each of the districts into which the county was divided for
this purpose there should be a sufficient number of different
rates to suit the resources of all or nearly all sorts of parents,
and in general fees tend to be fixed at a figure which will
attract enough fee-payers to keep the school full.

[1] Board of Education, Educational Pamphlets, No. 50.

One disadvantage of this, which is a really important disadvantage, is that where a number of schools are more or less equally accessible the more well-to-do parents tend to flock to the more expensive schools. They think that they secure a better education because they pay more for it, and the sense of social distinction which is one of the plagues of education reinforces their credulity. If there were no other argument in favour of the total abolition of fees, the chance of dealing an effective stroke at this state of mind would make it worth trying. Only it must be done thoroughly. I wish to pillory nobody, but it ought to be said that an education authority which is content to have half a dozen free secondary schools and one where fees are charged may be aiming at the production of an intellectual aristocracy, but is certain to be fostering those delusions about the moral value of money which we all deplore, especially in those who are better off than ourselves. Since one of the relevant facts about the day school, as part of the system of public education, is the fact that hardly anybody pays in fees for what he gets out of it, the question whether it would be better to make it wholly free cannot be disregarded. The answer must be a matter of opinion, since it depends upon the effects that the change would produce. Ultimately we have to consider not only whether it would be a good thing in itself—if there is anything connected with education that can be so described—but whether the community is ready for it.

The same question arose twenty years ago when the Free Place regulations were invented. I remember looking in at the office of Special Inquiries and Reports at the Board of Education not long after the issue of those regulations. I was told that a letter had just been received from the headmaster of a grammar school in a provincial town. It was a day school with provision for boarders, and the boarding-house had for many years been comfortably filled, largely by the sons of those who were in the habit of coming in from the country-side to the town for various purposes of business. The headmaster stated in his letter that owing to the impression made by the Free Place regulations upon the imagination of the parents he had just said farewell to the last of his boarders, all of whom—and all the prospect of there ever being any more—·had now been transferred to a proprietary school in the town which had previously all but perished of its own inefficiency. Well, that was a tragedy, and there were others like it ; but they were not fatal either to the Free Place system or to the schools, in the long run. And for all the dogged persistence with which we cling to our social distinctions and the incredible number of fine shades that can be discovered by those who look for them, the Free Place system has been a great leveller, and has made the day schools in particular a powerful instrument for pooling the intellectual and spiritual resources of all sorts and conditions of men.

There is one set of figures to which I wish to draw attention before I come to the general reflections that I have in mind. One of the most striking developments in day school education—hardly realised, I think, by those who are not in actual touch with it—has been the growth of the mixed school. The reader will notice that the proportion of mixed schools to boys' schools in the figures given above is almost exactly as 7 to 8, and the number of boys educated in them a little less than 2 to 5. The geographical distribution of the mixed schools is of some interest, because the most obvious characteristic of the day school is that it serves a particular area, and it is natural to ask whether the difference between one area and another in this particular has any significance. The complete figures are as follows :

			Boys.	*Mixed.*
Bedfordshire ..	..	..	1	1
Berkshire ..	..	..	2	2
Buckinghamshire	..	..	0	5
Cambridgeshire	..	..	3	0

				Boys.	Mixed.
Cheshire	..	..	..	9	8
Cornwall	..	..	..	5	8
Cumberland	..	..	..	2	7
Derbyshire	..	..	..	3	14
Devonshire	..	..	..	9	11
Dorsetshire	..	..	..	1	8
Durham	..	..	..	9	13
Essex	..	..	..	8	8
Gloucestershire	..	..	..	8	16
Hampshire	..	..	..	7	13
Herefordshire	..	..	..	1	4
Hertfordshire	..	..	..	5	0
Huntingdonshire	..	..	..	0	3
Kent	..	..	..	15	2
Lancashire	..	..	..	38	33
Leicestershire	..	..	..	5	8
Lincolnshire	..	..	..	7	6
London	..	..	..	40	3 [1]
Middlesex	..	..	..	14	18
Norfolk	..	..	..	2	2
Northamptonshire	..	..	..	3	1
Northumberland	..	..	..	10	5
Nottinghamshire	..	..	..	2	5
Oxfordshire	..	..	..	3	3
Rutland	..	..	..	—	—
Shropshire	..	..	..	5	2
Somersetshire	..	..	..	7	5
Staffordshire	..	..	..	11	5
Suffolk	..	..	..	2	9
Surrey	..	..	..	21	0
Sussex	..	..	..	6	1
Warwickshire	..	..	..	15	3
Westmorland	..	..	..	0	2
Wiltshire	..	..	..	1	10
Worcestershire	..	..	..	4	5
Yorks, East Riding	..	..	3	2
Yorks, North Riding	..	..	3	8
Yorks, West Riding	..	..	34	26

[1] Including the Lycée Français de Londres.

It is difficult to draw any general conclusions. Buckinghamshire, Derbyshire, Durham, Gloucestershire, Hampshire, Lancashire, Middlesex, Suffolk, Wiltshire, and the West Riding appear to like mixed schools; Kent, London, Northumberland, Staffordshire, Surrey, and Warwickshire appear not to like them. In Lancashire, 25 out of the 33 are under the County Authority; in the West Riding, 23 out of 26; in Durham, 11 out of 13; in Gloucestershire, 13 out of 16; in Hampshire, 11 out of 13; in Derbyshire, the whole 14; in Devonshire, 10 out of 11. Clearly the origin of most of them, whether as new schools or as old schools remodelled, was due to convenience, including financial convenience; but the interesting point about them is the growth of a belief in them on educational grounds, and the remarkable success of their work. A spirited expression of this belief is to be found in a little pamphlet written by the headmaster of Holt School, Liverpool, and published in 1923 by the Headmasters' Association.

"At the present time," says the author, "educational writers group together the schools of a newer type where individual freedom is cultivated, where outdoor education is encouraged, and where boys and girls are educated together, as belonging to the vanguard of educational progress." And again—"In the social education of young England the mixed schools are the pioneers, and if the schools are to be judged by the men and women they have produced, these schools are well content to be judged by their products. They have produced men and women capable of serving their country in time of crisis, and capable of working sensibly side by side in the professions or in business, and—a very high test— capable of meeting in friendliness and without frivolity in intelligent recreation." [1]

At the end of the Board of Education's Educational Pamphlet No. 50, in which the late Chief Inspector, Mr.

[1] "The Case for Co-education in Secondary Schools."

W. C. Fletcher, surveys that recent development of secondary schools which owes more to his wisdom and enthusiasm than I can here even try to describe, two questions are asked : " First, are the schools doing their obvious and necessary work of teaching with reasonable efficiency ? Second, are they in the main such places as their pupils will look back to with respect and affection, and to which they in their turn will wish to send their children ? " These questions have to be answered by every kind of school ; and the day school may at least claim its part in the satisfaction with which Mr. Fletcher answers for the secondary schools as a whole. Any one who wants to understand the grounds of that satisfaction should study the pamphlet ; what we are concerned with for the moment is the Idea that determines the meaning of the questions, where the day school is concerned. I have already turned for help to Professor Ker ; I turn to him again—and I beg you not to be upset by the suggestion that what is true of a kind of poetry may be worth considering in relation to a kind of school. " What," says Professor Ker, " is the truth about Ballads ? The truth is that the Ballad is an Idea, a Poetical Form, which can take up any matter, *and does not leave that matter as it was before*." Is not this just what is at the back of the mind of that most pathetic figure among parents, the parent who says, " I have brought him to you because I do want him to grow up a little gentleman ? " An aspiration not to be despised, if it were understood. We do expect schools not to leave their material as it was before ; we have no right to expect them to transform it, though even that does sometimes seem to happen, but we expect them, each in its own way, to cherish and protect and inspire those for whom they are responsible, and thus not merely to carry out their " obvious and necessary work " but to become places commanding and deserving the devotion of their scholars and doing great and lasting service to the community.

" Each in its own way "—what, then, is the way of the

day school, that gives it its special opportunity of service ? One answer is obvious enough : it brings the home into education ; the converse is less obvious but equally important —it brings education into the home. The boy's family and his school are necessarily in partnership—some would say in a conspiracy against him, and there is something in that disrespectful way of putting it ; when there is, it provides a good reason for sending him to a boarding school, since a boy who is too efficiently shepherded by his elders may never learn to have a soul of his own. This, however, is not a very common danger ; on the other hand, the value of a really understood partnership between home and school seems to me to be still imperfectly appreciated. There are still far too many parents who are content to believe that the schoolmaster knows more about their boys than they do—or than anybody has a right to expect them to. There are still schoolmasters who say that parents are a nuisance, which may be true, and who keep them at the greatest possible distance, which is flat treachery to the Idea. What this partnership does for the boy is to give him a chance of learning all the time how to be a son and a brother as well as learning how to be a schoolboy ; what it does for the parents is not only to keep them in touch with their son's education, to enable them to interest themselves continuously in his work and his friendships, but to educate them continuously in the art of being parents ; what it does for the schoolmaster is not only to enable him to meet his boys " new every morning with the sun " or thereabouts, conscious that at least somebody else shares with him the blame for whatever mischief they may have been up to since he saw them last, but in a word to domesticate him. It is, or should be, impossible for the headmaster, or for any master in a day school, to forget that he is an element in the home life of every boy in the school, any more than he can forget that every boy's home life is an element in the school's efficiency.

These characteristics of day-school education are sufficiently obvious : the other main characteristic, also obvious
enough, but not yet made enough use of to enable the
school to do all that it might do for the common good, is the
fact that a day school serves a particular and, generally
speaking, a limited area. In London, and in large cities
generally, two or three or more schools will be found to
serve the same area, or at any rate there will be a certain
amount of overlapping ; but even in these cases it will
seldom be found that the day school is not primarily the
school of its neighbourhood. Surely, then, it is one of the
functions of the school to be a centre of civilisation for the
area which it serves ; and if this is true it is the duty of those
responsible for the establishment and the equipment and
the government of schools to see that both the material and
the spiritual conditions are such as to make that function
easy to perform. So far as the schools are concerned, a
great deal is done in this direction all over the country ;
there is even sometimes a danger that it may be overdone.
The headmaster of to-day has not only to be ruthless in
filling his wastepaper-basket with appeals to get his pupils to
subscribe to every sort of society and movement that wants
money, but to decide how much the school as such can do for
the entertainment or even the enlightenment of the neighbourhood without spoiling the work which must be his
prime care, or without boring everybody concerned to tears.
What he has to do is to get the respect and affection of his
neighbours for their school by showing that in the fullest
sense of the words it looks after their sons ; and whatever
else he may do, it is what those sons feel that the school
has meant to them that will be his chief witness.

But if the school is to be a centre of civilisation it must be
allowed both to look like one and feel like one ; and perhaps
nothing in the future of the day schools is more important
than the measure in which those who establish, equip, and
administer them understand and meet these two needs. Of

administration there is this to be said, that no degree of
official comfort—even though called by those who enjoy
it " ease of administration "—no adventures in search of
economy ought to be accepted as an excuse for failing to
respect and cherish the claim of every school to have a
personality of its own. The precise form of government
may vary according to the circumstances ; the education
committee of a local authority may be imbued with the
right spirit and may have its officials sufficiently well in
hand to see that the right spirit informs its actions ; but the
surest guarantee that the personality of a school will be
continuously respected and not blown about by the changing
winds of political doctrine is the presence on the governing
body of a strong and permanent element devoted to the
interests of that particular school. I will give two examples
of the sort of thing that ought to be impossible, one from the
recent past, one from actual existing practice. After the
War a certain local education authority devised a form of
commemorative album in which each school should record
the names of its scholars who had fallen, together with a
particular kind of hole in the wall, protected by a particular
kind of glass door, and locked with a particular kind of key,
in which the album should be kept. Any school could
have all this for the asking, but no school which preferred
its own artistic expression of its own feeling could have a
penny towards the cost of it. And at the present moment
there are education committees under which no school
can change a textbook unless all the others, with the consent
of the Director of Education, change it too.

So much for the soul of the school ; but as Aristotle
observed, προσδεῖται ὁ εὐδαίμων τῶν ἐν σώματι ἀγαθῶν,
Happiness cannot be complete without material equipment.
The whole of the passage in which these words occur is
appropriate.

" No activity," he says, " is perfect if it is impeded, and

the happy man needs bodily comforts and external conveniences and some measure of good luck if the absence of these things is not to hamper him. But those who declare that a man will be happy while he is being broken on the wheel or plunged in great misfortunes, provided that he is good—whether they mean it or not these people talk nonsense."

Yet letters are written to the *Times* every now and then about schools—usually, it is true, about elementary schools —which recall nothing so much as Blake's lines :

> The Angel that presided o'er my birth
> Said, " Little creature, formed of joy and mirth,
> Go, love without the help of anything on earth."

And my last word is a plea for a fuller recognition of this truth. Fine buildings do not of themselves make a fine school ; but what I have called the romantic appeal of the schools does gain very much from association with what is in itself dignified and beautiful—and beauty and dignity are not necessarily more expensive than what is mean and ugly. Nothing that has been done to raise the standard in every sense of the University of Bristol is likely to have a more permanent effect than the character of the buildings with which it has just been endowed ; and any one who has had to do with schools, above all with the day schools in great cities, knows the value of the impression produced by some element of beauty in an uninteresting or even sordid environment. I do not believe that authorities and governing bodies are indifferent to this. The character of many of the new schools shows that they are not. What is still imperfectly understood is the necessity for playing-fields— and when I say playing-fields, I mean at least an acre to every thirty boys. I know the difficulties. Want of forethought has made them, even in the case of our greatest day schools, extraordinarily baffling. When, for example, St. Paul's moved from the Churchyard to West Kensington, thirteen acres, including the ground occupied by the buildings, was thought enough for a school intended for 1,000 boys. But, at any rate, there is no excuse to-day for acquiescing in a standard like that ; and if the day schools of this country are to be what they might be, mean what they might mean, and play the part in national education that they ought to play, no amount of care and forethought, devoted to this and every other aspect of their development, is to-day either unprofitable or superfluous.

Much more might be said. Some of it, I hope, may be inferable from what I have tried to say. At any rate, like the White Knight, I have tried to say what the song is ; and you will not suspect me of claiming that the tune is my own invention. It is an old tune, capable still of many variations, and on the manner in which we show ourselves able to compose and to perform those variations much of the happiness and the prosperity of this country will depend.

I might put it more strongly than that. The question whether a particular boy or girl goes to a boarding school or to a day school has many possible answers, some of which have very little to do with education. I do not think that it can be doubted that the net result is, apart from anything that happens in the schools themselves, a profound difference in the contribution that can be made by the two of them to the life of the nation. The philosophy—I can think of no better word for the sum of the influences and ideals and general outlook upon life which I have in mind—the philosophy of the boarding school is on the whole a philosophy of the well-to-do. The rough draft has been worked over by many hands, and some original and eager minds have made of it from time to time a more enlivening and inspiring thing than might have seemed possible ; but that, in its merits and defects, is what it fundamentally is ; and I do not see how any probable measure of change will make it anything else. I do not undervalue—at least I hope I do not—its merits, and in particular the effort, which

I

is one of its striking features to-day, towards a broader view of education and a broader sympathy with all sorts and conditions of men ; but the well-to-do look out upon life from a fortress, and recruit as we may from outside, the spirit of the fortress endures.   It is a fine spirit, admirable in many of its manifestations, but it can never really bring to the nation as a whole that sense of being essentially the same kind of people which is what this nation needs perhaps more than anything else if it is to survive.   I believe that so far as schools can help to do this service, it is mainly from the day schools that help will come ; and, therefore, I believe that few things matter more to the happiness and prosperity of the nation than the growth of an appreciation of the nature and a devotion to the spirit of the day school.

REFERENCES

ADAMSON, J. W.   A Short History of Education.   Cambridge, 1919.

ARCHER, R. L.   Secondary Education in the XIXth Century.   Cambridge, 1921.

CHOLMELEY, R. F.   Secondary Education in England.   Smith, Elder, 1913.

CHOLMELEY, R. F. (AND OTHERS).   The Next Step in National Education. Univ. of London Press, 1927.

COOKSON, C. (editor).   Secondary Education, Essays.   Clarendon Press, 1898.

FARRAR, F. W. (editor).   Essays on a Liberal Education.   Macmillan, 1867.

LINDSAY, KENNETH.   Social Progress and Educational Waste : A Study of the " Free-place " and Scholarship System.   Routledge, 1926.

NORWOOD AND HOPE.   Higher Education of Boys in England.   Murray, 1909.

WATSON, FOSTER.   The Old Grammar Schools.   Cambridge, 1916.

School Histories : e.g. McDonnell's St. Paul's School, and (a chapter in) Winchester : its History, Buildings, and People.   P. G. Wells, Winchester, 1921.

CHAPTER VI

By Cyril Norwood

It is impossible to deal with the public boarding school apart from its history, so interwoven has it become with the whole stream of the national activity, and so unparalleled is the influence which it exerts over those who have passed out into life through its portals. To call oneself Old Etonian, Old Wykehamist, Old Harrovian means something definite, something more definite than the claim to membership of a school society means in any other country. Those who think that the distinction is valued for social prestige only, and that it is really based on snobbery, make a mistake— which, although it is common, is none the less profound. The school stands, and continues to stand, in the conscious-ness of its Old Boy for his better self, and it remains a tie through life which he will not lightly dishonour.

Whatever theories may be held as to the prevalence and the character of education in the Middle Ages, I shall claim that the English public school system was founded in 1382, when William of Wykeham founded Winchester College. In that foundation, at the very beginning, he established certain characteristics which the schools have never wholly lost. In the first place, he founded the school in close connection with New College, Oxford, for which its business was to be to prepare students. In the second place, he established a rudimentary prefect system, for he placed eighteen of the most advanced boys in a position to exercise control and to give instruction. In the third, he established a corporate life to extend to all occupations and to all amusements. Fourthly, and perhaps its importance is not least, he made the formation of character the main object of the life and education of the place, by his famous motto that " Manners makyth man." Lastly, and this is a direction in which his plans have never fully developed as he may have wished, he founded Winchester for poor scholars, choristers, and a certain number of paying scholars chosen from the sons of noble and influential persons. He therefore contemplated a certain mixture of classes as desirable, and intended his school to be an avenue through which talent of whatever origin should emerge into opportunity and performance.

A common life, a common ideal of character-formation as the chief end, a tradition of sound learning as generally understood, and a close connection with Oxford and Cambridge—are the marks of the " public school " at the start. The idea that it should give opportunity to all classes is also strongly marked : for the early foundation of Eton as well as of Winchester, and in the same spirit that of Harrow, indicate the existence in the view of the founders of the theory that the education provided for poor scholars was a privilege, for their share in which the rich would be willing to pay. The scholars have indeed usually remained a feature of the schools, though they have ceased to come from the sons of the poor, if indeed they were ever drawn in the main from the class which we should call poor. But the sons of the rich soon outnumbered them, and brought their own standards into the schools. Difficulties of travel, isolation, and deadness of public conscience all played their part in the seventeenth and eighteenth centuries. The nineteenth century awakened indeed the public conscience, but England had become a very different society from that which William of Wykeham or John Lyon ever contemplated. Problems could no longer be solved by old solutions, and the old foundations could no longer play the same part. Whether they can again be made vehicles of opportunity for the poor, how far it is desirable, and in what way it can be done, are questions which I propose to defer to a later portion of this chapter.

The example of Winchester was widely followed in Tudor times, and the coupling of schools with Oxford and Cambridge colleges went on apace, especially when the grammar schools were refounded. But the fair dawn was soon overcast. The schoolmasters were underpaid, and the schools were understaffed. There was a natural temptation, seldom resisted, to make financial profits by under-feeding the scholars and by appropriating endowments. Corruption soon spread through all the old foundations, and the only thing of which you can be reasonably certain, when you examine the history of a school in the seventeenth or eighteenth century, is that the foundation is being exploited, and wrested from its proper purpose, by some individual or individuals, who have got themselves into a position of privilege and are unchecked by public opinion. It is not my business, nor have I the space here, to give a history of those dark days. The boarding schools were few in number, and they became the close preserve of the aristocracy and of the landed classes. They did not contain many boys all told. Yet, in spite of the general corruption, the bad food, gross bullying, excessive corporal punishment, stupid teaching, and narrow curriculum, they did preserve somehow or other the tradition of what the boarding school might be.

It is at first sight difficult to see why the reforming spirit in the early nineteenth century did not sweep all these corrupt schools away, as they disappeared in Prussia and elsewhere on the Continent. But the reason is to be found in the work of one man, successfully accomplished at a moment when a host of influences were beginning to work in favour of the sort of school which he reformed. Arnold of Rugby is not a myth. At the right moment he showed what could be made of the boarding school. He attracted to it a new class, the sons of that upper middle class which was beginning to enter public life, and demanded for its children the same training as that of the aristocracy. He made religion a living force, and found in the school chapel and pulpit his chief opportunity. He dominated his Sixth, who became at once his Prætorian Guard and his apostles. He widened the curriculum, and he taught in a living way. He created a school whose influence was rapidly felt in all directions, and reacted at once on the other great schools of the land. He showed that the reformed boarding school could be what William of Wykeham had dreamed that it could be, a mighty instrument for the training of character.

No sooner had he done this than the introduction of railways made travel infinitely easier than ever it had been. At the same time there was a very great increase in the number of individuals earning an income of £500 to £1,000, and the smaller country gentry and the clergy began to find that a boarding school was not beyond their means. The Empire grew and extended, and with it the necessity of parents living abroad to have their children educated at home. The local schools had sunk to the lowest depths of inefficiency. It is not to be wondered at that an enormous demand for a boarding-school education on the model of Rugby sprang up, for it was incomparably the best education that was then to be got.

The demand was met in two ways. First, by reviving old grammar schools, and throwing them open to a wider recruiting area than that of the immediate locality. Examples of this are Uppingham, Repton, Sherborne, Sedbergh, and Tonbridge. Secondly, by starting new foundations not for profit, but to promote a particular kind of education, often for a particular class, like Marlborough in 1843 for sons of clergymen, Wellington in 1853 for sons of deceased officers,

and others. Some were wholly for boarders, some for a
mixture of day boys and boarders, like Clifton and Cheltenham. Most were free from a strict denominational basis,
though of Anglican foundation. But some from the start
had a definite sectarian colour, like Radley and Lancing on
the one hand, or Mill Hill and the Leys on the other. If
you except Eton, Harrow, Winchester, Westminster,
Charterhouse, Rugby, and Shrewsbury, it will be found that
nearly all the rest in one way or the other are the product
of this great movement of the middle of the nineteenth
century.

The number of schools thus provided was sufficient for
the demand until recent memory. But after the war a
number of causes began again to operate, prominent among
which I place the democratisation of the secondary and
grammar schools, and the redistribution of wealth. At the
present moment all the public schools are full to the point
of inconvenience, and new boarding schools have made their
appearance only to be filled at once. Stowe, the Wrekin
School, Canford, and others, are in my opinion only the
vanguard of a new wave of foundations, which will have
various objects and varying curricula, but will all be built
on the basis of the public school tradition. When allowance
is made for fashion, snobbery, and all the other unworthy
motives which are sometimes cast in the face of the supporters
of the boarding schools, it has, I think, to be admitted that
there is strong *à priori* evidence that the nation thinks that
the system has something good to offer. Let us turn to the
consideration of what a public boarding school has to offer
at the present day.

In curriculum and organisation of work the great
boarding school does not now differ very much from the
other great secondary schools throughout England. Latin
holds a stronger and more assured position, and Greek is
more commonly taken : on the other hand, science is begun
later, and at the middle age of sixteen stands at a definitely

lower standard than that of the secondary schools. The elementary work in practically all the boarding schools is dominated by the School Certificate, in the sense that it is designed to lead on to that examination, and to meet its exigencies. It therefore falls into the three groups or categories of subjects : English and its allies, scripture, history, and geography ; the foreign language or languages (two usually being offered, Latin and French) ; and mathematics and science. Most of the great schools pass a hundred or a hundred and twenty boys through this examination in the year, and take it from the lower fifth form.

It is, of course, an examination of great importance for the type of boy who goes to the boarding school. It is necessary for him if he is to sit as a regular candidate for the Army. It admits him to Oxford, Cambridge, and the other universities. It opens the door to entry into various professions. But it is an examination well within the compass of the average boy, and it has already had a profound effect, on the whole for good, on the work of the public schools. Some masters of the old school, and among them some of the best teachers, will be found to deplore the mastery which this external examination has gained over the whole curriculum. They sigh for the days when old and famous masters of their youth spread themselves at large on the things that interested them, and gave, to the select, teaching that was most stimulating and most valuable. This sort of teaching, they say, since it has no examination value, is now wholly a thing of the past. On the other side, I may perhaps quote without a breach of confidence the joint opinion of a strong team of inspectors, given a very few years ago. They wrote that they had not observed in the school in question (and it had been their experience also in other schools of the type) the existence of the sort of class which had been common in the years before the war, consisting of boys who had failed to learn, had lost all hope and all interest, and were a nuisance to themselves and to all who tried to teach them. They remarked that it was an interesting question where these boys had gone to, for it was certain that in these and other schools they had ceased to exist. My own opinion is that they have ceased to exist as a class completely, just because there is now open to their efforts an examination which is within their compass, and has given direction and a sense of achievement, however humble, to their work. The School Certificate, which has established its hold in the public schools only since the war, has undoubtedly to a certain extent limited the freedom of teaching, but has equally to a certain, and indeed a very definite, extent raised the average standard of performance.

In the stages which follow the School Certificate the boarding schools are in a strong position, and compare favourably with the great bulk of the other secondary schools, simply because they keep the majority of their pupils to a more advanced age. If you were to compare a boarding school of 600 boys with a day school of a similar number, you would find far more boys above the age of seventeen in the former than in the latter. How long this will be so is uncertain. I have heard that the average age of those in attendance at secondary schools rises by a month every year. But at the present moment the boarding school has an advantage at the higher ages, and, though it does not talk in terms of " advanced courses," it will be found that most of them can present advanced courses in all the types recognised by the Board of Education. A boy can usually specialise in classics, mathematics, history, modern languages, physics, chemistry, and biology : he can work for Woolwich, he can often take economics and geography to an advanced stage. He will not find himself solitary in any of these courses : there are enough boys at the top to make up forms of a satisfactory size in them all. There is no question, as in some of the smaller secondary schools, of a boy being forced into a line of study not really suitable for him, merely because an advanced course exists in that study and not in others, so that it has to be filled, and the right teaching power cannot be provided for other kinds of advanced work. There are some who think that specialisation has been carried too far in the boarding schools. But certainly no one can now allege with truth that the boys are bound by a narrow and obsolete curriculum, or that their studies suffer from any tyranny of tradition. The forms are small and they are handled by competent scholars. We are very far from the days at Eton when Edward Coleridge was one of the 198 boys in the headmaster's division, and none who taught mathematics could have the full status of an assistant master.

In out-of-school activities the boarding school is very favourably placed, because it has the command of the whole time of the boys. No time is cut to waste by travelling, and the evenings are available for profitable use. Many things which in the day school can only be done by definite effort and some real inconvenience can be done easily and naturally in the boarding school. There has certainly been, for instance, in the last twenty-five years on the whole a marked advance in the standard of music. There have been of late some notable achievements, based not merely on the excellence of the few, but on real musical appreciation by the whole school. Most boarding schools have again made advance in art. They have generally good art schools, and they give exhibitions from time to time which show interest and some achievement in a good many lines of artistic activity, not always the conventional. And there usually exists behind these some society of masters and boys devoted to criticism and to æsthetics. For societies of all kinds, long-lived and ephemeral, there is of course ample opportunity : I need not go into a description of them all. But I may point out that, since the boarding schools are very commonly in the country, they have usually natural history societies of long standing, and that these have never been more flourishing than they are to-day, nor the school museums, which are their foundation, more efficiently conducted.

It is perhaps unnecessary to speak at this moment of the part which games and athletics play in boarding-school life : it will come in more fitly when I deal with the criticisms which are commonly levelled against the system. Here I shall be content to say that they play a great part, and that the day is so arranged that every boy can usually change and get exercise in the open air for one or two hours every day. Change, exercise, and the bath are part of the daily order, and it is a rule which makes for freshness and for health.

Every boarding school of the ordinary type has its Officers' Training Corps contingent, and this institution, which arose from the old and sometimes derided Cadet Corps, though it dates only from 1908, is now an integral part of the school institutions. It has never made for militarism, nor does it do so now. It does not fill the ordinary boy with enthusiasm, but the work is done from a sense of duty, and it has proved its value to the nation. The old members of the Officers' Training Corps provided the first thousands of young officers for Kitchener's Army, and they were not found wanting. And now, if another struggle were to break out, there are existent in this country an even larger number of young men than there were in 1914, with some knowledge of arms, and some notion of how to lead a platoon. This work is done quietly, and it is not stressed : Jingoism is not inculcated, nor war made attractive. It is not even done for the sake of discipline, or for the opportunities of command and responsibility which it brings with it. It is done as a part of citizenship, and in my opinion it is a fine piece of work : much is it to be desired that in other directions our country could get so solid a return for so small an expenditure of public money.

The basis of the corporate life remains what it has been,

that so far as possible the boys shall be responsible for the good order of their life in " houses " and out of school. I have heard a public school defined as a place where the boys educate one another, while a certain number of scholars, more or less distinguished, called masters, look on. This exaggeration has its kernel of truth. In the good boarding schools the authority of house captains, dormitory captains, and games captains is real : the term " games master," foisted upon them by the Press, and the analogy of the games mistress, apt to be rampant in girls' schools, is a term of abhorrence. The new boy is a creature with no privileges and few rights, but little by little he is given his responsibilities, and they are never artificial : if he does well, he gets more. The merit of the system is that the boy has always to be thinking for others, and some of the positions to which he may rise, such as the captain of a game in a big school, or the head of a house, call for a good deal of organising ability, and the power to make and stick to decisions which are not easy. On the other hand, I do not think I am wrong in saying that the old system of monitors and prefects, of which so much is often made, tends, as the years go by, to become more honorific than real : it is difficult to attach much reality to the duties of a school prefect, and it has now become the reward of good service and a sound record—a distinction rather than a duty. In the days of Arnold the boys came young to school, and they came wild. They were as a rule not very well fed, not very well looked after out of school, not expected to be civilised : there was very little friendship between masters and boys. Now they come at a considerably later age, after being well broken in at their preparatory schools, where all has been ordered in imitation of the bigger school to come. They know what is expected of them. Their time is very well filled. Organised games and school and " house " societies occupy their leisure. They are filled with a strong " house " spirit. The days when the headmaster dominated the Sixth, and used the Sixth to dominate the school, are simply gone by ; the position which faced Arnold or any headmaster of the middle of the nineteenth century exists no longer, partly because Arnold and his contemporaries showed the right way to deal with the problem, but also, and largely, because of the growth of those preparatory schools which are the subject of another chapter of this book.

That which distinguishes the boarding school very markedly from other types is the possession of a school chapel and the use which is made of it. There is much noise and dust of controversy about what is called public school religion. In this controversy nearly every one generalises from the particular, and indeed it is hard to do otherwise. It would be necessary to live for a space of years in a large number of schools at the same time in order to arrive at a position from which an authoritative verdict could be delivered. All the authority that I can claim is that I have known two great boarding schools from the inside, have preached in the chapels of a considerable number of others, and have had the opportunity of sharing in di cussions with those who have to carry the same responsibilities as myself.

That the public school masters should directly concern themselves with the whole religious training of the boys is a comparatively modern development. The first chapel at Harrow was built in 1839, but the boys continued to go to the parish church for some years. At Shrewsbury the governors ordered that the boys should go regularly to the parish church in order to counteract the irregular influence that might be exerted by the preaching of the headmaster, Samuel Butler. Arnold was the first headmaster to be chaplain of Rugby, and he was the real pioneer. He insisted first and foremost that a headmastership was a cure of souls, and even though to-day the majority of headmasters are laymen, there are few who would deny the responsibility.

At the present time you would find in most boarding schools that there is one sermon a week. If it is worth hearing, it is intently listened to, and keenly discussed ; but the boys will not listen if it is dull, and they sharply resent being preached down to. Boys are an inspiring and quick audience, quicker than adults ; but they are critical, and not easy for strangers to address. Many strangers think themselves fit to do it, but few are so in reality. I can only say, after listening to many sermons in school chapels, that their level is markedly higher than that of those heard in the average church, as indeed it ought to be. There are many examples both from recent and more distant times of boys being influenced for life by what they hear from the school pulpit.

The service itself is apt to be inspiring. The standard of music has risen of late years, and there is a great corporate feeling in the singing both of psalms and hymns to which it is hard to find a parallel elsewhere. Attendance at holy communion is on the whole good, and it would please and embarrass the ordinary vicar if as large a proportion of his parishioners presented themselves at eight o'clock on an ordinary Sunday. Boys are reverent and well-disposed : without bothering much about it, they take all seriously. Finally, it is probably safe to say that a great deal more trouble is taken over confirmation, and the whole preparation is taken more seriously, than was the case in former days. Housemasters and headmasters alike give a great deal of time and thought to the work in order that, whatever it is, it may not be a merely formal and conventional act in a boy's school career.

It is argued that the whole system is a failure, because the boys who were regular worshippers at school become almost at once regular absentees from their parish church or their college chapel ; that in reality it is a specious sham, formal and compulsory, with no underlying reality ; that headmasters ought to be in holy orders, or appoint a chaplain to full control of the religious life of the school ; that there is no real churchmanship. I shall not attempt to discuss this question in full, for it would require a chapter all to itself. Much depends upon what we mean by religion. If by religion we mean a faith that the basis of the world is spiritual, that the eternal values are truth, goodness, and beauty, that these are revealed in the life of Christ, and that what matters is conduct, then I think that religion is presented and taught in the public schools, and that even the average boy leaves with some elementary sense of these truths. If by religion we mean the necessity of individual conversion, or the acceptance of verbal inspiration, or a particular attitude of mind towards the eucharist or the importance of confession, or if we believe that a choral eucharist is necessarily religious, and matins is not, then there is a failure to teach religion in the boarding schools generally, and I personally hope that the schools will continue to fail.

For the rest, I would say that I do not think that the element of compulsion matters a bit if the services are not too many, and that boys would never have grumbled at compulsion at any time if the idea had not been put into their heads by injudicious elders. As to the vexed question of schoolmasters and holy orders, I have heard one bishop say that the lay headmaster is a disaster, for the boys think as soon as he enters the pulpit that the sacraments obviously do not matter—an idea which as a matter of fact never enters their simple minds. I have heard another bishop say that schoolmasters in holy orders are a disaster, because the boys say at once to themselves that they won't be half-timers like him. Whichever course the schoolmaster takes, he is therefore not likely to escape all episcopal censure. It is best for him to go straight ahead, and do his work with earnestness, and the hope that critics outside will in time cease to be so ready to demand from children in their teens evidence of advanced religious experience, and cease to press for that very dangerous type of training which consists of turning the schools into religious hothouses.

I turn from this subject to another group of criticisms, which really hang together, for they fasten on the same malady, though they ascribe its cause to various reasons. It is asserted that the boarding schools fail to awaken intellectual or æsthetic interests ; more, that they actually deaden them, and mould boys to a type ; that they send forth their products ignorant of politics, social history, music, and art, interested only in athletics. Pathetic pictures are drawn of the bright boy interested in all the world about him arriving at the boarding school, and ossifying, first gradually, and then rapidly, as he falls into the grip of the machine :

> Heaven lies about us in our infancy !
> Shades of the boarding school begin to close
> Upon the growing boy.

Now the first question to ask is, whether the boys do arrive at thirteen and a half trailing clouds of glory ? After studying them carefully over a great many years I have emphatically to reply that they do not. They arrive with a belief that games matter most, and that lessons are a duty to be done, up to a degree, so long as unreasonable demands are not made. Learning they regard as something connected with examinations. If they arrive with these ideas, they certainly do not get them from the public school in the first instance, though the public school may reinforce them. Nor would I push the responsibility on to the preparatory school entirely : parents and homes and the whole national system and character must bear a share. The picture is, of course, exaggerated : there are plenty of boys who arrive with keen intellectual interests and keep them. But we have to think, we ought to think always, in terms of the average boy, and there is enough truth in the allegations to make us reflect seriously.

I hold the personal view that much harm is done by the

Common Entrance Examination to the boarding schools. It is an immense convenience ; the examination is taken three times a year at the preparatory schools, and travel by young boys is thereby rendered unnecessary. Expenses are saved, and risk of infection avoided. A level of intellectual attainment, approximately equal, and the same for all schools, has been arrived at. But in following the line of convenience to the preparatory schools, and convenience to parents, both of them admirable objects, we have, like Sinbad, bound on our shoulders an old man of the sea, whom we cannot shake off. A great many of the preparatory schools direct their teaching wholly to this examination, for they cannot afford to have their boys fail. There are some who instruct—I cannot use the word educate—wholly by means of old examination papers. In any case, the object aimed at is to give a boy of thirteen the faculty of putting down knowledge in snippet form on all the subjects which he learns, in rapid succession during a space of two days, and he naturally regards this as the intellectual end of education. The end is not to learn Latin, or history, or mathematics, but to do a paper on them ; hence drill has to be substituted for interest, and cram for teaching. I do not myself believe that anybody ought to be examined before he is sixteen years old, save by his own teacher, and I think that Junior Locals and Preliminaries of all sorts have done a lot of harm. But they have not done the immense harm which the Common Entrance Examination has done, and is doing.

Of course, it is easy to say to the preparatory schools, " Forget all about the examination, don't let the boys think about it ; just teach, and all will be well." That, I am certain, is true ; but only a few believe it, and act upon it. The rest see the doors of the boarding schools rather too narrow for those who would enter them : they fear the imperious pressure of parents, and they have the places in their own schools to fill, now becoming rather too many for

K

those who are available to sit at them ; they therefore take no risks. The examination paper is definite and calculable, and it dominates curriculum and teaching. Of course the process is deadening, and renders real education impossible. Here lies the worst feature of the boarding-school system of education at the present time.

Reform is extremely difficult. Yet I believe that the right course is to abolish the written test, and to rely on a curriculum, agreed on between the boarding schools and the preparatory schools, by which the preparatory schools in their top forms would overlap the bottom forms of the boarding schools. The sole test for passing from one to the other should be oral, and take place at an interview ; due weight should be given to the word of a responsible preparatory schoolmaster that a boy is up to a definite standard. It would be a system of far less convenience ; it would mean bringing up boys for inspection ; but it would render possible much better teaching, and the retaining of freshness of intellectual interest. Yet in saying this I do not think that I am expressing the opinion of a majority of those who are concerned with the system, and do not ask you at present to regard me as more than a voice crying in the wilderness.

It is impossible to generalise fairly as to what goes on inside the boarding school when the boys get there. It is wrong to say that the boys are not appealed to, and their intellectual and æsthetic interests are not aroused, both inside and outside the classroom. Music, art, natural history, politics, debate, social science—there are opportunities for all in most schools, and they are freely taken. It is wrong to say that there is intolerance, a forcing to type : the schools are now quite tolerant of many different sorts of boy. The purely artistic nature will be unhappy under any system of discipline whatever : it will always fret its wings. But these natures are rare, and when parents have brought such a rarity into the world, they should not submit him to a system which is manifestly unfitted for him, and then criticise that system because the *rara avis* does not fit in.

A tendency to produce a type will always be there, as will always be the case where a community lives together : the main thing to aim at is that the type should be good, and not intolerant. The danger of intellectual deadness, I believe, threatens the masters more than the boys. The schools are often self-contained communities, isolated from the main currents of the national life. Masters have in some cases known nothing else save for a brief interlude at Oxford or Cambridge. The system they have known satisfies them, and they do not know what is going on outside, because they neither read nor visit. These grow into the second-rate obstructives of the boarding schools, of whom there are still too many. They regard themselves as the custodians of the most valuable traditions of the past, and their ignorance of the rest of the national system of education can be gathered from the fact that they think that a secondary school is a kind of what they still know as a " board school." But the numbers of these gentlemen decline, their influence declines still more : they are valuable only as examples of what a boarding-school master should strenuously endeavour never to become.

It is urged again that the cause of lack of intellectual interest is that all alike, masters and boys, think far too much of games and athletic distinction. People argue as if the public schools alone were guilty of this enormity, and there is a great deal of what I must call cant talked about it. In the first place, physical training, physical games and achieve-ment have always been held highly desirable : half the educational system of the Greeks was devoted to its attain-ment. We are bidden to admire the result by those who forget that the athlete was placed by the Greeks on a pedestal far higher than that which the public schools award him. Physical training, excellence in all martial and athletic exercises, was again a main part of all the training of knighthood in the Middle Ages. Its absence from the schools of the seventeenth and eighteenth centuries was a grave defect : in its place vice and cruelty flourished. When Arnold and his contemporaries introduced games as the organised occupation of leisure time, they were not introducing something new, they were going back to something old, and they were deliberately fighting some very evil things which were entrenched in the schools. In the contest with those evil things, by which I mean expressly drinking, bullying, fighting, poaching, and stealing, organised games have proved successful. Not only that, they have contributed something definite to the *morale* of the whole education, and have had an influence on character for good which cannot be disputed.

All this tends to be forgotten by the opponents of compulsory games. They hold up hands of horror because schoolboys honour most the captain of the XV, in a world which outside the schools sends thousands of professionals into the football field every Saturday afternoon, and assembles in hundreds of thousands to see them ; which goes a hundred thousand at a time to see greyhounds race, and gives a large fortune to a champion pugilist for a display which is as brief as it is frequently inglorious. You cannot expect schools not to reflect the public opinion of the whole nation, but I am prepared to maintain that the boarding schools are not so unbalanced about the place of games in life as the newspapers which represent the views of people at large. I am prepared to maintain further that the schools do not give as large a place to the mere athlete as they did a generation ago, and that they still play games as games, for the sake of the game, and with a high standard of honour. And I maintain lastly that the influence of games played thus is beneficial, and that in any national well-balanced system of education, which takes into account the whole of human nature, games ought to play a great and definite part.

I shall speak very briefly of an argument which is sometimes advanced that the segregation of one sex leads to
immorality, and that the public boarding school is full of
vice. Quite bluntly I say that this is a beastly libel. I have
no hesitation in saying that the standard of personal morality
is higher among any five hundred boys at a good boarding
school than in any other group of five hundred that you
could take from any social class of the community. I do not
say that vice never exists : that would be absurd. But so
far from blaming the public schools for being hotbeds of
iniquity, they ought to be praised for being in this respect
so clean as they are. For they certainly deserve it.

Finally, critics touch on a very serious danger when they
point to the segregation of the public boarding schools.
They are segregated in place, for whether they are in or
near towns, the pupils are segregated from their own homes
into a separate self-sufficient community. They are
segregated in social class, for none but the well-to-do can
make use of them. Expenses range from £150 to £300 a
year, according to the school. But this is preceded by a
course at the preparatory school, which is as long and quite
as expensive, and nearly all boys take it. It is true that
there are scholarships, but they are won by boys of exceptional ability who have suffered an intensive training. The
founders of the schools in nearly all cases contemplated the
growth of an education, which their foundation's income
would pay for in the case of the poorer, while the rich would
be glad to pay fees to share it. It has not turned out so,
and it is nobody's fault : the founders never foresaw the
growth of facilities of travel, the growth of cities, the entrance
of wholly new classes into political power and their demand
for education.

Moreover, the position has become worse of late years,
in that it has become more sharply defined. Until 1902
many boys of good material circumstances and good social
classes went contentedly to their local day schools, and

their parents were satisfied. But changes then began, and when the free-place system was introduced, the extrusion of this well-to-do type became marked. Such a boy was sent off to the boarding school, and this more than anything else is the cause of the boarding schools being overcrowded at a time when the birth-rate has been falling. Increase and greater diffusion of national wealth have had something to do with it, but the mixture of classes in the day schools has had more. The war came, and added to the prestige of the boarding schools ; they officered the first armies with material that stood the test well. There followed a movement in which snobbery, and a sense of real merit in the training offered, have played fairly equal parts, and we have now a clear-cut separation. The independent schools, which are almost wholly boarding schools, are now segregated as concerns both masters and boys, and the two sections of the nation, which need to work together throughout their adult lives for the general good, are being educated in isolation from one another.

The boarding schools are not, and have not been, insensible of the dangers and disadvantages of the position. A generation ago, when the problem was much simpler, almost every school started a school mission, and most of these survive. They represented opportunities by which boys could get into contact with those less fortunately situated, learn sympathy, and offer help. Since the war there has been a development of clubs and camps, in which the boys are brought into contact with those of other classes, and of these the best known is the Duke of York's Camp. Excellent as it is, it does not offer the means of permanent friendship and association. At most schools outside speakers visit and speak to the Sixth, or a society, or the whole school, and aspects of our social problems are continually presented. All this, however, fails to move anything but wrath in the minds of the class-conscious, who assert that the public boarding-school system is designed to produce " bosses "; they would like to end it, and not mend it, and in so doing they would destroy something which is of very great value to the country.

The obvious proposal to meet the difficulty is that the schools should be made accessible to more than one social class. But the proposal is not so simple to carry out in practice as it looks. If boys are taken from the elementary schools, they must first of all be sent to the preparatory schools, since the attainments demanded from the public school entrant at thirteen and a half are far in advance of what can be taught in the primary stage of education. I confess that it seems to me almost impossible to select at ten or eleven years old the sort of child who will, coming from a poor home, be fit for a boarding-school education. The qualifications required are by no means wholly intellectual, and those who are physically weak and mentally precocious can never come to much. There are immense difficulties, too, in dealing with the preparatory schools, nearly all privately owned, and not very likely to pull together. If you try to select the boys for a four-year course at the age of fourteen, you must take them from the secondary schools. But these see in the scheme a subtle attempt on the part of the boarding schools to rob them of their best material, and they show such hostility that there is no chance of the teaching profession ever elaborating an agreed scheme. The attempt has been made, and it has failed.

Yet the jealousies of schoolmasters ought not to be allowed to prevail over the general interest of the nation, and some scheme ought to be imposed upon the schools to break through the cast-iron barrier of segregation which now divides type from type. It is not in the least necessary to rob the secondary schools of their best intellectuals, for that is the type that would do better at the day school. But I submit that there are boys of strong character and physique in the day school who would do better in the boarding school : at any rate I saw plenty of them during the fifteen years in which I was working in schools of that type. But the scheme which I would suggest, in the national interest, and in the interest of the boys themselves, is that the boarding schools should offer free tuition, and the state should pay the boarding-fee together with a bursary, where necessary : that the boys should be selected by interview on a basis of school record : and that the qualification for election should not be intellectual pre-eminence in an examination. Such a scheme can have no chance of success unless it emanates from the Board of Education, and has the government behind it. But after it had worked for a short time, all would settle down to it, and it would create no friction. It is the only scheme of which I can think—and I have often reflected on this problem—which offers the chance of success, and would go some way to break down the barrier of moneyed privilege which now fences off the boarding school.

As I draw to the end of this chapter I am conscious that I have been far from fully covering the ground. But I hope I have made clear my own faith that the boarding schools are a living expression of our national genius, an outgrowth from our national life. I have, I think, frankly admitted their difficulties and dangers, but the attacks that are commonly made on them I believe to be either exaggerated or ignorant, sometimes, indeed not infrequently, malicious. I believe that great as have been the individual achievements of particular schools in days gone by, the general level of the boarding schools has never been higher than to-day. That is not to say that they cannot improve still more, as I hope and believe that they will. I trust that they will always maintain their independence, and all that makes for individuality, while they break down, or break through, all that makes for isolation. And that being so, they have a great part to play in the building up. of that educated democracy, with which the future rests ; which has indeed not come into existence yet, and can only come into existence, if all schools, for girls as well as for boys, play their part worthily, and work together in a single system and in a single spirit.

REFERENCES

ARCHER, R. L.   Secondary Education in the XIXth Century (chs. iii and viii).   Camb. Univ. Press, 1921.

BENSON, A. C.   Cambridge Essays on Education.   Camb. Univ. Press, 1918.

Histories of individual schools : *e.g.* Winchester (A. F. Leach), 1899 ; Rugby (Rouse), 1909 ; Charterhouse (Tod), 1905, etc.

Lives of Headmasters : *e.g.* Stanley's "Arnold," 1844 ; How's " Six Great Schoolmasters," 1904 ; Parkin's " Thring," 1898, etc.

CHAPTER VII

THE GIRLS' SCHOOL

By DOROTHY BROCK

I HAVE sometimes wondered whether girls' education has suffered more from those who have taken it too seriously or from those who have found in it a subject for inaccurate levity. That women should be educated is in theory assumed in this century as axiomatic. The school attendance officer knows no distinction of sexes. But the product of that education—and especially the successful product—is still regarded with some suspicion, and the cartoons of *Punch* have left their trail over our thinking. It is not without significance that at prize-givings in girls' schools Kingsley's relentless alternatives of virtue and intelligence are still presented with conviction and the consolation is administered to those who do not reap a material harvest of prizes that at least they will be the better wives and mothers.

But will they ? Is that, after seventy years of the secondary education of girls, the considered verdict of this nation ? When a mother says to me, *à propos* of the continuation of her daughter's school life, " But supposing she marries . . . ? ", leaving me to supply the rest of the sentence—" it will all be wasted," I wonder sometimes whether her daughter, or her granddaughter, will say the same. For, after all, the whole thing is still so new and young, and the girls' secondary schools in this country—there are 537 represented in the Head Mistresses' Association to-day—have had so comparatively short a time in which to cover the ground which the boys' schools have covered in centuries of more gradual evolution. My predecessors in this volume, Mr. Cholmeley and Dr. Norwood, could speak in centuries where I can speak only in decades. Yet in that same rapidity of growth there is, I think, much promise for the future.

For indeed the story of the girls' secondary schools in this country is a wonderful story. With its main outlines the reader will be familiar. Let him cast his mind back over the history of the last seventy years.

First came the colleges—Queen's College, London (the training ground of Frances Mary Buss, Dorothea Beale, and Elizabeth Day), in 1848 ; Bedford College (where Sophia Willock, Mrs. Bryant, was a student), a year later ; Girton (in the house at Hitchin), in 1869 ; Newnham, in 1871. Miss Buss's school was already founded ; and in 1858 Miss Beale had gone to Cheltenham, which had been established five years before. There were also some good private schools ready by 1865 to take advantage of the success of Miss Emily Davies' efforts for the admission of girls to the Cambridge Locals. While examinations were eagerly sought in those early days, as affording an external test and stimulus, it is a little comforting to find even Miss Davies writing in 1868 " The ideally perfect examination has yet to be devised."

The findings of the Schools Inquiry Commission in 1867, which, thanks to the efforts of Miss Davies and Miss Buss, extended the scope of its investigations to include the girls' schools, not only played a great part in the foundation of the Cambridge women's colleges, but also roused public opinion on the whole question so effectively that the next few years saw the opening of the first schools of the Girls' Public Day Schools Company in 1873, and of independent high schools, such as the Manchester High School ; and the establishment of the Endowed Schools Commission, which secured financial help for girls' education, led to the foundation of the King Edward VI.'s Girls' Schools in Birmingham, the Bedford schools, and others, such as my own school in South London, which was opened in 1877. When Miss Buss founded the Association of Head Mistresses in 1874, eight head mistresses attended that first meeting in her house at Primrose Hill, and passed a unanimous resolution " that no school can work satisfactorily unless the head mistress be entirely responsible for its internal management." To that, whatever other limitations of their freedom changed conditions, and especially the state control of education, have brought, her successors have remained faithful.

There are two more notable stages in the story : first, the growth of the boarding schools (for example, St. Leonard's in 1877, Roedean in 1885) organised on the model of the boys' public schools, with their house system and prefects and games, all features of school life which were later adopted by many of the day schools ; and secondly, the springing up all over the country, as a result of the 1902 Education Act, of the county secondary schools, many of which have recently been celebrating their coming of age. Some of these were new schools, others were old higher grade schools, altered and improved, and others were high schools taken over by the local authorities. In Miss Burstall's introduction to a series of papers called *Public Schools for Girls*, published in 1911, there is an interesting passage on the changing situation and the problem of the preservation of individual liberty and variety of type under a system of state control ; and I think we can say that her faith in our power as a nation of combining apparently incompatible principles has in great measure been justified. Of the special problems of these county secondary schools and of others, such as the " aided " schools in London, whose school population is akin to theirs, I shall speak later. One thing at this point I want to make clear about the policy of the pioneers—for that policy is, I think, still misrepresented ; and it is essential to understand it, and particularly its bearing upon the growth of the curriculum, if we are to understand the position in the schools to-day. It was not the first concern of the pioneers to prove that women were as good, intellectually, as men. (I can imagine that some of them might, if challenged in the heat of the conflict, have stated the case more strongly than that !)   But a passage in a paper read by Miss Emily Davies in 1864 on " Secondary instruction as relating to girls " puts the issue quite clearly : " We are not encumbered by theories about equality and inequality of mental power in the sexes. All we claim is that the intelligence of women, be it great or small, shall have full and free development. And we claim it not specially in the interest of women, but as essential to the growth of the human race."   And again : " It may be that the curriculum most commonly pursued, or at least professed "—there is a tang in much of Miss Davies' writing—" is as good as any that is likely to be devised, and that we only want better methods and more encouragement. On questions of detail we are not in the least inclined to dogmatise. It would be rash indeed to fix upon any particular course of instruction as absolutely the best for girls, while as to that of boys, on which so much more thought has been bestowed, we are still in a state of confusion and bewilderment."   When the perfect scheme of education has been produced, she suggests, it will probably be found that " the same course is in the main best for both boys and girls, the object being substantially the same, that of awakening and strengthening and adorning the human spirit."

That was the spirit of the leaders.   They were primarily concerned with throwing open to girls the doors of know-ledge. " Their aim," said one of the early students at Newnham, speaking at the Conference of the Head Mistresses' Association last July, " was not to ape the education of boys in the education of girls. But many of

the rich fields of intellectual knowledge had long been fenced
off and reserved for the masculine intellect ; and there was
an intense desire on the part of women and girls to learn
these subjects." In other words, Latin and mathematics
and the rest came into the girls' curriculum because they
were subjects worth learning, not solely, or primarily,
because they were in the curriculum of their brothers. It
is for that same reason, and for no other, that certain other
subjects have since been included in the curriculum, and it
is on that basis that they lay claim to equal respect.

Before 1850 the difference between the education of
girls and that of boys had been based on the assumption of
sex inequality and on difference of social function ; for the
gentler sex accomplishments were sufficient, helplessness
was a recommendation and intelligence a matrimonial
handicap. Those were days when a girl was " finished "
before her education had begun, and when many of the
subjects now in the curriculum were regarded as dangerous
and unwomanly, or were still suspect for such curious
reasons as those given more than two centuries earlier in
the Verney Letters, where Sir Ralph Verney writes :

" Let not your girls learn Latin nor Short hand ; the
difficulty of the first may keepe her from that Vice, for soe
I must esteeme it in a woeman ; but the easinesse of the
other may be a prejudice to her ; for the pride of taking
Sermon noates hath made multitudes of woemen most
unfortunate."

The alleged unwomanliness of certain studies has always
been a curious psychological study.

Then from 1850 onwards came the second stage—the
struggle for equality of educational opportunity, when not
humanistic motives only, but vocational and economic
considerations all tended towards identity of curriculum.
It was inevitable ; for the education given in the boys'
schools was " education," the only education known and

recognised as such. We who more than half a century later plead the cause of what are known as the " Group IV " subjects—that rather heterogeneous collection which includes, together with certain subjects, practical and æsthetic, which have no assured place in the older intellectual tradition, those other subjects, housecraft and needlework, whose womanliness is unimpeachable—know what would have been the fate of girls' education as a whole if Miss Buss and Miss Beale and the other pioneers had pursued " differentiation of curricula " in the 'sixties. It was not until 1920 that the Consultative Committee of the Board of Education began to investigate that subject officially, publishing in 1923 a Report to which this chapter is much indebted. It is one of the few official documents which I find myself re-reading, not for the value of its conclusions, which are usually inconclusive, though to two of the most definite I shall have occasion to refer, but for its unbiassed consideration of evidence, for its appendices and above all for its admirable introduction.

Identity of curriculum, then, based on the assumption of intellectual equality, was a necessary stage. That it brought in its train certain dangers and problems is true. But the end of the story is not yet ; and, as the Report suggests :

We may now be entering on a third stage, in which we can afford to recognise that equality does not demand identity, but is compatible with, and even depends on, a system of differentiation under which either sex seeks to multiply at rich interest its own peculiar talents. . . . In such a stage there might again be difference, but there would still be equality. . . . But this third stage, if it should be one of ready recognition of differences, whenever and wherever they exist, must also be one of a no less ready recognition of similarities at all times and in all places in which they are to be found.

Of the plea which follows for latitude in choice of subjects and for freedom in progressive experiment, I shall have more to say later.

So much, then, for the history of the girls' secondary schools and the growth of the curriculum. That curriculum in a normal girls' school to-day includes :

Scripture : increasingly taught by specialist mistresses or by those who have made themselves familiar with the results of modern scholarship.

English Literature and Language and *Composition.*

English and European History ; and some *World History :* that rather curious but attractive creation of Mr. Marvin and Mr. H. G. Wells, in which young minds sometimes lose the trees in a premature attempt to grasp the entire wood.

Geography : still trying to decide whether it is humanistic or scientific—and often more successful for girls when it stresses the former side.

Foreign Languages, Classical and Modern : the latter often treated more seriously in the girls' schools than in the boys' schools, and the former—so there is reason to believe—gaining ground.

Mathematics.

Science : i.e. Chemistry, Physics, and especially Botany—in a few schools Zoology—and some Physiology.

Domestic Subjects : Cookery, Laundry Work, and Housewifery.

Needlework and other handicrafts.

Commercial Subjects, in some cases—usually only for girls who have passed the First Examination stage.

Physical Exercises and Hygiene ; Dancing ; and Organised Games : Rounders, Netball, Lacrosse, Hockey, Tennis, and Swimming. About one game Miss Beale's desire has been fulfilled : " It is to be wished that croquet could be abolished. It gives no proper exercise." The school medical work deserves a chapter of this book to itself, as a piece of national service.

And finally there are included those two subjects which are so often spoken of as if they were a kind of hyphenated hybrid, that one almost visualises them written as such : " Music-and-Art."

I have often wished they could be separated, for they have quite different functions, although they are alike in being creative and in being not quite respectable. But what the examining bodies have joined let no woman venture to put asunder. Both are regarded by those who do not know very much about them as " soft options," and both are suspect among men, and sometimes among academic women trained in the old tradition, partly because they were not included in the traditional curriculum, and partly because they are enjoyable, and because many girls do them rather well. In music especially the girls' schools have done pioneer work, often giving to the language and literature of music a place in the curriculum right through the school. The educational value of music, when it is well taught (and music badly taught deserves all that even the headmasters can say about it), its power of developing the intellectual as well as the creative and æsthetic sense and of teaching concentration is no longer a matter of vague theory. We know it for a fact of experience.

Those schools which are happy enough to possess preparatory departments include also in their curriculum the subjects which initiate small children into the kingdom of knowledge. These departments are not only efficient ; they are delightful and happy places, whose value perhaps only we can realise who see our girls go right through the school from four or five to eighteen or nineteen. That the parents value their work has been brought home to some of us when, in the various economy campaigns which have swept over us and left us unbeaten, the fees of these departments have been doubled or even trebled, and they have nevertheless refused to succumb according to programme.

It is a full curriculum, indeed ; though not all schools,

L

of course, teach all these subjects and obviously they are not all taught at all stages. Many girls' schools have sixth-form work in modern studies, mathematics, and science, some in classics, and a few in art and in music and in domestic subjects. Here there is much differentiation and a complicated sixth-form time-table; in my own school, for instance, in a sixth form of sixty-two there are actually thirty-four varieties of time-table, and the secretarial sixth has yet another.

This variety is expensive, on our present inadequate staffing rate; but it is worth while at almost any cost, even that of big middle-school forms, to let girls in the last year or two of school life follow their own bent. Greater variety of choice at an earlier stage—at about fourteen—would, I believe, solve the problem of overpressure. But it cannot be done to any extent on the present allowance of staff, since it involves smaller divisions and more teaching power. It is interesting to find that as early as 1877 the head mistresses at their conference were discussing " The arrangement of a curriculum so as to secure width and thoroughness without overwork." Their successors discuss it still.

So much for the main lines of the curriculum. But there are many other sides of school life and education besides work and organised games—such as " houses," clubs and societies of all kinds, girl guides, and various forms of social and philanthropic work. In these out-of-school activities staff and girls work together in a sane and healthy comradeship which has largely superseded the sentimentality of a bygone generation. The modern schoolgirl is not really a sentimental person, and the modern schoolmistress does not encourage her to be one.

A modern school, then, is a complex organism—yet it is usually a good and happy and friendly place, whose manifold activities do not necessarily imply fuss and busy-ness and strain. For complexity is a danger, but it is not in itself a vice; and it is not always the biggest or most complex school which is the most feverish. And perhaps to knock up against all kinds of people, and to learn in a busy place to keep one's head and do one's own work without getting in their way and without fuss or self-importance or self-pity, is no bad training for a girl to-day, provided that her school life contains spaces of quietness and leisure, is penetrated by courtesy, and has time for humour. But a big library, quiet and well-stocked and pleasant, should be the first necessity, not the last luxury, for every school. "A library," said Victor Hugo, "is an act of faith." But an act of faith should not be turned into a classroom, and any schedule of accommodation which reckons it as such stands condemned.

I do not propose to trouble the reader with many statistics. Those I wish to quote come from the Board of Education Report for 1925–1926. In the grant-earning secondary schools in that year (which include, of course, the mixed schools, which are outside my terms of reference) there were 157,064 girls, and another 26,053 were in non-grant-earning schools recognised as efficient. In the 537 schools in the British Isles which are represented in the Head Mistresses' Association there are approximately 150,000 girls.

In the brief space at my disposal I can hardly go into the differences between the various types of day and boarding schools. I must rather deal chiefly with what is common to all. And, since my personal experience has been confined to day schools I speak chiefly of them. But I do not forget the special contribution of the boarding schools, with their fine public school tradition ; and the day schools owe much to those trained in them, who passed on that tradition to the schools in which they taught. The problems of the boarding schools are more complex than of old ; for though, in the nature of things their pupils come mainly from the wealthier homes, wealth no longer implies a certain standard of culture and education, and there is no longer a common home background on which the school can depend. The boarding schools have not to contend, as the day schools must, with the competing claims of home upon a girl's strength and time ; yet they miss that partnership between home and school which can enrich both so much. They offer many advantages and they have a fine record. Perhaps the two main criticisms which can be brought against them are first, that they are sometimes too much dominated by games, and secondly, that by filling every moment of a girl's day with a set programme of work and play they may fail to train her to plan for herself her own work and leisure.

Of private schools I cannot attempt to speak. They are of all varieties, ranging from those which are conducted on public school lines, many of which are on the Board's list of " efficient " schools, to those which are known to some of us by their fruits and which far from giving secondary education do not apparently give any education at all.

The editor of this book has invited its various contributors to consider three questions " without "—so runs the re-assuring postscript—" necessarily feeling compelled to find an answer to them." They are :

1. What place does the institution for which you speak hold in the English educational system ?
2. What is the main or the characteristic contribution which it makes to the national life ?
3. In what way might this contribution be made more complete and more effective ?

With the first I have attempted to deal. What, then, of the second and third ? Here, I think, two factors need to be borne in mind. One is the war and its after-effects, and the other is the change in the population of the schools since the 1902 Act, and especially in the large number, both urban and rural, which take a percentage (up to as many as 40 per cent.) of scholarship and free place holders. Some of these scholars come from homes with little or no cultural background, some from homes where economic problems—

unemployment, difficulties of housing, domestic help, nursing in time of illness in the home, and the like—are reacting very heavily on a generation of schoolgirls already handicapped in childhood by shortage of suitable food during the war, by the nervous strain of war conditions, and in London especially by the effects of the air-raids. It is wonderful to realise the difference between the prospects of these girls, many of them of great ability and promise, and the restricted opportunities which would have been open to them twenty years ago. " The educational ladder " is no longer a safe phrase to use ; but the thing which it stood for is real and, so far as it goes, it works ; and we are proud to have a share in its working. Then, too, the school population includes girls from educated homes, and others from homes where greater comfort and opportunity and leisure sometimes bring their own temptations. For the " flapper," in all forms and in all classes of society, is our problem, and we have not disposed of her when we have written about her follies to the *Daily Mail*. All these different types, with their very different background, the schools have to handle together and to equip for life and for livelihood in a world which is not too easy for women. " The coiled perplexities of youth " are common to both sexes ; but I think that the world is harder to-day for a young woman than for a young man. For one thing, there are so many more of them—two million are " surplus " women—and for another, their economic and social position is not so assured. Incidentally, the mere fact that the school population in many of our schools is socially so mixed and that it mixes so extraordinarily well, is in itself no small contribution to a better mutual understanding and the breaking down of social barriers.

Then, too, we have to take into account the change in the whole pace of living ; while, with the new opportunities open to girls, there are heavier demands on the schools to supply a training which shall be a sound foundation not only for the three great careers of women, homemaking, teaching, and nursing, but also for industry and commerce (a vital question to-day), for medicine and law, for politics and social service, for colonial and agricultural life, and for many others—demands which sometimes take a curious form. It cannot be too strongly emphasised that the business of secondary, as distinct from technical, education is to educate *people*—not primarily to supply the fluctuating requirements of the labour market or even to solve the servant problem ; and that after all the result of education is, as Aristotle suggested, " a sort of educatedness." It makes a difference in people, who by their impact on it will make a difference in the world. But what *is* that difference ?   Does the type and standard of education which we understand by " secondary " give something of real worth ?   As I attempt to answer that question for myself my memory goes back to a personal experience during the war.   In the early years of the war, when I was teaching in Birmingham, I spent my out-of-school hours helping in the clerical work of an office which administered the Prince of Wales' Relief Fund in a very poor district in that city. The organiser in charge staffed the office entirely with voluntary helpers, both men and women ; and I used also to take from school in turn detachments of girls of fifteen or sixteen from my own School Certificate Form.   The work was, of course, entirely new to them ; they had never filled in a government form in triplicate in their lives, and they had not the advantage which the other workers had of knowing the district and the names of streets and shops. Yet, with very few exceptions, they were the best people we had, simply because they brought to their work certain qualities which their education had given them—not accuracy only, nor adaptability to a new task, nor the power (and it is curiously rare) of reading instructions and carrying them out, but also a certain quality of mental endurance and a sense of responsibility and an understanding of teamwork, which they had learnt at school. Our books were balanced at an earlier hour on the days when we had them in the office ; and I found myself reinforced in my faith that the trained mind is after all an asset in man or woman. Right living depends on right thinking, for both sexes. Women are naturally intuitive ; I say that, remembering that a speaker (not a woman) at the British Association this year put the " intuitive reliability " of men slightly higher than that of women. But intuition—or shall I say, leaping to conclusions ?—is generally conceded to be one of the things in which women excel. Now the training in the schools in clear, logical thinking, in " hard, uncoaxed, uncomplimented work," has reinforced intuition. It is not sufficient to be intuitive about a Latin declension or a chemical law ; and the girls in our schools have at least begun to learn that there is a difference between knowing and not knowing, and that they produce different results. That is no small part of the equipment of a citizen of either sex under a democracy, which exacts from the rank and file powers of clear thought and vision which in old days were required only from the few. Mrs. Grey, whose name is perpetuated in the Maria Grey Training College, in her historic speech at the Albert Hall in May, 1872, pleaded the right of women " to have their reasons trained to form just opinions upon the circumstances around them." That necessity is not less in 1927.

In citing the instance which I have chosen from the years of the war, I do not forget that other women, of all types and all classes, rendered other forms of service in those years ; nevertheless it is true that it was in virtue of all that their education had given them, and of their power to lead and to bear responsibility, that the special contribution of these girls and women was effective in many fields of unaccustomed service. In spite of many shortcomings, the training of the girls' schools, no less than that of the boys' schools, was tried in those years and was not found wanting.

In those years—yes, and before, and since. I gave one illustration, but it could be multiplied indefinitely. Take the *Jubilee Book of the Girls' Public Day School Trust*—which I mention with honour, as in private duty bound—and its record of service rendered in many fields by its Old Girls. Or take the records of any one school celebrating its jubilee or its coming of age, and study not only the academic record, but also the varied public service of its past pupils ; or get to know, as we who are really intimate with one school know them, the homes which owe much to the wider outlook and the quickened appreciation and the trained mind of a woman whose school days gave her that knowledge which " maketh a woman to be a friend to herself " and keeps her spirit fresh. It is not the academic nor the professional woman only whom the right sort of education can enrich.

Or think of the most obvious instance of all—so obvious that I do not dwell on it— the contribution of the secondary schools to the teaching profession in all its branches. According to the Report of the Departmental Committee on the Training of Teachers, 6,000 women will be needed annually for the teaching of little children alone, a branch of teaching which seems likely to pass entirely into the hands of women—and most of them must come from the secondary schools.

Professor Dover Wilson in his opening chapter notes the close connection between great political movements, such as those of 1832 and 1867, and landmarks in the history of education. That connection of political and educational history has, of course, always characterised the women's movement ; and now, at a time when civic responsibilities are being increasingly extended to women, the training in citizenship which the schools give is no small contribution to national life. That training may be given in part directly by the teaching of civics and history and economics. But, since the only way to learn citizenship is to be a citizen, it is the training in the life of the school community which is most valuable. That, too, is not peculiar, I know, to the schools of which I speak ; but, inasmuch as ours is the privilege of keeping our pupils through the years of adolescence, often until eighteen or nineteen, those last years of school life, with the experience which they bring of holding office as prefects, games captains and the like, have developed in many girls not only the desire for service but also the qualities which efficient and intelligent service and leadership demand, both in voluntary fields, such as care committee work, women's institutes, and club work of all kinds, and in paid social and philanthropic work. An audience of schoolgirls such as that which the Prime Minister addressed last month at the annual meeting of the Union of Girls' Schools for Social Service, which has a membership of over 150 schools, is rich with possibilities ; and there are few schools where some form of work for others is not part of the school's own life—not a matter of giving money to a collection, but of knowledge and understanding ; a turning away from self-interest to service, and a corrective to the prevalent individualism. Such work has always been vaguely regarded as women's sphere, but much well-intentioned effort in the past has been ignorant and patronising and misdirected. Now thought and knowledge are kindling imagination and bringing right desires to good effect. And as the Prime Minister said at that meeting, " a sense of social duty is in itself a religious education in the best sense of the word."

That expression " religious education " covers a wide field ; and the head mistresses are not unmindful that theirs, too, is a cure of souls. They seek to discharge that duty in many ways—by direct teaching, by frank discussion, by the nurture of all things that are pure and lovely and of good report. And, though it is only the larger boarding schools which have their school chapels, the school prayers of many of the day schools have a very real part in the life of the community. They are not just " school assembly," but rather a corporate act of worship definitely relating the whole of the work of the school to the purposes of God and the service of men, and presenting life in terms of spiritual values. There is nothing about which head mistresses think more and talk less.

And again, the outlook of the schoolgirl of to-day is not limited by the confines of her own country. She discusses everything in heaven and earth in her debating societies— for this generation has views on everything, and is not afraid to state them. And in days when the world is being daily knit more closely together, it is well that a woman, no less than a man, should realise her world-citizenship and be able to read the foreign news in the papers with intelligence, should know something of the work of the League of Nations and the progress of disarmament, and should understand the manifold sources of that food-supply with whose purchase and preparation for her family she will be expected to deal efficiently all her life by that sex which still refuses domestic science a place in her examinations.

Now in saying all this I do not ignore the patent defects of the girls' schools, though I plead their youth as in some measure responsible. For example, the lower average standard of certain subjects, such as classics, mathematics, and physics, is in part due to a shortage of teachers equipped themselves with a sufficiently high standard of scholarship. After all, the colleges themselves were growing side by side with the schools, and their output was absolutely insufficient to meet the demand for teachers. It is true that there were many women in the early days whose paper qualifications were almost non-existent, but whose culture was something in the presence of which the young college graduate of to-day might well feel humble. But they were not, and are not, all such. " Nobody can teach," says a character in a recent novel, " but any firm female can make children learn " ; and in days when the repressed complex had not yet been discovered—or invented—firm females did their worst with many of us.

But still worse were the incompetent dilettantes, survivors of the older " governess " type, who taught because they could earn their living at nothing else, dictating endless notes to us and stemming the torrent of interested questions for reasons which we were not slow to discover. The girls' schools have suffered from the teaching of those who did not know, and who were ignorant of the fact that they did not know. They are not alone, though, even in that ; and they can claim, on the other side of the account, that it is in them that training for teaching has found its most ardent and consistent adherents.

But there are other defects besides deficiency of teachers. " The special danger of girls' schools," says the Differentiation Report, " is that they may become excellently organised and conscientiously loyal groups, composed of mediocre and uniform units." I have a feeling that that sentence was written by a man ; it does not fairly describe the schools which I know and in which I have lived. I do not really believe girls are always more imitative and " uniform " than boys ; the tyranny of tradition in a boys' preparatory school, for instance, is one of the most cast-iron tyrannies in the world. And I sometimes wonder whether the impression that girls are so monotonously " conscientious " is not an out-worn cliché. But there is more truth in the criticism that the knowledge the girls' schools give is sometimes unreal and unrelated to life, or that, as Dean Inge puts it, a girl is trained, not to be a good housewife or a literary and artistic person, but a teacher. Here again the girls' schools are not the only ones where knowledge may fail to grow into culture and the love of knowledge and the power to use knowledge may never be imparted in spite of the many branches of knowledge which are included in the curriculum. We all know the " clever " woman, who lacks intellectual sincerity, whose knowledge has never become

part of herself.   She is an unlovely creature, in part created
by the examination system, which encourages her on all
sides, by the too academic trend of our education, and by
our own faulty scale of values.   The genuine scholar, even
the bookworm, is one-sided, but she is sincere, usually
humble-minded, and has her place in the scheme of things.
She contributes something to her generation.   But the
intellectual sham is our worst failure ; and the pity of it
is that we have sometimes produced her as our greatest
success.   Nor is she our only failure.   During the last ten
years or more the head mistresses have been increasingly
conscious of other types whom the rather stereotyped educational system we have inherited has neglected.   Our
consciences were stirred afresh, I think, on this matter by
the realisation that during the war certain individuals who
had been failures at school had proved themselves the most
capable citizens.   For it is in terms of individuals that
women naturally think ; that, by the way, is one reason
why they should be on all educational bodies ; for where
men think in terms of systems and groups and " average "
pupils, women think, for good or ill, in terms of people,
seeing (shall I say) Joan Smith and Marjorie Brown, aged
sixteen, before them, faced with that paper which seemed to
dons and schoolmasters so entirely within the power of that
" average " pupil of sixteen in terms of whom we are told
we must always think.[1]   That picture of " the average boy "
and " the average girl," so convenient and so mythical, does
sometimes need to be exposed to the illuminating test of
the actual.   The two views are complementary to each
other and both are useful.

One of the things which inspired the pioneers was
their resentment of the waste of women's gifts, a passion
for the development of each individual woman's powers of
service.   But the pioneers were mostly in the nature of
things academic people—as are we, their successors ; and

[1] *Vide*, p. 128.

yet with the rapid extension of the sphere of the schools and the change in the school population it is obvious that many of our pupils are of the non-academic type. The head mistresses began, I remember, by talking years ago about " the dull girl." But we soon found that these girls were not " dull "; they are really different. And, as Tacitus said, " A thing is not worse because it is different " [1] —a good motto for all examining bodies. Some of them are practical; and often these are among the very best people in our schools. They are educable, too, by the interaction of hand and brain, by that craftwork which is really brainwork. Some are domestic, homemaking girls, whose contribution this nation assuredly needs to-day. Some are artistic and æsthetic—and we do ill to ignore or to leave untrained those who in days like these can see and create beauty. These girls, and others who do not quite fit into the traditional scheme, are found at the bottoms of classes, or herded together into " C " forms, incapable of ever taking a school certificate, that sign and seal of a secondary education, and in many cases therefore debarred from the scholarships which would make continued school life possible. Yet we who have taught them those Group IV subjects of which I spoke, or have experimented in the teaching of the more orthodox subjects by unorthodox methods, have found a response and an " educable capacity " which have often astonished us. There is a truth in the story of the small boy's reassuring reply when his father reproached him for being bottom of his class : " It's all right, father ; they teach the same to both ends." We have taught the same to both ends too long. The boys' schools seem in the main to have been content hitherto with that educational policy, with the exception of a few rebels like Sanderson of Oundle. Yet different minds are trained by different exercises and nourished by different foods ; and segregation of types at the school age would be a

[1] " Nec statim deterius esse quod diversum est," *Dialogus*, ch. xviii.

disaster in a country most of whose troubles have arisen not from ill-will but simply from the failure of one type of mind to understand another.

And so, in trying to answer the editor's last question [1] —how can the contribution of the girls' schools be made more effective ?—I make two suggestions. They are not new. As a matter of fact, both are to be found in the recommendations of the Differentiation of Curricula Committee. The first is that Group IV—Music, Art, and (the head mistresses would add) Domestic Science and Handicrafts— should be on a parity with Groups II and III in the First School Examination. In the chapter that precedes this Dr. Norwood speaks of the beneficent effect of the " domination " of the curriculum in the lower forms of the public schools by the School Certificate Examination, since it gives to the boys (who, it must be remembered, have previously suffered an intensive culture in the preparatory schools) " an examination which is within their compass, and has given direction and a sense of achievement, however humble, to their work." [2] The girls' schools do not find that domination so uniformly beneficent. Their experience is that the direction is too narrowly academic to suit all types, and that, inasmuch as at least 50 per cent. of those who leave over the age of sixteen leave without a school certificate, there is for them no sense of achievement, but rather of failure. This policy about Group IV is no new craze of a fanatical few ; it has been pressed by the Association of Head Mistresses since 1918, and is at the present time being urged upon the Secondary School Examinations Council by a majority of 95 per cent. of the members of that association—a remarkable unanimity, when one remembers the varied types of schools in which their experience has been gained. It is being urged simply because such freedom of choice would enable us to educate girls of these " different," non-academic

[1] *Vide*, p. 148.   [2] *Vide*, p. 121.

types in the last years of school life in the subjects in which they have proved to be educable, instead of forcing upon them a curriculum which does not suit them in order that they may pass—or try to pass—an examination which was never framed to meet their needs, but which is now so firmly rooted in the educational system and in public opinion that every one, from the Board of Education, the Local Education Authorities, the parents and the employers, down to the girl herself, expects an " average " girl to take it. We are told that such a modification of the examination system (which, by the way, would probably leave the work of three-quarters of our pupils unaffected) would be risky. But it is less risky than a policy which lays secondary education open to the charge that it is an avenue to the scholastic and clerical professions only, and that it has no meaning and no value for other types of life ; and we believe that if we had this freedom of choice, if, that is to say, examinations followed curricula in reality and not only in aspiration, the contribution of the girls' schools to the nation in the next ten years might be enriched beyond measure. For the nation needs—and is not getting—the varied gifts of varied types of women, developed and disciplined.

And the other suggestion, also in the 1923 Report, is perhaps even more revolutionary—" that women should be adequately represented on all committees and examining bodies which deal in any way with girls' education." It sounds so obvious ; yet is it taken seriously ? Is it ungracious to suggest that the proportion is usually more like that which is found in the space allotted to girls' schools in this volume ? And although the effectiveness of the women members of a committee—as of a government—is not always in proportion to their numbers, yet not all the courtesy with which we are heard, nor the sincere desire to include girls in the deliberations, can compensate for that understanding of girls which women alone can give, or for the loss of that sharing of experience which

women need if they are to take long views and form states-
manlike judgments.   We have owed much to the men who
helped us in the early days.   Now, after seventy years, we
have served our apprenticeship ; is it too much to ask that,
at this stage, we might help to forge the machinery which
is to govern both boys and girls, instead of spending our
strength later in laborious adaptation ?   I shall always
remember with affection the persistent and courteous
efforts of one committee on which I sat—often as the only
woman present—to change the word " boys " now and then
in the Report to the word " pupils "—the chief result being
immediate dislocation of the grammar of the rest of the
paragraph.   Nor shall I forget my feeling of helplessness
a few weeks ago when pleading the cause of cookery to a
committee almost wholly masculine, whose scholastic experience had been limited to other forms of applied science, the
products of which are not usually consumed.

There are two other things which would help us.   One
is material—equipment, books, libraries, laboratories, playing-fields ; the other is non-material—a sympathetic and
enlightened public opinion, and richer opportunities for
those engaged in the education of girls to make and to
preserve contacts with the wider world outside the schools
to which, after all, their work must be related.   If girls'
schools, and the people in them, are still too much of one
type, too narrowly academic, too little human, it is partly
because the schoolmistress is rarely asked to public or
social functions, save to meet others of her kind.   She is
far more cut off from the stream of the nation's life than are
those women engaged in political, social, or commercial
work, for whom, be it not forgotten, the educational pioneers
opened the doors.   And yet it is chiefly a question of habit,
I think—the lingering blue-stocking tradition ; for the girls'
schools are not really without national value in the thought
of our leaders.   " I am amazed and rejoiced," said the
Prime Minister the other day, " by the spirit that is running

through the girls' schools and colleges to-day, making them seek, as those who enjoy great privileges, to recognise the obligations that those privileges entail." Perhaps the time will come when amazement will give place a little more to rejoicing, and then to our more universal acceptance as comrades in national service.

We may regret the passing of the Victorian woman. She had many graces, as had the age which produced her and which she adorned. At her best she was gracious and beautiful ; at her worst she was empty-headed, silly, and boring. One thing is certain : she would never have survived transplanting to such an age as this. She could never have coped with its pace or its complexity. And one is tempted sometimes to wonder what would have happened if the girls' schools had not been there, to send out into the world her Georgian successors, with their so obvious faults and their splendid virtues—their independence of spirit, their pluck and initiative and resource. For the nation to-day cannot afford either economically or spiritually to carry the deadweight of its women ; they must be in all senses contributory members of the commonwealth. For that they need—and especially those who are to lead others need—all that the best and most varied education can give to develop their varied powers.

Is it too fond a faith which makes one wonder whether in years to come, when the history of this amazing century comes to be written by those who stand sufficiently far away from it to see things, as we cannot see them, in their right perspective, it may be said of the girls' schools, as it was said of one gallant woman in story—" Who knoweth whether thou art come to the Kingdom for such a time as this ? "

REFERENCES

Association of Head Mistresses :
(a) Reports on the Annual Conferences held in 1919, 1922, and 1927. (b) The Book of the Jubilee Conference. C.U.P., 1924.

BURSTALL, SARA A. English High Schools for Girls. London. Longmans, Green & Co., 1907.

BURSTALL, SARA A., AND M. A. DOUGLAS. Public Schools for Girls. London. Longmans, Green & Co., 1911.

DAVIES, EMILY, LL.D. Thoughts on some Questions Relating to Women, 1860–1908. Cambridge. Bowes & Bowes, 1910.

MAGNUS, LAURIE. The Jubilee Book of the Girls' Public Day School Trust. C.U.P., 1923.

RAIKES, ELIZABETH. Dorothea Beale of Cheltenham. London. Constable & Co., 1908.

RIDLEY, ANNIE E. Frances Mary Buss and her Work for Education. London. 1895.

ZIMMERN, ALICE. The Renaissance of Girls' Education in England. London. A. D. Innes & Co., 1898.

Differentiation of Curricula between the Sexes in Secondary Schools. H.M. Stationery Office, 1923.

CHAPTER VIII

TECHNICAL SCHOOLS, EVENING SCHOOLS, AND DAY CONTINUATION SCHOOLS

By E. Salter Davies

When I rashly undertook to contribute a chapter to this volume on the subject of technical institutes, evening schools, and day continuation schools, I had not fully realised the difficulty of the task. Other chapters have dealt with, or will deal with, such subjects as the public elementary school, the public secondary school, the training college. Each of these subjects has its own peculiar difficulties, but each conveys a meaning which is more or less clearly defined and generally understood. The subject allotted to me is so large, so chaotic, and so little explored that it is difficult to deal with it intelligibly and adequately in a single chapter. It includes whole-time and part-time day technical schools, junior technical schools, evening schools, and day continuation schools. Each of these sub-divisions deserves a chapter to itself. I originally proposed to arrange my remarks under three heads—the history of our technical institutions, their present position, and their future development—but I soon discovered that anything on such a scale was out of the question. The attempt to be comprehensive had therefore to be given up. I shall have something to say under each of these three heads, but I shall not attempt to trace the full story of the development of our technical institutions, nor to give you any complete picture of them as they exist to-day. What I shall try to do is to examine certain phases in their development, and to draw from such examination some conclusions as to the lines on which they may be expected to develop in the immediate future. I should add that, for the purposes of this paper, I have drawn to some extent upon an article which I contributed on the subject to the *Journal of Education* in September, 1926.

In the introductory chapter of this volume it is pointed out that the educational institutions of our own country are of ancient lineage. Oxford and Cambridge are older than the state. There were schools at Canterbury and York before England was a nation. Throughout the centuries of our national growth we have developed a common culture, and to that development nothing has made a larger contribution than that force which expresses itself in and through our educational institutions. These institutions themselves reflect the political and social ideals of their time. The history of English education is—in a sense —the history of the English people.

Organised technical education is the product of the nineteenth century. So far as this country is concerned it may almost be said to be the product of the last fifty years. In it are fused two traditional forms of education—that of the school and that of the workshop. This fusion took place during the revolution in social and economic conditions, brought about by the application of steam to industry and locomotion. This, in its turn, was the result of the application of science to the problems of industry and commerce. The development of technical education is due to a continuous effort to adjust the training of the worker to a changing industrial organisation, and its history, like that of the other educational institutions whose story has been told in the preceding chapters, carries us back to the beginnings of our political and social life.

In the earlier stage of that development there appear to be four main phases. Each of these suggests certain ideas which are of interest and significance in regard to the present position and the future development of technical education. These four phases are represented by :

1. Apprenticeship under the Craft Gilds ;
2. The rise of the Mechanics' Institutes in the early part of the nineteenth century ;
3. The establishment of Working Men's Colleges just before the middle of that century ; and
4. The activity in technical education, stimulated by the Great Exhibition of 1851 and its successors.

In the old days the craftsman was naturally and inevitably not only a producer but a teacher as well. The apprentices were recruited from those who were born and bred in the atmosphere of craftsmanship. The earliest apprentice followed the calling of his father. The smith " sitting by the anvil and considering the unwrought iron . . . will set his heart upon perfecting his works and he will be wakeful to adorn them perfectly " [1]—and he taught his son to do the same. Thus, the apprentice learned the " art, craft, and mystery " of his future occupation through participation in productive work under the tutelage of a master-craftsman. " The master first sheweth his apprentice what he is to do, next works it himself in his presence, and gives him rules, and then sets him to work." [2] In due time, the various crafts were organised into gilds, each of which was responsible for the supply and training of its own recruits. The gilds had three classes of members, apprentices, journeymen and masters, and most members passed through all three stages. The lengthy apprenticeship prescribed by the gild was not only a technical training and an initiation into the secrets of the craft, it was also a preparation for the very real and onerous duties of citizenship in a mediæval city, as well as for posts of responsibility in the government of the gild. The master to whom an apprentice was bound was

---

[1] Ecclesiasticus xxxviii. 28.
[2] Walker, *Of Education*, p. 9. (Oxford, 1687.)

further charged with what we should now call the care of the moral development of the young persons through adolescence into adult life. Thus, the apprentice " must do all the servile offices about the house and be obedient to all his master's commandments, and shall suffer such correction as his master shall think meet." [1] The ideals of the old system of apprenticeship are embodied in the stories which tell us how the industrious apprentice married his master's daughter and became Lord Mayor of London.

The gild system succeeded in maintaining a high standard of craftsmanship and helped to produce worthy citizens. It involved, however, two important presuppositions. In the first place, the system assumed that skill in craftsmanship was in no way dependent upon the scientific study of the craft, as, indeed, in those days, it was not. Thus, no attention was paid to the development of the intellectual interests of the learner. The need for the study of scientific principles in connection with industry was not yet apparent. In the second place, it postulated a certain leisureliness of life and stability of industrial conditions which are, unhappily, absent from the world of to-day. Modern industry is characterised by a feverish instability, due to the rapid evolution of new methods and new processes in old industries and to the continuous emergence of new industries. Handmade products are being ousted by machine-made goods and the craftsman replaced by the machine-hand.

The actual period of transition presented infinitely greater difficulties than are known to-day. In those industries where apprenticeship died out, it suddenly became necessary to supply a new form of training appropriate to the radically changed conditions. In those industries where it, in some measure, survived, it became equally necessary to provide a supplementary form of training. The changes in industry had been wrought by the application of science. It became essential, therefore, to give, as part of any training

[1] Lipson, E., *Woollen and Worsted Industries*, p. 29.

for industry, some education in the scientific principles underlying the particular industry concerned. It was not realised that the workers generally were quite unqualified by their previous experience to grasp and absorb such scientific ideas. The seriousness of the problem was intensified by the prevalent atmosphere of political unrest—an unrest largely created by the absorption in repetition work of an ever-growing proportion of a rapidly increasing population.

The first experiment which sought to provide a training suited to the new conditions marks what I have called the second phase in the history of technical education in this country. The movement began in 1823 with the opening of the London Mechanics' Institute, and by 1841 over two hundred such institutes had been established in various places. Their aim was to " instruct the members in the principles of the arts they practised and in the various branches of science and useful knowledge." [1] They provided a valuable means of self-improvement to the more intellectually inclined minority, but made no appeal to the general body of workers. It must be remembered that this experiment was attempted at a time when the great majority of working men and women were without any educational grounding, and were suffering from grave physical discomforts both in the factory and the home, due to the changed conditions of industry. As yet, the Factory Acts which were so to limit the working hours of the worker as to make possible education after working hours, were still to come. These institutes failed not only because of the hostile circumstances, but also because they made no intimate contact with the daily work of their members. They relied on general lectures given largely by people acquainted with the scientific principles they were explaining but ignorant of the industries in which their hearers were

[1] Cf. *Manual for Mechanics* (1846), p. 35 ; also Hudson, J. W., *History of Adult Education*, p. 56.

occupied. In the words of a contemporary Committee of the Society of Arts, " the whole scheme was pitched far too high to be of general use." [1]   At the same time, it left some permanent results. It was responsible for a considerable development of working men's clubs and mutual improvement societies, and prepared the ground for the work of the Science and Art Department in the latter half of the century.

The third phase began with the opening of the People's College at Sheffield in 1842. This movement marked a reaction from the ideas which had led to the establishment of the mechanics' institutes. The latter aimed at educating the workers through a scientific training directly connected with their work in the factory. The working men's colleges, under the stimulus of a desire for social and political reform, sought rather to equip the working classes with a knowledge of the general social and economic principles conditioning their lives, and so to prepare them for the duties of citizenship. This aim was to be achieved not through the medium of lectures, but through the development of classes and a tutorial system designed to bring student and teacher into close personal relationship. The purpose was not only to supply the deficiency in general education, but to open out a way of life. In these respects the movement anticipated the modern development of the Workers' Educational Association.

Working conditions were still hostile to the successful development of technical education. An address of the Working Men's Association to Queen Victoria in 1837 contains the following passage :

" But by many monstrous anomalies springing out of the constitution of society, the corruptions of government, and the defective education of mankind, we find the bulk of the nation toiling slaves from birth till death—thousands

[1] Cf. *Manual for Mechanics* (1846), chap. x.

wanting food, or subsisting on the scantiest pittance, having neither time nor means to obtain instruction, much less of cultivating the higher faculties and brightest affections, but forced by their situation to engender enmity, jealousy, and contention, and too often to become the victims of intemperance and crime." [1]

These conditions were still prevalent despite the passing of the Factory Act of 1833. The ideals which inspired the working men's colleges are illustrated by an address which Professor Huxley gave to the first London Working Men's College in 1868.

Life, said he, "is a game which has been played for untold ages, every man and woman of us being one of the two players in a game of his or her own. The chess-board is the world, the pieces are the phenomena of the universe, the rules of the game are what we call the laws of Nature. The player on the other side is hidden from us. We know that his play is always fair, just and patient. But also we know, to our cost, that he never overlooks a mistake or makes the smallest allowance for ignorance. To the man who plays well the highest stakes are paid with that sort of overflowing generosity with which the strong shows delight in strength. And one who plays ill is checkmated—without haste, but without remorse." [2] The opponent is a calm strong angel who is playing for the love of the game, as we say, and would rather lose than win; and education, Huxley suggests, consists in learning the rules of this mighty game.

Working men's colleges sprang up in various parts of the country, and, at first, appeared to give a satisfaction which the mechanics' institutes had failed to give. Nevertheless, they, too, failed to achieve permanency, owing to the fact that the wider principles which they sought to inculcate could not be grasped by workers who had gained

[1] Bland, A. E., Brown, P. A., and Tawney, R. H., *English Economic History : Select Documents*, p. 641.

[2] Huxley, T. H., *Science and Education*, p. 82.

their early training not in the schoolroom nor under any educational influence, but in repetition work in the factory.

This was a time when all the formal education many received was through the medium of evening classes, or in connection with a Sunday School, where an endeavour was made to supply the elementary grounding which should have been given in the day school. Even for the more fortunate who attended day schools, two or three years' schooling was deemed amply sufficient at a time when there was a pressing demand for child labour. The passing of the Factory Act of 1844 did something to remedy this state of affairs. By this Act the employment of juveniles was limited either to seven hours a day or to ten hours on three alternate days, provided that on the other three days the young people attended school.

The Exhibition of 1851 foreshadowed what I have called the fourth phase. It brought home to those interested in industrial development in England the progress which had been made in certain continental countries in the application of science to industry, and the need for increased attention to technical education if British trade was to hold its own. It would be untrue, however, to conclude that the modern development of technical instruction in this country is wholly due to foreign influence. Undoubtedly, the Great Exhibition introduced new ideas. These ideas fell on ground well prepared by the two experiments of earlier date, by the movement towards better conditions and shorter hours for juveniles, and by the growth in the number of primary schools. Had it not been for the mechanics' institutes, the working men's colleges, and these social and educational developments, the Exhibition of 1851 would probably have had little result upon technical education. As it was, under the fostering care of the Science and Art Department, which was constituted in 1853, schools of art and of science arose in various parts of the country—the forerunners of the movement towards the establishment of a national system of education.

Recognition should be given to the invaluable service rendered in the earlier part of this phase by the Prince Consort, who had been deeply impressed by the development of technical education in Germany, and, in later years, to the service rendered by King Edward, as Prince of Wales. His influence was of first-rate importance, during a critical period, in the building up of a system of technical education in this country.

It was during this last period that the foundations of a system of Junior Technical Schools were laid. From the year 1852 onwards, trade schools arose in connection with the Mechanics' Institute at Manchester, the Islington School of Science and Art, and at Liverpool, Bristol, and elsewhere. The object of these schools was to prepare boys for apprenticeship in the engineering, building, and manufacturing trades, "by supplementing the work of the elementary school with instruction in practical mathematics and physical science" as applied to industry. These schools were the direct ancestors of the junior technical schools of to-day, though these also owe something to the organised science schools which were founded in the 'seventies. These science schools, after 1903, became secondary schools, division A, and took their present shape, after 1907, under Article 42 of the Regulations of the Board of Education for Further Education.

In securing the closer touch between education and industry which we all desire, the junior technical school, which is a near relative of the German Realschüle, has important lessons to teach. It cannot be doubted that this type of institution owes much of its success to the regulation which provides for the inclusion on the staff of a certain proportion of teachers with workshop or other industrial experience. The issue by the Board of Education of Circular 1389 towards the beginning of 1927 has made

possible, for the first time, the partial extension of this
provision to other types of school.

Junior technical schools generally provide a two- or three-
years' course of instruction from the age of thirteen or
fourteen. Their purpose is to provide not specific vocational training, but rather a course of general education with
a bias towards a particular industry or group of industries.
The curriculum is designed to suit the circumstances of
each particular school.   Where boys leave to enter a number
of occupations, the curriculum is less specialised than
it is where the course of instruction is definitely recognised
as part of the pupil's apprenticeship—as it is, for example,
in the printing and furniture trades.   The junior technical
school of a general type has a curriculum which devotes
something like a sixth of the whole time available to each of
the following groups of subjects : English, mathematics,
science, technical drawing, and workshop practice ; the
remainder of the time being given to religious knowledge,
physical training, and art.   Where a modern language is
taken, as it is in all such schools in Kent, the time given
to all the other subjects is slightly reduced.   The inclusion
of a modern language in the curriculum of a junior technical
school is an interesting development.   It is not intended
that the teaching should follow the traditional secondary
school method.   It is recognised that it will be impossible
to teach the pupils to write French or German prose or to be
fluent conversationalists.   The main object is to give them
such ability to read the language as will form the basis
for fuller knowledge, if that is required later, as well as to
bring them under the widening influence of the study of
another tongue.   The more specialised school gives, roughly,
a quarter of the time to workshop practice in the first year,
a half in the second year, and two-thirds in the third year.
Corresponding schools are provided for girls, particularly
in connection with the needle trades.   These, generally,
provide a course which lasts for two or three years.   Approxi-

mately, one-sixth of the time is devoted to English, one-sixth to mathematics, drawing, or science, and three-fifths to trade instruction. While the trade school is necessarily limited to large centres of population where particular trades are congregated, the junior technical school with a more general curriculum furnishes a valuable alternative form of educational provision in any industrial neighbourhood.

Each of the four phases in the earlier history of technical education has definite lessons to teach, for it was during the period which they covered that the problems of technical education which still await solution emerged. They showed that industry in its modern development requires that its workers shall be trained both in handicraft and in science. They showed also that a sound general education is an essential preliminary to technical education. They, further, forced upon the community the realisation that the efficacy of such education was dependent upon a shortening of the hours of work in the factory and a general improvement in working conditions. Finally, to those who have eyes to see, they showed that, without the continuous and active co-operation of educationist and industrialist, there can be no effective education for industry.

The old system of training for industry was simple in method and in aim. It was, more or less, a family affair and aimed at teaching skill in craftsmanship. Modern industry tends more and more towards standardisation and central control. The proportion of skilled workers to unskilled decreases, and there is a growing need for men and women trained in the duties of management. Our system of technical education has failed to adapt itself with sufficient rapidity to the changed conditions. Such failure was perhaps inevitable. It could have been avoided only if the old intimate association between the school and the workshop which existed in the days of apprenticeship could have been maintained. The function of our technical institutions, our technical schools, our technical colleges, and the technical departments of our universities, is not merely to provide an output of men and women fully equipped with the technical knowledge required in the various industries. It is their function, also, to meet the demand for experts in the science of management and for a constant, though limited, supply of skilled workers. It is obviously desirable that the output of such trained workers shall be adequate to but not in excess of the demand, and this end can be secured only by the maintenance of close touch between the educationist and the industrial employer and worker.

The modern phase of the movement for technical education may be said to have begun with the formation of the City and Guilds of London Institute in 1880. This was followed by the opening of the Regent Street Polytechnic in 1881, and of the Finsbury Technical College in 1883. In 1887 the Association for the Promotion of Technical and Secondary Education was established, largely as a result of the Report of the Royal Commission on Technical Education which appeared three years earlier. Then came the passing of the Technical Instruction Act of 1889 and of the Local Taxation (Customs and Excise) Act of 1890. The councils of any county or borough or urban sanitary authority were empowered to aid and promote technical education up to the limit of a penny rate. A considerable number of authorities availed themselves of these powers and, helped by grants from the county councils from the " whisky " money, proceeded to establish technical institutes. This led to a growth in evening technical instruction, and was responsible for such development of day technical work, as, for example, took place at the Municipal School of Technology at Manchester. The era of technical instruction, as we understand that phrase to-day, had begun.

It has already been pointed out that some of the earliest steps to promote technical instruction in this country failed owing to the absence of a national system of elementary education. As the movement for technical education grew, it was realised that the more advanced forms of technical instruction could be founded only on the basis of secondary school provision.

The Education Act of 1902, which laid the foundations of a national system of higher education, and the " Fisher " Act of 1918, which opened the way to the full development of such a system, did much to bring about improvement in the standard of the work in both day and evening technical classes. The Act of 1918, for the first time, clearly established the principle that a sound education of secondary grade is the essential foundation for specific vocational training.

There is a growing recognition that recruits for the great industries require, under modern conditions, a preliminary education of a higher standard than that which was formerly needed. In the engineering industry, for example, candidates for trade apprenticeships are often admitted now about the age of sixteen instead of at fourteen.

Some firms have given up admitting boys from secondary schools as premium pupils about the age of sixteen or seventeen in favour of post-graduate pupils who come in about the age of twenty-one or twenty-two. Many of the larger engineering firms provide a systematic course of instruction for trade apprentices, as well as a regular and comprehensive course for pre-graduate pupils. Some have appointed an educational expert who advises students and supervises their work. Such firms usually look to the local education authority to supplement such internal courses of instruction by external work in the classrooms, laboratories, and workshops of the local technical college The proportion of external to internal work, of course, varies greatly according to local circumstances.

It is difficult to decide how far the education of the worker should be a charge upon the employer and how far upon the local authority. Full co-operation between them is, however, an essential condition of success. Since the time of Robert Owen, enlightened employers have realised the importance of the education of their workers. The Bournville system is only a modern edition of what has been attempted before. When this spirit has permeated the whole body of employers the problem will be solved.

In some areas advisory committees of employers and working men have been set up to assist in the development of local schemes for technical education. The more general creation of such bodies in connection with our technical schools would do much to bridge the unfortunate gap which now exists between education and industry. National advisory committees in connection with our great industries are also needed, like those which were established in connection with the Joint Industrial Councils which came into existence during the Great War.

In this connection, the important part to be played by the trade unions and other associations of working men must not be overlooked. In certain trades, at any rate, they have an important voice in matters connected with apprenticeship and the training of apprentices. Such co-operation is of vital importance in building up suitable forms of training for young men entering the different industries. It must not be forgotten that working men collaborated in the establishment in London, in 1873, of the Trades Guild of Learning, which was succeeded by the Artizans' Institute, the pioneer institution in the modern movement for teaching technology as distinct from science and art. It was the success of this institute and of its classes in bricklaying, masonry, plumbing, and so forth, that opened the way to a wider and truer form of technical education than had been envisaged by the Science and Art Department. It is interesting to remember that this exclusive attitude on the part of the Science and Art Department was upheld by scientists like Huxley, who urged that classes in technological subjects ought not to be supported from public funds but should be provided by such bodies as the Guilds and Companies of the City of London. Mr. Millis, in his valuable book on technical education, quotes a speech made by Huxley at the Society of Arts on December 3, 1879. His opening statement was, " The Science and Art Classes were not meant to teach people to saw."

Technology has had to fight hard for recognition as a necessary part of technical education. From the establishment of the Science and Art Department in 1853 until the passing of the Local Taxation (Customs and Excise) Act, in 1890, the work of the institutes was dominated to a very considerable extent by the system of " payment by results," since the only money generally available from public sources was by way of grants made by the department in respect of individual successes in approved subjects. The position was somewhat improved in 1880 by the formation of the City and Guilds of London Institute, the main purpose of which was to foster classes in technology which the Science and Art Department refused to recognise. The opportunity for another step forward came with the establishment of the Local Education Authorities after 1902. In 1911, Circular 776 was issued by the Board, abolishing the elementary Science and Art examinations. This step encouraged schools to develop their own syllabuses, framed to meet the educational needs of the students, and their own systems of examinations. There followed a considerable extension of the work of such bodies as the Union of Lancashire and Cheshire Institutes, the East Midland Educational Union, and the Union of Educational Institutes. A further development is now in progress which seems likely to result in an arrangement by which these and similar combinations of education authorities, together with examination boards formed by large single educational authorities, like those of the West Riding of Yorkshire and Kent, will retain their position as examining bodies, but will be linked together under a national board of assessors which will endorse certificates, awarded locally as a result of an approved examination.

Most of the technical institutes and colleges of to-day provide a great variety of courses for day and evening students of widely varying needs and capacities. The bulk of the students are represented by those young persons who have left the elementary school at the age of " fourteen plus," in order to enter industry. These, for the most part, attend evening classes. The larger institutes and colleges have also to provide for one or more groups of day students who require either full-time day instruction or part-time day and part-time evening instruction.

A few institutes have taken another road and have concentrated upon preparation for a single industry. Examples of this type are the London School of Printing, and the Shoreditch Technical Institute, which prepares for cabinet-making and the allied trades. The majority of institutes have, however, developed a curriculum of extraordinary complexity. The technical institute, too often, is a congeries of classes rather than a school. Something is done by means of students' clubs, associations, and so forth, to create and maintain a corporate spirit, but the strength and sureness of touch that come from a clear objective are, in some measure, wanting.

One obvious difficulty which hampers the development of the technical institute is that, so often, both students and teachers have done a full day's work before the class begins— " An evening school," as someone has said, " is an assemblage of tired students taught by tired teachers." When the work consists wholly or mainly of evening classes, it is difficult to secure a thoroughly efficient staff. This difficulty grows less as the proportion of day to evening work increases. It is then possible to engage a proportion of whole-time teachers whose working-day can be apportioned between day and evening classes.

The publication by the Board of Education in the early part of 1917, when Mr. Fisher was acting as President of their Draft Regulations for continuation, technical, and art courses in England and Wales, appeared to mark a new era for technical education in this country. The regulations urged " the need for a complete and systematic plan of further education in each area, properly related to elementary and secondary schools and universities, adapted to local needs, and particularly to industrial needs, and offering to every student facilities for a graduated and progressive course of instruction suited to his or her requirements." They foreshadowed the development of local colleges for technical education and defined the work of such colleges in the following terms : " A local college should fulfil two main functions in the educational life of the area which it serves— it should supply technical instruction for all local industries for which such instruction is necessary and desirable, on the basis of a careful and complete investigation of the industrial needs of the area, and it should provide facilities for disinterested intellectual developments by means of classes in literature, history, economics, and other humane studies which make for wise living and good citizenship." It was provided that " in the more important colleges a reasonably large proportion of the full-time staff should have the experience necessary to enable them to undertake original research and to direct the research of advanced students, both in day and evening classes." It was further laid down that " in all full-time departments care should be taken to develop school conditions, including organised games, and all those amenities which are found in well-organised secondary schools." It was realised that " in the case of evening students, the growth of the corporate spirit is a matter of greater difficulty, but much may be done by means of lectures on general subjects, and the establishment of clubs and societies with technical, social, and recreative objects." [1]

Most unfortunately, these regulations failed to receive official recognition. There can be little doubt, however, that, if technical education is to take its true place in our national scheme, there must be development along the lines laid down in the Draft Regulations of 1917.

The successful development of our technical education depends upon the effective recognition of three principles. In the first place, a closer relation must be established between the technical institutions and the other parts of our educational system. Technical education not only must be founded upon a sound general education, but must be developed, in all its stages, in close association with the other branches of post-primary or secondary and university education. It is our administrative practice to divide education into three systems—elementary, secondary, and technical—each distinguished by its own set of rules and regulations, and until recently each controlled by a separate department of the Board of Education. The development of three systems was natural enough, as the problem of education had to be attacked piecemeal. That such a division hampered educational growth was evident even before the Act of 1902. This Act, far from breaking down barriers, probably strengthened them. The results could hardly have been otherwise, seeing that the Act established two kinds of administrative authorities, the one concerned almost entirely with the problem of elementary education, while the other, though responsible for developing all forms of education, was limited in its expenditure on higher education to the product of a two-penny rate.

The Act of 1918, though it removed this limit, though it faced for the first time the problem of universal education

---

[1] Draft of proposed Revised Regulations for Continuation, Technical and Art Courses in England and Wales (February, 1917).

up to from sixteen to eighteen years of age, and though it sought to include within the existing administrative system all forms of educational activities, left intact the three systems —elementary, secondary, and technical education. The result has been a constant struggle to lessen the gulf which at present separates elementary from secondary and further education, in regard to standards of accommodation, equipment, staffing, and salaries. A step in the right direction was taken by the Board when, shortly after 1918, it amalgamated its three departments. But it can be laid down as a postulate that the organisation of our educational system cannot be carried out effectively until we can get rid entirely of our present artificial barriers and realise that the senior elementary school, the junior technical school, the secondary school, and the technical institute are not things different in kind, but that they all provide alternative forms of the same thing—post-primary education. A great obstacle in the way of such a consummation is caused by the existence of separate education authorities for elementary and higher education—and these, except for pious admonitions as to the duty of co-operation, were left untouched by the Act of 1918. Such an arrangement can be defended only if we are prepared to admit that education in an elementary school and education in a secondary school are things different in kind. If we are to have a unified system, this system of divided control must be brought to an end.

In the second place, our conception of technical education must be widened in scope. It is generally recognised that it is the function of a technical institute to teach skill in handicraft and to enable the worker to supplement his daily work in his craft by practice in the workshop or the laboratory under skilled supervision. It is also recognised that it is a part of the function of a technical institute to give instruction in the principles underlying the application of science or of art to industry. It is not yet recognised so clearly that a technical institute must provide also for the development of the social and intellectual interests of the worker. It is the function of the modern technical institute to prepare for leisure as well as for livelihood. An authority like the London County Council is able to make such provision through specialised institutions, like its Literary Institutes. The ordinary provincial institute tends more and more to include in its curriculum not only such subjects as aim at the development of technical knowledge, but also those subjects which, by a false antithesis, are called cultural, like history, literature, and economics.

It will be observed that through the whole period of the development of technical institutions there has been a continual shifting of emphasis. At one moment stress has been laid on the promotion of the industrial efficiency of the worker ; at another on the development of his interests as citizen. One movement has emphasised the formal and utilitarian aspects of technical instruction ; another its social and recreational function. In an ideal society there would be no such conflict. The worker would find in his daily occupation scope for his physical and mental energies. The occupations of his leisure hours would be merely supplementary and recreative. Under modern conditions, the worker, too often, feels no joy in work, no freedom in service. It is only in his leisure hours that he feels able to realise himself. The education of the worker must, there-fore, aim not only at increasing, so far as that is possible, his interest in his work. It must also provide for the develop-ment of his " higher faculties and brightest affections," so that, even if he feels his work to be narrow and limiting he may yet return to it refreshed and strengthened. It should be the aim of technical education, not only to instruct but also to re-create the mind of the worker.

Tribute should be paid to the University Extension Movement and to the Workers' Educational Association for the efforts which they have made in this direction. There is a danger, perhaps, in the fact that such movements have so far concerned themselves almost entirely with what may be called the humanistic side of education. It is not every worker who finds salvation in history or in economics, or in literature. In this respect, it is possible that the Workers' Educational Association may have something to learn from its sister movement, the Federation of Women's Institutes, which has done so much to brighten the lives of the women of the countryside. Though the Women's Institutes rightly lay stress on literature, on music, and on the drama, they lay almost equal stress upon the development of handicraft, and so make their appeal, not only to those who are interested in the former things, but also to those whose primary interest is in handicraft—those people who " pray best with their hands." The technical institute of the future must enlarge its outlook, so as to embrace in its purview—not necessarily to bring under its control—such movements as these, while these movements themselves must widen their conception of Adult Education so as to include its technical aspect. Otherwise, there will be grave danger of a disastrous cleavage between the technological and the humanistic aspects of the education of the worker.

In the third place, and lastly, there must be a determined attempt to bridge the fatal gap which at present exists between the school and the workshop. Success in such an effort demands a change of view on the part both of the educationist and of the industrialist. In our justifiable reaction against the idea that the child should be considered merely as a future cog in the industrial machine, some of us have rushed to the other extreme, and have sometimes argued as though vocation had no bearing upon the education given in our day schools. We have shut our eyes to the fact that the most effective appeal to the adolescent comes often from the close association of his school work with the industrial work to which he is looking forward. We have overlooked the fact that secondary schools and universities are largely training grounds for the professions, and to that extent vocational. We have forgotten that the trodden path of academic culture is not the only way to a liberal education. On some young persons I believe that a stronger educational influence would be exercised by entry into industry, coupled with attendance at the part-time day continuation school, than by the prolongation of their full-time education.

Hitherto, there has been little incentive for pupils terminating their whole-time education at fourteen, to continue to pursue a part-time course of instruction, because of the divorce which exists between the day school—both elementary and secondary—and the institute for further education. This point was emphasised in a statement on the report of the Consultative Committee on *The Education of the Adolescent* made to the County Councils' Association in March, 1927, by Lord Eustace Percy :

" We have," he said, " to consider the closely related question of part-time education. I said recently that the time had come when we ought to think out afresh the whole question of technical and vocational education, and, if we are to do this, we ought to do it in the closest connection with post-primary full-time instruction. As you know, this close connection already exists in the case of what are now called junior technical or trade schools, which are themselves often an integral part of polytechnics or technical institutes conducting evening or part-time day classes."

The Education Act of 1918 required that " appointed days " should be fixed after which young persons who had not continued under full-time instruction until the age of sixteen would be under a statutory obligation to attend for part-time at day continuation schools. Nothing would, in my judgment, prove more effective in establishing the right relations between education and industry, and in helping us to discover the right curriculum and methods for the post-primary school as the putting into force—perhaps in a somewhat modified form—of the suspended provisions of this Act.

It is a matter of profound regret that the Consultative Committee, in considering the education of the adolescent, were debarred by their terms of reference from including in their purview day continuation schools. This fact has had the unfortunate result of directing the attention of the country to the question of the raising of the school-age to fifteen to the neglect of what seems to many the more important and more urgent question of the continued education of the adolescent in part-time day classes until the age of eighteen. I wish to see the school-age raised to fifteen. I believe that this reform will come. I am afraid that its coming may mean the indefinite postponement of the compulsory day continuation school. If that is so, it will be bought at too high a cost. On the other hand, the establishment of the day continuation school would facilitate and hasten the raising of the school-age, and would enable the curriculum of the post-primary school to be adapted to the needs both of the adolescent and of industry in the light of experience such as we do not yet possess.

In April, 1920, when the establishment of compulsory day continuation schools appeared to be imminent, the Kent Education Committee issued a memorandum on the organisation and curriculum of day continuation schools for young persons between the ages of fourteen and sixteen. From it I quote the following general paragraphs :

" The immediate aim of the Day Continuation School is to take the practical life of boys and girls in the workshop, the office, and the farm, and endeavour to give it a new social value and a new meaning, leading them to participate in it more fully and more worthily and helping each to make the most and best of himself. The young people who attend these schools will remain under educational influences throughout the period of adolescence. A course of education, wisely planned, should enlarge their interests, widen their outlook, and enrich their understanding of life, both during their working hours and during their leisure time at home.

"The teaching should be essentially practical in character. A variety of interesting handicrafts will be one of the main ways of developing the pupils' powers ; and physical education, including organised games, should be a prominent part of the school life. Class libraries and workshops for handicrafts and practical science, or in the case of girls, domestic rooms, should be essential features of every school.

"The school should be a community, a corporate entity, and not merely a procession of transitory classes without common interests. It should become the social centre of its neighbourhood. It should develop a strong recreative and social side with clubs and societies, as far as possible under the responsible control of the pupils themselves. Indeed, the fullest opportunities should be given for the development of healthy self-government not only in the outside enterprises, but also as regards the more formal business of the actual school hours.

"A Continuation School should be a centre of spontaneous activity. Under the wise and kindly guidance of their teachers and tutors, boys and girls will be free to develop their own chosen interests, for the most part through private study and self-organised occupations. The school should foster and develop not only those interests which, if they have been fortunate, the young adolescents will have brought with them from their earlier school days, but also that lively curiosity and that sense of exploration and adventure of which they are conscious in the larger world which they have now entered. It must reveal to them not only their place and their responsibilities in the world of to-day, but also their heritage from times past in history, literature, and art. It must provide worthy and acceptable ideals for their leisure time."

If there is a need for a change of attitude on the part of the educationist towards industry, there is also need for a radical change in outlook on the part of the employer. As the report of the Departmental Committee on *Juvenile education in relation to employment* has said, the age of adolescence must be " brought out of the purview of economic exploitation and into that of the social conscience. The conception of the juvenile as primarily a little wage earner " must be " replaced by the conception of the juvenile as primarily the worker and the citizen in training." It must be " established that the educational purpose is to be the dominating one without, as well as within, the school doors during those formative years between twelve and eighteen."

It is not only in the case of the adolescent that some change of outlook is needed. The other day, a visitor was taken over a modern factory where the process of scientific management, or " rationalisation," as the Americans call it, has been carried to an extreme degree. The visitor duly admired the perfection of the organisation, and asked, " Is there any point of weakness ? " " Yes," was the reply ; " the weak point in our system is that about which we know least, the nervous system."

In his book *Science and the Modern World*, Professor Whitehead writes :

" In regard to the æsthetic needs of civilised society the reactions of science have so far been unfortunate. Its materialistic basis has directed attention to *things* as opposed to *values*. The antithesis is a false one, if taken in a concrete sense. But it is valid at the abstract level of ordinary thought. This misplaced emphasis coalesced with the abstractions of political economy, which are in fact the abstractions in terms of which commercial affairs are carried on. Thus all thought concerned with social organisation expressed itself in terms of material things and of capital. Ultimate values were excluded. They were politely bowed to, and then handed over to the clergy to be kept for Sundays. A creed of competitive business morality was evolved, in some respects curiously high ; but entirely devoid of consideration for the value of human life. The workmen were conceived as mere hands, drawn from the pool of labour. To God's question, men gave the answer of Cain—' Am I my brother's keeper ? '; and they incurred Cain's guilt. This was the atmosphere in which the industrial revolution was accomplished in England, and to a large extent else-where. The internal history of England during the last half century has been an endeavour slowly and painfully to undo the evils wrought in the first stage of the new epoch. It may be that civilisation will never recover from the bad climate which enveloped the introduction of machinery." [1]

In the modern factory the machines are watched and tended with scrupulous care. The human organism is more complicated than any machine, more liable to get out of order and, if neglected, as certain to produce catastrophe. Of all natural forces it is the most difficult to understand and to control. From the time of the industrial revolution onwards, there has been a growing tendency towards the dehumanising of industry and the neglect of human values. To counteract this tendency, local education authorities and many employers, with the help of the industrial psycho-logist, are doing what they can by means of welfare work, vocational selection, vocational guidance, and after-care. What is needed, however, in the case of the adult as in the case of the adolescent, is a change of view. We have to recognise that, in the long run, the effectiveness of the worker does not depend merely upon the speed and accuracy with which he repeats his allotted task in the factory. He cannot work effectively if he takes no interest in his work, and if in that work there is no room for the exercise and development of his mind.

The author of *The Mind in Action* observes : " The use of machinery has stimulated production and has con-ferred many benefits on men, but it has undoubtedly in many cases made it impossible for the workman to feel interest in his work. This is one of the main problems of industry at the present moment : ' How can work be arranged so that the workman is able to find the maximum possible interest in it ? ' " [2] The evil can be mitigated but

---

[1] *Science and the Modern World*, by A. N. Whitehead, pp. 291–292.
[2] *The Mind in Action*, by George H. Green, chap. iii.

not removed by shortening the hours of labour. Leisure is a necessary supplement to work which absorbs the physical and mental energies of the worker. It is no effective substitute for it.

The instruction and training which are given in our technical schools and colleges are only one form of the spiritual process which we call education. Professor Whitehead, again, has said that " Wisdom is the fruit of a balanced development. It is this balanced growth of individuality which it should be the aim of education to secure." [1] In such development, school and workshop, hours of work and hours of leisure, play their part.

> Slow o'er the dial the shadows creep.
> So many hours for food and sleep.
> So many hours till studies tire.
> So many hours for heart's desire.

The worker is not merely student nor merely craftsman. He is a human being with a natural and social inheritance of ideas and emotions.

The prosperity of industry does not depend alone upon the manual skill of the workers, nor upon their scientific knowledge. It depends, to an extent which has never yet been fully realised, upon that common understanding between employer and employed which can be based only upon a common culture. Craft Gild, Mechanics' Institute, Working Men's College, Polytechnic, Trade School, Tutorial Class, and Women's Institute—each has made its own contribution to our conception of the meaning of technical education. Not until that conception is wide enough to include all these separate fragments of truth will our technical institutes take their due place in our educational scheme, and play their full part in the common educational task, the building up of a community of men and women both able and willing to serve the commonweal.

[1] *Science and the Modern World*, by A. N. Whitehead, p. 284.

190 SECONDARY EDUCATION

REFERENCES

BALFOUR, GRAHAM. Educational Systems of Great Britain and Ireland. 1903.

CREASEY, CLARENCE H. A Technical Education in Evening Schools. 1905.

DAVIES, REV. J. LLEWELYN. The Working Men's College, 1854-1904. 1904.

DOBBS, A. E. Education and Social Movements, 1700-1850. 1919.

GODARD, JOHN G. George Birkbeck. 1884.

HOGG, ETHEL M. Quintin Hogg. 1904.

HUDSON, J. W. The History of Adult Education. 1851.

MAGNUS, SIR PHILIP. Industrial Education. 1888.

MILLIS, C. T. Technical Education—its development and aims. 1925.

MOORE SMITH, G. C. The Story of the People's College, Sheffield, 1842-1878. 1912.

PARRY, R. ST. JOHN. Cambridge Essays on Adult Education. 1920.

ROBERTS, R. D. Education in the XIXth Century. 1901.

SADLER, M. E. Continuation Schools in England and elsewhere. 1907.

WYATT, CHARLES H. Manual of Continuation Schools and Technical Instruction. 1892.

A Manual for Mechanics and their Institutions. 1846.

Board of Education. Humanism in the Continuation School (Ed. Pamphlets No. 43), 1921.

——. Annual Report, 1908-1909.

Report of the International Congress on Technical Education. London, 1897.

Report of the Royal Commission on Technical Education, 1880-1884.

The Directory, South Kensington.

The Journal of the Society of Arts.

The Record of Technical and Secondary Education.

The Reports of the City and Guilds of London Institute.

CHAPTER IX

THE BORSTAL SCHOOL

By C. A. SIEPMANN

THE fact that education in Borstal institutions should figure in this series of studies under the heading " Secondary Education," is a sign of the times, and indicates in striking fashion the development which is taking place in modern theories both of crime and education. I hope to show that these institutions have not only an interest and a romance of their own, but a bearing on the future of education as a whole which no wise thinker can afford to overlook. I propose therefore to tell their story in outline, and to forecast within the limits of one's present vision the future course of their development.

On a high hill, overlooking the Medway and one of the loveliest valleys in the south country, were erected late in the last century the grim buildings of a convict prison. The developments of twenty years have seen the removal of the convicts and the destruction of almost all the buildings on this site. In their place now stand the four houses of His Majesty's Borstal Institution. This was provided for by Act of Parliament just twenty years ago. The contamination in gaol of boys still in their teens by hardened and experienced criminals was at that time the subject of general concern, its prevention the slogan of reformers. This dread of contamination led to the foundation of our first Borstal institution. It led equally to the early limitations and defects of the system. The public at that time was ill-informed. The average man knew little of his neighbours, even of such as were respectable ; and criminals, young and old, were left by the virtuous to the tender mercies of prison authorities, dulled by a crude tradition and embittered by long contact with an ugly system of reform and a brutish type of criminal humanity. The boy delinquent was regarded as belonging to a species different from the normal, and therefore to be differently treated. It was an age of educational catchwords. General principles of treatment were applauded with little reference to the appropriateness of their application, and the drab uniformity of dress in prisons further induced a view of prisoners as undifferentiated units of a single species. A man who passed within prison walls parted with personality even as he bade farewell to liberty. Discipline, hard work, constant—too constant—supervision comprised, with long hours of confinement in separate cells, the staple diet of our first Borstal institution.

We have not lived on into these post-war days to decry discipline or to disparage industry. But time and a new knowledge of ourselves and of our fellows has taught us how much interpretation matters, how discipline can mar as it can make ; and other chapters in this book will tell no less how much the timely aid of a new science has advanced our knowledge of the means to educational achievement. The four years of the war induced in the Borstal system a disastrous *status quo*. Its end heralded an inspired advance.

This volume has been termed " a study in renaissance." It is a cause of pride to those who work to-day in Borstal institutions that they are carrying out their arduous but inspiring duties within sight of a great rebirth—a rebirth of which they are themselves an element, and to which they are themselves contributing. It is of recent developments in the principles which underlie the system of our present institutions that I wish to speak. Borstal to-day is visibly and fundamentally the antithesis of its own past.

There are now three Borstal institutions for boys and one for girls ; and while there are minor variations, desirable and necessary in each, the general system is more or less the same in all. The boy who has passed through the courts and has waited at Wandsworth Prison until final arrangements have been made for his disposal, is sent to one of the three institutions at Borstal, Feltham, and Portland. In the institution where he is to spend the next two years he starts at the bottom of a ladder, the top of which is well within his range of vision. He is allocated to a house, whose colours he will wear, and in whose interests he will be taught to work and play and think. He will have opportunities, through good conduct and exercise of public spirit, of rising through a system of grades with an increasing range of privileges, and a gradual extension of his personal liberty. In his first weeks he will be set to carry out the necessary menial work of the institution ; he will be employed to scrub the floors and tables of the halls in which he and his fellows live, under the guidance of officers chosen for their insight and sympathy, who will watch and note the elements of character which the monotony of uncongenial work reveals. In these first days his record will have been examined and his fitness for any particular vocation studied. In time he will be consulted as to a choice of trades to which he will be asked to devote himself during the remainder of his time in Borstal. The daily routine in Borstal institutions involves an early rise at six o'clock, morning drill and exercise, breakfast at seven, and with an interval for lunch, an eight hours' day of labour in one or other of the various trade parties. Boys in these parties, painters and plasterers, plumbers and carpenters, have had their share in the construction of many of the houses and buildings which you may see to-day. In eight hours of daily work the boy learns, perhaps for the first time, the secrets of a skilled trade, and the discipline and virtue of regular and un-flinching labour. By five o'clock this element of his training

o

is over and the evenings are given to recreation and to
" school classes."

In the friendly rivalry between houses, in games and
house matches, and in his own house as member of a
" group " or " section " under a boy leader, pitted in
rivalry against other sections in service and good conduct,
he learns the pride and pleasure of being the useful member
of a social community. Every day of his life he will come
under the influence of a housemaster and a staff of officers,
whose chief duties are the study of his character and the
pursuit of a relationship which at its best attains to friendship. Of the " school classes " it is difficult to give a
concise account. The education of a community varying
in age between sixteen and twenty-three, and in educational
attainment between that of the illiterate and of the secondary
school boy, presents a problem of bewildering complexity.
Add to these difficulties the fact that few members of the staff
are trained classroom teachers, and it will be realised that
the task of the education officer, himself a housemaster, is
one providing scope for an ingenious originality. The
absence of certificated teachers is not on the whole a serious
matter. It is to be remembered that boys at Borstal are the
failures of all previous systems of training, the renegades of
all influences hitherto exerted on them. The schools have
not proved sufficient, and the young man of twenty is not
to be brought back to classroom methods without offence
to his self-esteem and the risk of repeated failure. It is for
Borstal to find new ways of influence, to initiate new methods
of approach. Hence the difficulty of a concise account of
class-room education. The syllabus constantly varies as
experience proves this or that element to be unsatisfactory.
In Borstal, education is to be found a process of empirical
development still in its first and most exciting stages.
Discovery is imminent, and term by term in method and
subject-matter fresh failures, fresh successes inspire the
activities of those who level these unbeaten tracks in

adolescent education. As I have hinted, it is fatal and foolish to attempt to set back the hands of the clock and to recall a lad of twenty to the methods of elementary schools. The independence of spirit and the enlarged experience of these boys must constantly be borne in mind, and education in the limited sense of academic instruction must be related to the current interests and aspirations of those for whom it is provided. Housemasters and officers (the one-time armed and uniformed warders) now share in the work of education, and the syllabus has developed from compulsory instruction in the three R's to the provision of handicrafts, the development of musical and literary societies, and the organisation of classes on a basis of voluntary choice.

The details of educational progress, the fascination of original achievement and discovery, the scope for enterprise and the astonishing effects on individuals of personal influence and sympathy, are subjects on which, did space permit, I would enlarge, but I must turn to consider what is significant in the post-war renaissance in Borstal institutions, what are the principles of faith and action that seem to denote elements of permanent worth.

There is a tendency in modern thought to view with growing anxiety the problem of post-primary education. The government report on *The Education of the Adolescent*, published in 1926, dealt with this problem from the angle of the schools, and the extension of the school age to fifteen or to sixteen will no doubt contribute to its solution. Nevertheless the extension of any scheme of education not modified to meet the needs of those for whom it is provided will be worse than useless—will indeed invite disaster and the expenditure and waste of sums of public money which it is urgent should be saved. The whole problem of adolescent education is a new one and there are few signposts along the road ; but in the Borstal system may be found certain first principles for students of adolescent education which experience is proving to be fundamental. I have suggested earlier that Borstal to-day is visibly and fundamentally the antithesis of its own past. The new teaching is based on the realisation, born partly perhaps of war experiences and partly of new observations in psychology, of the essential likeness of us all. Crime and the criminal have lost a good deal of their exotic and unhealthy fascination as men's knowledge of themselves and of each other has increased. The ordinary boy at Borstal is not essentially different from the boy of our own past. He is a boy in difficulties, and those at Borstal have set themselves the task of discovering and disposing of his stumbling-blocks.

It must be remembered that psychologically the adolescent is in a state of acute and perilous transition, that the conditions of his home environment are too often not such as will help him to assimilate or to control the instincts and impulses stirring within him. Further, he is potentially a worker in an industrial world where absence of skill will materially affect his chances of employment. I have stressed the deficiencies of environment. It is important that any scheme of education, anything taught, any new interests aroused, should be related to the environment and the conditions under which the boys and girls of this industrial age are forced to live.

It is in the light of these and similar considerations that the Borstal system has been developed. It is at the moment the only complete system of education for the adolescent, unique in that it provides that complete training for life which was the ideal of Platonic philosophy. The very routine of the day which I have outlined is a replica of the day of work and leisure in ordinary life. There must be no sudden break, no violent contrast in the environment to which, on completion of their training, the boys pass on. There is inevitably a contrast, a difference between school life and home life. No system of education can wholly dispose of it, but it is urgent, especially among adolescents, in whom the practical bias is so strong, that this distinction be as far as possible obliterated, that the relation of education to life itself be plainly understood. The outline which I have given of a Borstal day should prove that this fundamental principle of adolescent education has been grasped. Vocational training must find its place in the curriculum, but of no less importance is that education in the uses of leisure to which the evening classes are devoted. The games, the spirit of rival sections, the constant presence and interest of housemasters and their assistants, all these are elements in a great scheme of education in that sense of membership of a community to which I have previously referred. What is at once so heart-rending and so inspiring is the freshness of these ideals in the experience of these boys. Daily new planets swim within their ken—new loyalties, a new sense of obligation to others, and of responsibility and self-respect ; most potent, perhaps, of all, a new realisation of the value of home influences and a desire to better home conditions by personal effort and example.

And what of the future ? It will be built on the experience of the present ; the faults and the deficiencies of our inspired to-day will become clearer in the cool retrospect of a to-morrow still beyond our view. The Borstal system will extend and grow. One hopes that the imprisonment of any person under twenty-one will not be tolerated much longer. There will be new Borstal institutions. New helpers will be required, men of character and education, ready to learn as well as to instruct. For students of adolescent education I know no better training ground, no field of research so varied in its appeal. For the duties of a housemaster or an assistant housemaster are no sinecure. On his influence and understanding depends in large measure the future of some ninety boys. He must so have studied and assimilated the past record and history of every member of his house as to be capable of gauging what method of approach is likely best to win the confidence and mould the future conduct of each individual. Mixing in easy friendliness with them at play and during the hours of association in the house, he must learn first to see life from their point of view (the root of all good teaching and of any lasting relationship), and thereafter by patient example win them to a finer and prouder conception of life and of their place in it. As education officer, librarian, games master, etc., he will have institution duties to perform as further claims upon his time and interest. He will have under him a staff of officers whose sympathy by tact and understanding and inspired example he must win for the development of his ideas. Here is room for the scholar and the athlete, for all manner of men, provided they have in them the milk of human kindness and a right sense of human relationship.

But no improvement in the system of Borstal training should obscure from our minds the fact that the existence of these institutions is a grave reflection on the state of our society. We cannot nowadays view with anything but impatience the notion that delinquency is a necessary evil. Poverty and unemployment, the lack of sound and helpful influences at home, amongst other influences combine with an incomplete education to create an atmosphere in which natural and healthy development is not to be expected. The extension of the Borstal system is certain. It is wise and necessary that such a course of training be extended. But I envisage the time when Borstal institutions will have discarded that implication of reproach which now attaches to them as places of correction. It is as models of a future system of adolescent education, brought within the reach of the many who need not correction but the completion of their training as citizens of a liberal state, that the Borstal institutions of to-day claim the attention of all who have at heart this great renaissance in the schools of England.

REFERENCES

BURT, CYRIL. The Young Delinquent. University of London Press, 1925. (An indispensable handbook to the whole problem, and a first-rate analysis of the causes of delinquency.)

GODDARD, H. H. Juvenile Delinquency. Kegan Paul, Trench, Trübner & Co., 1923.

GURNER, RONALD. C3. Dent.

HALL, W. CLARKE. The State and the Child. Headley Bros., 1917. (A study of the system of children's courts.)

HALL, STANLEY. Adolescence. Appleton & Co., 1905. 2 vols.

HEALY, WILLIAM. The Individual Delinquent. Little, Brown & Co., 1915.

SWIFT, G. J. The Psychology of Youth. Scribner & Sons. (A Study of school methods in America.)

Board of Education, J.O.C. Report on Juvenile Delinquency, 1920.
The Education of the Adolescent, 1926.

There is as yet no first-rate book on the Borstal system itself. For those who are interested to trace the development of public opinion with reference to the treatment of offenders, young and old, the following are recommended :—

HOBHOUSE AND BROCKWAY. English Prisons To-day. Longmans, 1921.

WEBB. English Prisons under Local Government. Longmans.

THE TRAINING COLLEGE

CHAPTER X

THE TRAINING OF TEACHERS

By HERBERT WARD

THE training colleges do not belong to the primary, or to the secondary, or to the university organisation. They have affinities with all three, but they are not entirely associated with any one. Nobody seems to have suggested that training colleges may be a species of technological institution, though the idea is not wholly absurd. They are anomalies, then, obnoxious to the minds of those who will be content with nothing short of a logical system capable of being displayed in a neat diagram. Like other anomalies in English education (and the training colleges do not stand alone), they are not on that account haphazard, nor did they arise incidentally and by inadvertence. It is the purpose of this chapter to show how they came into being in response to a need, and how their development is intimately bound up with the development of education—elementary, secondary, and university education alike. It will attempt to remove some of the fog which in the eyes of the outside public surrounds the training of teachers, and indicate a few of the unsolved problems which embarrass those whose business it is to conduct training colleges.

The temptation to detail the quaint beginnings of training colleges in England and Wales must be resisted. Let it suffice to say that by 1860 an intelligible system was fully established. It had arisen because elementary education was rapidly spreading, and the two great societies, the

National Society and the British and Foreign School Society, which stimulated and directed the benevolent founders of schools, from the first had felt the absolute necessity of preparing teachers to set up the new schools. The government chose to aid the voluntary agencies instead of themselves instituting state colleges as in France. The supply of students was assured by the pupil-teacher system, which by 1860 was in full working order. Most of the present voluntary colleges, diocesan and other, were then in existence. For thirty years, save for insignificant internal changes, there was no disturbance in the scheme.

It is this stable period of thirty years, from 1860 to 1890, to which I wish to draw attention, partly in order to have a basis of comparison with present conditions and partly because certain prevalent conceptions of training, of institutions for training, and of the certification of teachers were formed in this period. The ideas which then arose have obtained so firm a hold on the minds of people who speak and write about education that it is difficult to persuade them that any substantial modifications have since occurred.

For thirty years the training-college system was a definite and exceedingly tidy organisation. Uniformity was its principal characteristic. The colleges were all under voluntary management, supported by religious societies or by committees which took up the undenominational position. They were all residential. With very few exceptions all the students had been pupil-teachers, that is, bright scholars in the elementary schools, apprenticed for four or five years. The studies of the pupil-teachers during each year of their apprenticeship had been directed by syllabuses issued by the Education Department, which examined them annually. Success in the final examination of the series, which became known as the Queen's Scholarship Examination, made them eligible for entry into a training college. In college the course was also laid down by syllabus and was the same for all, with some differences between men and women, and a few unimportant options. The college was examined at the end of each year of training, and if the student passed the examination at the end of the second year, he was entitled to the teachers' certificate.

The whole of the work of the students, both in their apprenticeship and at the training college, was little more than an expansion of the curriculum of the elementary school. It was designed to prepare the future teachers for the work they took up on leaving college in the elementary school. So the training colleges for thirty years were quite clearly part of elementary education with no recognised connections with either secondary school or university. When we look back upon it, the training seems to us very narrow, illiberal, and inadequate, as it has often been declared to be by those who passed through it. Interested observers from outside, like Edward Bowen of Harrow, were apt to shudder at it, and to pray Heaven that they should never be expected to become certificated teachers.

There is, of course, another side to the picture. If you reflect that the thirty years, during which the training colleges were stabilised, were the years when elementary education in England and Wales really took shape, covering the whole country and becoming compulsory for those who were not under other forms of instruction, and remember that this gigantic evolution was effected quietly, and in its way efficiently, and certainly without breakdown, you will have nothing but admiration for the men and women who were the chief instruments in the change. The same tribute of respect will be extended to the large number of pupil-teachers who through want of accommodation or want of means could not enter training colleges, but prepared themselves by assiduous study for the same examinations and also gained the certificate.

As a matter of sober fact, teaching in elementary schools became in this period a new career, a career with special attractions for the vigorous and ambitious children of those members of the community to whom the avenues of approach to secondary schools were few and difficult. Young people who themselves felt a thirst for further education, or whose parents felt it for them, had hardly any other means of procuring it, and few other outlets than teaching for its exercise when it had been obtained. The result was that a large number of vigorous men and women became elementary school teachers. The narrowness of the course of training through the pupil-teacher and college years did not quench the energy of these virile people or turn them into mechanical pedagogues. The generation trained between 1860 and 1890 has now nearly all passed out of the schools. As one who has had the amplest of opportunities for knowing them in their maturity, I am bound to testify my high appreciation of the work they have accomplished.

By 1890 it was clear that the colleges were growing unequal to the demands made upon them. They were not sending out enough teachers for the expanding elementary school service, and there was little hope that the deficiency would be supplied through voluntary agencies. Moreover, the prescribed syllabuses were too narrow and too easy for the better educated pupil-teachers who were now entering the colleges. The Education Department, therefore, following the recommendations of the Commission of 1886, made some striking new departures. Selected students might read for degrees, and for that or for the purpose of study abroad might be kept for a third year. Further, universities and university colleges were authorised to establish training departments, in which students could stay three years and gain both a degree and the certificate. In this volume it is appropriate to remark that the first institution of university rank to set up a training department was King's College, London.

These changes introduced a period of development which at the present day is not complete. The simple organisation of the older kind of training disappears ; the central authority begins to relax the strictness of its control, and the certificate no longer testifies to a uniform training, clear and unmistakable in its outlines. A further complication adds to the growing confusion. The new graduates were to liberalise the elementary school. But the able young men and women who took degrees were to a large extent absorbed by secondary schools, training colleges, and the newly-instituted pupil-teacher centres. Hitherto there had been no very regular flow of trained teachers into secondary schools, though from time to time elementary schoolmasters had found places in these schools. But from 1890 the flow becomes steady, and it is not too much to say that almost inadvertently the training of secondary teachers begins.

The Education Act of 1902 made possible the next significant change, the replacement of pupil-teacher apprenticeship by education in secondary schools. Only a rapid increase in secondary schools, such as took place after 1902, and in consequence of the powers conferred by that Act, could have made feasible the transfer of what is now called the preliminary education of intending teachers from private instruction and pupil-teacher centres to the secondary school. From this time, although pupil-teachers continued, and even exist to-day in some areas, the training colleges have an increasingly intimate connection with secondary schools, from which all but a few of their students now come. This change loosened also the tie between the curriculum of the training colleges and that of the pupil-teachers ; it could be looked upon not as the completion of an advanced type of elementary education, but as the continuance of the education of the secondary school. At the same time from the new secondary schools there proceeded an increasing number of students capable of reading for degrees at the university or in the training college.

The Act of 1902 also brought into relation with training colleges the new local education authorities. For they were not only empowered, but encouraged by building grants, to establish colleges of their own. The voluntary colleges were not able to meet the demand for teachers, and the supply from the university training departments was too small to make up the growing deficiency. The local authorities have not only provided fresh accommodation but are making their influence felt in the training of teachers as a whole.

Since 1902 there have been certain changes to be noticed. In 1911 the period of training in universities was extended to four years, and the rule established in them that the professional side of training, that is, the study of the principles and practice of teaching, should be generally relegated to a professional year to follow the years during which the students prepare for the degree. The " year of training " comes to have this special meaning. Since 1902 also the Board of Education have by degrees relaxed their control over the curriculum and the examinations in training colleges ; in the Regulations of 1926 the Board almost ceases to prescribe and control by approving what is held to be suitable. It was manifest that the old prescriptions in syllabus and the former detailed management of examinations could not exist when universities came into the field. Moreover, the colleges themselves became staffed with persons who were competent to decide upon their own courses of instruction, and could not be asked to follow uniform lines dictated by a central office. The successive stages by which colleges which desired it secured independence in curriculum and in examination need not be detailed. In 1925 the President of the Board announced that the Board would cease to examine teachers and intending teachers, and would utilise existing examining bodies or bodies to be specially created for the purpose. As these new bodies are not yet finally settled, comment would be impolitic. Later, in 1926, the Board removed all syllabuses and nearly all detailed rules regarding the content of the training course from the regulations.

The new regulations, now a slender pamphlet containing only the conditions of grant, also dispense with the perplexing distinctions between types of training and kinds of colleges, and for the first time in our educational history training colleges are treated as one kind of institution and training as one process. This simplification, which has received scanty notice in the educational press, seems to me to be a considerable step in advance. Forms of training may be varied and numerous, as they must be if they are to meet the numerous and varied requirements of the schools. But from 1926 onwards training is one function.

Space does not permit me to detail all the corollaries which follow from the principal steps in development so sketchily described. No better example could be adduced of the Spencerian law of progress, from homogeneity to heterogeneity. In 1890 a simple system with a definite end ; in 1927 a highly complex system apparently with different ends and a variety of ways, some direct, many by-ways, and numerous short cuts, to each of the ends. Universities, secondary schools, and elementary schools are all concerned, but their relations are far from manifest. Yet there is one gleam of hope at least. The various means and ends all tend to be merged into one ultimate aim, the training of all teachers for the service of teaching.

Is it so extraordinarily difficult to convey to the intelligent inquirer how a person becomes a trained teacher ? Let the attempt be made.[1] In order to become a trained teacher an aspirant must enter a training college, and the door of entrance is by way of one of the First Schools Examinations.[2] For most candidates this means education at a secondary school. The choice of a training college depends upon whether the candidate wishes to read for a

---

[1] *Cf.* the passage quoted on p. 12.
[2] *E.g.* the School Certificate Examination described in Chap. VI (p. 120) and Chap. VII (p. 158).

degree or does not. If he does, he must apply at a university or university college, or one of the other colleges where a degree course is recognised. He must expect to stay four years, as a rule, giving three to work for the degree and the fourth to professional training. If he does not wish to take a degree, he must go to a training college which is not a part of a university, and must stay two years. At the end of his course he obtains the teachers' certificate or, at the universities, a diploma of education, which includes a teachers' certificate. He is free to teach in any type of approved school, and is not earmarked for any. This bifurcation, in one direction towards a degree, with a certificate and a diploma, in the other towards the certificate without a degree, seems to me to be the leading distinction at the present time. All the alternatives are but variations of the main principles, dictated by common sense or the particular conditions of certain colleges. It is beyond my purpose to discuss whether the bifurcation is right or to prophesy how long it will remain. The formal contact with universities that will be established when the new examining bodies already mentioned are constituted may produce modifications. But as things are the system of training teachers is so near approaching tidiness that, if need be, it could be illustrated by a diagram, at least as clear as some of the educational diagrams by which we are expected to be instructed.

It will not be amiss to say something at this point upon the Board's certificate, concerning which there are misunderstandings in some quarters. Why, it is asked, is the elementary service barred to those who do not possess this particular certificate ; or if admission is not absolutely barred, why must all who are not certificated enter and continue in a quite subordinate capacity ? There is no specific qualification demanded in secondary schools or the various schools of further education, why should there be in elementary schools ? Is there any special virtue in the Board's certificate and in the preparation for it that could not be found in other qualifications, possibly more advanced ?

The answer broadly is that the certificate is a survival from an earlier condition of affairs, and that the time is not yet ripe for it to be superseded. During the initiatory period, when the nation was sincerely anxious to establish elementary schools accessible to all children who were not otherwise under instruction, it was of first importance to find teachers and to set up a standard of preparation and of attainment which would meet the situation. The result was the pupil-teacher system and the training colleges. Unlike France and Germany, the English government did not create training institutions through which all teachers in the public service must pass. They were content to admit persons who were partially trained by their years of apprenticeship—the ex-pupil teachers—and even auxiliaries wholly untrained—the supplementary teachers. It is to be remembered that the English system was at the bottom one of voluntary schools, not of state schools. But they did set up standards, not only a standard of attainment, but a standard of staffing. The responsible teacher in an elementary school was to be a certificated teacher. If the standard of attainment remained for a long time without modification, that of staffing developed and in the larger schools assistant teachers were also certificated. In the '70's and onward certification did not always mean training, but in the last twenty years the association has grown closer and closer, and in 1926 the last examination for the certificate without training was held. Henceforward the certificated teacher is also the trained teacher. Although we have not yet reached the consummation to which all the developments have been tending, we are nearing a time in which the term " elementary school teacher " means one who is trained and certificated. There are 169,000 teachers in elementary schools, and of these some 120,000 are certificated.

It is clear that this development, so slowly achieved, cannot be summarily checked merely because certification appears to the first glance of the outsider to be a bureaucratic or a pedantic device. The absurdities which it seems to entail are few and unimportant. It is true that Mr. Fisher, on retiring from office, humorously regretted that he could enter an elementary school only as an uncertificated teacher. But high graduates and fellows of their colleges have not displayed an overwhelming anxiety to teach in elementary schools. Moreover, some quite recent changes have done much to remove this anomaly. For a young graduate who is trained in a university training department or elsewhere, now automatically becomes certificated if he wishes to be so. If he is not trained, he can enter an elementary school, and by serving there under some supervision get the certificate on what to him should be easy terms. In fact the certificate is rapidly becoming, what it should become, a licence to teach. This licence to teach continues to be required for all new entrants into the elementary service, save for very subordinate positions, carrying low salaries. It is not required for secondary schools ; but out of 14,000 graduates in state-aided secondary schools, 7,000 are trained and certificated.

The line of advance appears to be, not for the Board at this stage to impose a kind of certificate upon persons wishing to teach in secondary schools, still less for the Board to relinquish its requirement of the certificate and training for elementary schools. They could not do the latter at any earlier point in the development of elementary education without the grave risk of depriving the schools of the serviceable staffs so gradually built up. Nor can they now. They have the responsibility of supervising the early education of about six millions of children, whose parents have no effective voice in determining the conditions under which their children should be taught. Moreover, the 120,000 certificated teachers now in the elementary schools constitute a profession with legitimate vested interests which cannot be light-heartedly set aside.

For secondary schools, and ultimately for all schools, the Board should require a licence to teach, not in the form of the present certificate, which, with all its varieties, does not suit the many specialist teachers that are necessary, but in the form of a wider licence. As they no longer prescribe in detail the content of the present certificate, they could not and should not seek to prescribe the exact conditions of a licence to teach. The teaching profession, in spite of appearances, is becoming more and more one profession ; and the time is rapidly approaching when it should be entrusted with the duty of settling the details of conditions of admission. The Teachers' Registration Council is the obvious agent. It is with this council, co-operating with the Board and with the employing authorities, that the business of determining the conditions of the licence to teach should rest. The licence itself must of course be given ultimately by the Board, as responsible to the state. The importance of training and the corresponding import-ance of training colleges in this connection need only to be mentioned in order to be perceived.

This review, mainly historical and explanatory, will have failed in its purpose if it has not revealed the interest of the nation in the training of teachers. In England we do not often evolve a logical system of meeting a national need and apply it at once ; we let things grow and take govern-mental action when we must. The elementary schools grew and the government had to create teachers for them. The method of training teachers developed unchallenged before 1870, and after the provision of schools became compulsory and attendance at them was obligatory on the mass of the population of children, it remained unchallenged. In the meantime, though even the fundamental principles of training do not escape criticism now, the nation has become increasingly conscious of the value of its schools and increasingly convinced that the teachers in them must be adequately equipped. Any proposal for relaxation in the standard of requirements, of which for elementary schools the symbol is the certificate, would be viewed with grave concern by the large public which sends its children to them. You cannot leave the education of six million children to chance, to the open market, and the Board of Education would fail in its duty to the parents if it did not maintain the standard. To impose broad conditions, elastic in detail, but solid in principle, is not to exercise bureaucratic control, but to fulfil a plain duty laid upon a state department by the laws of the realm.

All this, which I take to be undeniably true, is not to say that there are not serious problems in which the nation is intimately concerned. The most important is, how far should the state continue to subsidise the training of teachers ? The present subsidy takes the form of aiding those children in secondary schools who declare their intention of becoming teachers, and of aiding training colleges, including university training departments, by capitation grants on all recognised students, if we neglect a handful of private students and one or two unaided colleges. Critics point out that no other profession is assisted to the same extent, and urge that the salaries now paid are liberal enough to justify the hope that they alone would attract candidates for teaching who would pay for their own education entirely, as in spite of government grants, they do pay in part already. It is too much, it is argued, that a young man or woman should be substantially helped to gain a degree and have a year of training and then be able to earn a respectable salary, virtually guaranteed.

The question was very carefully considered by the Departmental Committee on the training of teachers for elementary schools, of which Lord Burnham was the chairman. In their report, issued in 1925, the majority recommended that the present system of recruiting teachers for elementary schools should remain practically as it stands. A minority reported against this recommendation. The question is discussed fully in the Committee's report, but I may perhaps give the main arguments in my own words. Teachers in elementary schools in the main come, as they always have come, from classes in society difficult to summarise under one name but fairly easy to distinguish. They are broadly the lower middle classes and the working classes : artisans, sometimes day labourers, shopkeepers, clerks of various degrees, small business men, ministers of religion. Broadly speaking, the parents are persons who cannot keep at their own expense all their children under instruction until the age of twenty or over, and who find it a struggle to educate one member of the family up to that age, even if they are able to take advantage of scholarships and bursaries. The argument is that if by a withdrawal of the present subsidies these classes are discouraged from sending their sons and daughters on to teaching, the supply of teachers will suddenly dry up at the source. The attractions of a good salary with a pension at the end, counterbalanced by the supposed disagreeable nature of teaching in elementary schools, will not in effect induce those who can afford to educate their children up to maturity to prepare them for teaching. Those who would be willing cannot afford. Those who can afford are unwilling. The Committee had a considerable amount of evidence of the neediness of intending teachers. There was also evidence that some such intending teachers did not require the monetary aid they received, and since the report was written the professor at the head of a large university training department has been heard to say that half of his students could have afforded to come to the university without the special teachers' grant.

There was agreement between the majority and the minority of the Departmental Committee on one point, that if subsidies earmarked for intending teachers were dropped, there would have to be a considerable extension of free places and maintenance allowances in secondary schools and of scholarships to universities and training colleges. But one party thought that the absorption of the special subsidies in a wider system of bursaries and scholarships not only would cost the Exchequer as much as at present, but would fail to secure an adequate supply of teachers. All agreed that the profession of teaching would gain in prestige if the approach to it were not so markedly sub-sidised ; and all hoped that some day the subsidy would come to an end. They differed as to the appropriateness of the present time to make the change.

Two methods of diminishing the reproach, such as it is, have been suggested. One is that, while the year of pro-fessional training should be liberally paid for, the grants given in aid of the academic side of training should be not specially allocated monies, but a part of the general system of assisted education. If the nation wants teachers to be professionally trained apart from academically educated, the nation should pay for it. The other is that special grants should be available only for those in real need of them. The best method of distribution for this purpose would be to pay a block grant to the training college and let the training college decide to what individual students financial help should be given. I can do no more than explain the position. No one seriously disputes what should be the ultimate outcome. The difficulty is to choose the right moment for change and to determine the exact stages by which it could be brought about without hardship and without endangering the supply of teachers.

In our discussion so far we have taken training for granted without defining it, and even, except incidentally, without describing the process. It may well be that the content of training is fundamentally of more importance than the precise organisation through which it is effected. At any rate, questions of practical policy cannot be really settled unless there is some agreement upon the aims and purposes of training and upon the methods of realising them.

There are two sides to training, an academic and a professional. Academic, because the teacher must be master of the subjects he is to teach ; professional, because he must know how to teach them. No one disputes that the teacher must himself be educated adequately for his work. There has not been and is not now a universal belief that the teacher needs to be trained how to teach. In the elementary sphere, it has been held, the teacher may be ever so learned, but it does not follow that he can teach. In the secondary sphere, it is assumed that a good scholar can somehow manage to teach. The reason for these divergent attitudes is not difficult to perceive. For on the one hand, teaching in elementary schools was a new craft in the nineteenth century, with no traditions : neither the hand-to-mouth teaching of the dame and charity schools nor the methods of the public schools or the private academies could meet the requirements of the large elementary schools that arose. The new craft appeared first as a mere routine or ritual, and during what I have called the stable period of training colleges, it was significantly called " school management." On the other hand, in secondary schools, the masters had themselves been taught as boys on traditional methods which were not difficult to remember and follow. So the idea that professional training is desirable beyond the elementary stage was for long generally scouted. But a change is visible. Apart from the large accession of trained graduates to the staffs of secondary schools there has grown a consciousness that principles and methods of teaching are not to be set aside as unimportant in secondary schools. Witness the controversies on the direct method of teaching foreign and classical languages and on the place of Euclidean geometry. Women teachers, in particular, take a serious interest in these questions and in training as a whole. Training for secondary schools is in fact established, though it is not universal, and though the desirability of it is by no means everywhere admitted. As we have already seen, in state-aided secondary schools, 7,000 out of 14,000 graduate teachers are trained.

There is space to draw attention to two problems only which arise in connection with the content of training. The first concerns the non-graduate students, the second the graduates, particularly those in university training departments.

The two-year colleges, those which do not prepare students for a degree, attempt a double task. They have to train the students in the principles and practice of teaching and also in some directions to continue their academic education. Now that the Board of Education has thrown the responsibility of devising a suitable curriculum upon the colleges themselves, prescribing nothing in detail beyond a certain period of practical teaching, the question of the proper content of training arises in an acute form. The professional training, which is to introduce the students to their future work and to instruct them in the elements of teaching, must occupy at least half of the time at college, and may occupy more. On the one hand, there are those who feel that the best guarantee of future success in a teacher is a good education, and that at all costs the students must go forward in advance upon what they have done at the secondary school. These look forward to the association with universities that will be formed through the new examining bodies, believing that under the new conditions the academic education of the training college will be less like school education and approximate more to a university type. On the other hand, some critics fear that the students will be further away than ever from the practical work of teaching in schools. The latter look back with approval to the time when the training in colleges bore specifically, subject by subject, upon the curriculum of elementary schools. The former claim that a highly educated person will have little difficulty in picking up the subjects he has to teach, and which in his earlier years he learnt himself, though he has temporarily forgotten them. This is the clash of opinion. Are we to have well educated school-masters who have not at their fingers' ends all the subjects a general practitioner has to teach, or less well educated teachers, who are as practically competent to undertake anything as the pupil-teachers of fifty years ago?

The report of the Departmental Committee offers a solution, which to some extent meets the difficulty, though it was not thought of merely as an adjustment of divergent views. It recommends that the student should pursue one favourite subject to an advanced stage for its own sake, in order to keep alive a scholarly interest in it ; and at the same time that the main subjects of the primary curriculum should be reviewed and studied afresh with teaching in mind. This is no pursuit of method *in vacuo*. Still less is it the learning of a set of trivialities, the dodges of teaching, or the minutiæ of a routine. It means the careful examination of the English, the arithmetic, the geography, and so on of a good primary school course from the point of view of teaching. Experiments already conducted indicate that it is quite possible to combine sound academic study with a training in the principles of teaching, with advantage to both. If such an alliance can be effected, the interest of students in training, now apt to be dangerously divided between their academic study and their professional work, will be united by the blending of the two under one common purpose clearly perceived and understood.

This solution goes far to meet the views of those critics who complain that the young trained teacher cannot teach the ordinary subjects of primary education. At any rate, they are not entitled to ask for more. Comparisons with the trained teacher of the 1860–1890 period are quite futile. He was, of course, familiar with school routine, because he had been immersed in it for four or five years before going to college. The period of direct training covered six years. Now it covers at most two. The introductory and prepara- . tory character of training, as it is now conducted in all training colleges, is emphasised by the action of the Board of Education in establishing a probationary year, as recommended by the Departmental Committee. This means that training extends at least a year beyond the training college. It means, further, that the responsibility for guiding the training of the probationary year rests upon the employing authorities and the teachers. If teaching were an art like that of doing some of the repetition work in the making of munitions, to be mastered rapidly by intensive application, a protest against the length of training would be in place. But, of course, teaching is not such an art. The critics to whom I am alluding have this justification for their attitude that, whatever else may have to be neglected, the training of a teacher must be in the closest connection with the schools and must be practical, in the highest senses of that much overworked word. Only in the schools can the teacher establish the subtle contact with his pupils which he must have ; and only there can he experiment with the substance of his teaching.

This argument appropriately introduces the special problem of the university training department. The professional year stands by itself and is a year of professional study, to be devoted entirely to training in teaching. So far, so good. There are no complications, for the academic study is over and the degree won. The way is clear for an introduction to the principles upon which classes are controlled and taught, and the principles upon which the matter of instruction is selected, arranged, and so placed before the pupils that they will themselves master it. The students are also to be made familiar with the conditions of the schools in which their future work lies, and to be aware of the questions that engage the thoughts of teachers as well as of the aims and ideals that inspire them. This outline of what training implies is applicable, of course, to all training colleges, although it stands out perhaps more markedly in the university training departments. It is a kind of apprenticeship to a highly practical art, with a technique and principles peculiar to it. It cannot be accomplished, as I have already said, without first-hand contact with schools. If you come to think of it, this kind of training is rather an odd enterprise for a university to undertake. In a sense it is technical education, and the workshops are not a part of the university but are schools that are independent of the university. The university training departments can quite competently, in the lecture rooms, discuss the problems of teaching, but for practical applications they have to go outside and sometimes a long way outside. They have met this awkward situation, of course, by setting up a working arrangement with neighbouring schools, and for the most part the schools have ungrudgingly assisted. But the embarrassment remains and cannot but give rise to difficulties in detail.

Besides giving due time and attention to technique and to practical teaching, the universities have instituted a diploma in education, for which their students are to prepare during the professional year. The diploma is of postgraduate standard, and indeed the university could be content with no less. At first sight the study of the theory of education which the diploma requires seems unduly severe for beginners even if they are graduates already. It is, however, stoutly defended by the professors in charge of the training departments. Their plea is somewhat as follows.

We urge, they say, that teachers should be trained to do their work, not following blind tradition, or even immersed in the particulars of technique, but with some knowledge of the philosophical bases of teaching and of education. It is exactly this kind of instruction in the ultimate principles of education that a university is best fitted to give, and if students do not get it during their year of training it is hard to come by in later years. We will try to be as practical as we can, and we are sincerely anxious to give our students adequate experience in actual teaching. But we cannot be satisfied to remain on the level of technique. After all, our students are men and women and not youthful pupil-teachers. If their education has been worth anything, they should be capable of rapidly seizing upon the essentials of a new study. A diploma of university rank is the natural reward for success in education as a university subject.

All this is cogent enough, but it does not get rid of the apparent incompatibility between the two aims of the training course, both to be accomplished within a short university year. The study of education as an organic theory and the technical preparation for the teaching of classes do not run well together. With much skill and devotion the training departments attempt to reconcile them, and they certainly succeed not only in giving their students valuable practice in teaching but in inspiring many of them with a genuine desire to pursue the study of the philosophy of their calling.

I venture to submit for consideration a double modification of the existing procedure. The schools should be taken into partnership even more closely than they are at present, and something like a real apprenticeship, or at any rate a period of probation, restored. Further, the high studies for a diploma in education should be begun in the year of training but not finished then. The university should substitute for the diploma a testamur or certificate of satisfactory work, which for employment and superannuation will rank as the present diploma and the Board of Education's certificate. The diplomas should be reserved and bestowed, after such tests as the university decides to impose, when the young teacher has proved his capacity to teach and has had some experience. This might be at the end of one year or more.

If the schools are to be brought into closer partnership, a change will be necessary in some of them. I have often wondered why teachers as a body, in elementary and secondary schools alike, do not demand a larger share in training. The trained teachers are to join their staffs, as assistants and colleagues. Yet, in effect, they are content to entrust the training to persons who, however skilled, are at the time outside the schools. Teachers in elementary schools are well used to taking students for practice, and, so far as they feel free to do so, are ready to help in the training. Teachers in secondary schools are willing very often, but shy. It will have to be an accepted duty in both kinds of schools to help to train the on-coming generations of teachers. It should be contended for as a right. Before this comes about, many teachers will have to shed prejudices and misconceptions. They will have no longer to shudder at method, as if it were some ritual invented by a remote theorist on education, but to regard it as a flexible instrument, open to be discussed, varying with the individual teacher and his class, though no doubt based on some principles upon which agreement will be easy. These teachers will have to get rid of a kind of self-consciousness which makes them unwilling to reflect on their own technique and to communicate it to others. And, finally, they must divest themselves of the shamefacedness of being seen at work. If teachers will regard their teaching in the light of a craft with a special technique, and consider that each teacher must find his own technique, they will be as free to discuss it and to reveal it to a beginner, mistakes and successes alike, as a craftsman, artisan or surgeon, may to a learner. Teaching is, of course, much more than technique : its ultimate effect depends upon personality. This " much more " cannot be trained or taught in a training college or elsewhere, neither is it a subject for discussion or for self-revelation. But technique can be and is : and in the ordinary day-to-day work in schools a great deal of teaching must be pure technique and little more.

The plea for closer association of schools with university training departments and with other training colleges will no doubt be accepted in principle. The practical application of the principle offers endless difficulties. But I do consider that it is in the directions indicated that advance should be made. If there is no advance, there is a danger lest training should become stereotyped, and the balance between theory and practice, philosophy and technique should weigh too heavily on the side of theory. Every teacher should have his own theory of teaching, and his own philosophy of education ; but they can be built only upon long experience and mature reflection.

REFERENCES

BIRCHENOUGH, C. The History of Elementary Education in England and Wales since 1800 (2nd ed.). Univ. Tutorial Press, 1925.

JONES, LANCE. The Training of Teachers. Oxford, 1924.

Board of Education *Annual Report*, 1912–13. (Chapter on "The History of the Training of Teachers for Elementary Schools.")

CHAPTER XI

THE WOMEN'S TRAINING COLLEGES FOR ELEMENTARY TEACHERS

By WINIFRED MERCIER

THE " hungry forties " did not constitute a hopeful period
for the foundation of a new type of educational institution.
England was a country of " two nations," the rich and the
poor; divided also by religious differences into the privileged and the unprivileged. Ignorance, selfishness, and
party spirit hindered movements for social improvement
and prevented the formation of national ideals.

In a period so inauspicious the first training colleges for
teachers were started.[1] They had a hard youth. There
was at the time no educational enthusiasm to expand them
and no educational traditions for them to inherit. Higher
education had virtually become the privilege of a class,
and no one imagined that the children who were filling the
new schools founded by the National Society and the
British and Foreign School Society, were to inherit any
traditions of national culture beyond the ability to read,
to write, and to count. The universities were aloof from
the new educational venture, and the merit—and high
merit it is—of discerning the need for the training of
teachers belongs (after Kay-Shuttleworth) to the religious
societies who were founding the schools. By 1850 sixteen

[1] As early as 1805 Joseph Lancaster was training lads to be teachers
in his school in the Borough Road.

training colleges were in receipt of grants, and by 1860 this number had more than doubled.[1]

The colleges, or normal schools, as they were first called, were thus for many years isolated institutions, little known outside the societies which had started them. When Bedford College for women was founded in 1849, few, if any, of those connected with this movement for the higher education of women realised that there were already in existence institutions for the education and professional training of women, which would in time to come cherish with a quiet pride their years of priority as women's colleges. In point of fact, the colleges paid to the full the penalty of pioneers. They were struggling to establish with inadequate resources a new type of education and training, which no one fully envisaged, and the effort was almost beyond their powers. A woman student of the seventies, reviewing her college days in later years, recalls that they were treated " sometimes as children, sometimes as nuns, and sometimes as convicts." [2] If this can be abundantly illustrated from the records of the older colleges, it must yet be remembered that, while advocates for the higher education of women in the main neither knew nor cared how teachers were to be secured for the ever increasing elementary schools, ministers of religion, and philanthropists, whose experience in community life was possibly of a somewhat arid type, were undertaking a task of an importance to the nation not easy to exaggerate. The isolation of the colleges was further increased by the fact that owing to the absence of any system of secondary or higher education for girls they were obliged to educate and train their staffs from their own students. Many of these proved to be women of ability and devotion, whose influence remained as a lifelong possession with those they taught. The principal in early years was invariably a man, but after 1904 the appointment

[1] Of these 10 and 17, respectively, were for women.
[2] Board of Education *Annual Report,* 1912–1913.

of women as principals was required by a regulation of the Board of Education.

The movements by which training colleges were moulded up to 1902 have been already described by Mr. Ward,[1] and it is not necessary to review them here. Although hampered by lack of money, by their isolation, and consequent narrowness of outlook, the women's colleges had by 1902 already achieved a great work. They had trained generations of teachers whom, it has been justly said, " it would be an impertinence to praise." [2] They had given to hundreds of women opportunities of education, in preparation either for the certificate of the Board of Education, or for the external degree of London University, which could not have been accessible to them in any other way, and they had accomplished this work without public recognition, except within narrow circles. From the first, the government inspectors were, as they have continued to be until this day, their staunchest friends. The Act of 1902 opens an important second chapter in the history of the colleges ; [3] not only were new colleges established, but the old were strengthened. The encouragement given to local education authorities to build training colleges and the well-known poverty of the older foundations gave rise to the expectation that " non-provided " colleges would gradually disappear or " be taken over." Quite the contrary, however, happened. The deep-seated loyalty they had inspired, so little known to the world ouside, provided as it were a source from which new life and new energy developed. It began to be perceived that institutions which had thrust such deep roots down into the heart of the teaching profession were worth preserving. They began to take on a new lease of life. The new " provided " colleges were better endowed with this world's goods.

---

[1] Chap. X, pp. 203–207.
[2] *The English Elementary School.*   Newton.
[3] Chap. X, pp. 207–209.

They started with wider resources and in more spacious and more humane days. Yet nothing has been more marked in the educational history of the last twenty years than the strengthening and development of all the women's training colleges, provided and non-provided.

In 1924–25 the Report of the Departmental Committee on the Training of Teachers for Public Elementary Schools reviewed all existing arrangements for training elementary teachers. Two alternatives to the existing two-year training college course were considered by the committee : on the one hand, a university course for all intending teachers, and on the other hand, one year of professional training following on a full secondary school course leading to the Second School Certificate.[1] If either of these alternatives had been adopted the two-year training college with its distinctive features would have passed away. Both were rejected, and thus the result of the departmental committee's work, so far as it can be at present perceived, has, in effect, been to bring the colleges before an educational jury, and to acquit them. The report, though disappointing in many ways, may in this respect be read as a charter of liberty bidding the colleges continue and develop their work, and acknowledging the fact that they have won an assured position in the national system of education.

It is now generally recognised that there are two main routes by which a teacher may reach her first post : the university route leading in the majority of cases to the teaching of older children, and the training college route leading in the majority of cases to the teaching of younger children.[2] The college course is at present much the shorter, being two years as compared with four, and it should undoubtedly be extended to three years as soon as

[1] Report of the Departmental Committee on the Training of Teachers for Public Elementary Schools, Chap. V.

[2] *Cf.* the division of the school population into primary and post-primary in the Consultative Committee's Report on the Education of the Adolescent.

the resources of the country permit of it. It is non-specialised, embracing within its scope all the elements of a young child's education, and thus contrasts with the more specialised university courses. It is, moreover, vocational throughout, whereas the university course is vocational only in the fourth year. The training college course is thus no pale reflection of the university course, but possesses its own genius and its own traditions, forming a considered and indispensable part of the national provision for the training of teachers. Third-year courses of a more special-ised nature can be taken by students who have passed through the two years' general training, and they give freedom to the individual and flexibility to the system. These courses cover a very wide range, and can take the form of preparation for a university diploma in such subjects as English, history, or biology, or they may provide more advanced work in art, the arts and crafts, music, etc. Other courses, such as those leading to a diploma in social science or psychology, or the more advanced study of educational methods and practice, are more suitable for teachers with some experience, and any third-year course can be taken continuously after the first two years, or deferred till after an interval of experience. Only a very few students are at present financially able to afford a third year of training.

" Diversity of gifts, but the same spirit " should surely be the ideal of every community, and in the two main alterna-tive forms of training, each embracing considerable variety, England possesses a rich inheritance. There is thus every reason to hope that, in proportion as the teaching profession grows in unity, it will embrace an ever-increasing variety of training and of outlook to meet the almost infinitely varied demands of a national system of education.

In such a spirit the women's colleges face what may well prove to be the third chapter in their existence. It would be premature at this time to write of the movement for the co-operation of the universities in the conduct of the final examination of the students,[1] but something more may perhaps be said of the outlook of the colleges on the eve of these important changes. Their ties with all parts of the educational system are close. Their students have been educated in the secondary schools, they return to teach in elementary or central schools, and they appreciate deeply the opportunity that now lies before them of a definite link with the universities. In the elementary schools they have found, and will continue to find, the mainspring of their work, and their closest ties of fellowship and of service. From the universities they hope to draw that special inspiration which association with a learned and learning body can give. Neither learning alone, nor social service alone, can make a teacher. Thus while the connection with the universities should foster sound learning, the training colleges may yet gradually prove to be the natural centre of training schemes for all those who in various ways seek to serve the child and find in the school the natural focus of their work. The practical bent of the colleges may also result in the development of new types of degree work in which courses of study and practical experience are pursued not wholly in the university, but also in the school, or in the workshop, or in the place of business, so that the teacher may reach graduation through a combination of academic study with well-proven experience of life and professional work.[2] If the post-primary education of England is to have humanity and broad culture, and to commend itself to all types of boys and girls, the nation must now help the universities and training colleges to explore every avenue by which teachers may learn the wisdom both of books and of life.

Reference has been already made to the fact that the training college course is limited in the very large majority of cases to two years. It is a short time. The students

[1] Cf. Chap. X, pp. 208, 218.
[2] Cf. the practical experience in Engineering and Medical degrees.

who begin their course in September are, with the exception of a sprinkling of more experienced candidates, between eighteen and nineteen. They are for the most part immature schoolgirls, and yet after two years they will be entrusted with the care of about fifty children for five hours a day. Those who criticise the work of the elementary schools may pause and consider after how short a preparation the young teacher is asked to undertake a task so important for the well-being of the nation. The curriculum of the colleges has for long been framed in accordance with regulations laid down by the Board of Education, so wide and elastic that each college has been able to express its individuality freely, and it is as true of courses of training as it is of buildings, government, and foundation that there is no " typical training college." [1] Three claims, in the deepest sense complementary, but sometimes conflicting on the surface, have to be met in framing the curriculum. The student must, no less than the university undergraduate, enter into her heritage of knowledge and culture ; the young teacher must show reasonable competence in her first post ; and the head teacher of the future must acquire by her training the power to go on learning throughout the intervening years of experience. These three objects must be reconciled in the central purpose of the whole course—to put the young person in a good heart about her life's work and to convince her that it is worth doing.

The two years' work will centre upon the practical study of how a child lives, and learns, and grows, in health and happiness, as a member of a school community. Practice in teaching a class must absorb three months in most cases. Child-study, both practical and theoretical, will be the basis of lectures on methods of teaching, and on school organisation and discipline, and on hygiene as applied to schools and to children. Demonstration lessons followed by discussions will elucidate both lectures and teaching-practice.

[1] Board of Education *Annual Report*, 1912–1913.

Visits to schools of all types, to clinics, to play-centres, etc., form an introduction to the wider problems of child life, which is frequently followed by participation in various forms of social work in the neighbourhood of the college. With the central interest is intimately connected the study of some six or seven subjects which are also represented in the curriculum of the elementary schools. French may be studied, but it is more usual to choose history, geography, science, or mathematics than a foreign language. In these subject-courses not only is the knowledge of the student carried beyond the school stage in further acquisition and in fresh interpretation, but the various methods of presenting them to children are studied. The curriculum of each college has at present some features common to all. Every student takes a course in physical training (which includes games and dancing), in English language and literature, and the large majority a course in divinity. Every student must also be prepared to teach arithmetic. As regards the remaining subjects, art or handwork (with needlework) or music must be included, and all three may be chosen. In the importance attached to these latter subjects part of the distinctive character of the training college course is shown. The music courses emphasise, naturally, singing and the teaching of singing and appreciation of music. The art courses are wide in scope, and in the handwork courses, pottery, weaving, bookbinding, woodwork, besides the simpler kinds of work with raffia, cane, etc., are enthusiastically pursued. By the development of work of this kind in the training colleges the reproach that the elementary schools are too bookish may eventually be removed. These courses do not, however, aim merely at deft manipulation. Each craft worthy of pursuit lies at the basis of a national industry and has played a formative part in the history of civilisation. To realise how much children may learn, and how much their creative power can be developed, not only through books, but through different types of work with their hands or bodies, or through experience of common life in watching a road mended or a hedge cleared, is a large part of the teacher's craft; and though the two years are short, a beginning may be made.

If it is objected that the training college curriculum compels the student to study too many subjects at once, the answer lies in the second claim suggested above. In her first post the young teacher will probably have to take a class of children in all subjects of their study, and her course must have prepared her to do this with reasonable competence. At first she will probably be far more successful in some subjects than in others. To attempt to prepare her to be equally efficient all round might (even if it were possible) completely destroy the two further claims the curriculum has to meet. A multiplicity of separate subjects and lectures would deny the student that which is necessary to every human being—space to grow. The difficulties inherent in this position may to a large extent be overcome by breaking down the artificial barriers between the subjects now separated in both college and school, and there is much need for experiment on these lines. A revision of the regulations of the Board of Education made in 1919 gave to the individual more choice than before in the details of her course, and nothing has been more remarkable in the colleges than the growth of intellectual interest since that date. To exercise the power of choice, to develop special aptitude, to fulfil an ambition, are essential parts of education after the school stage. If the individual is denied these opportunities, stagnation frequently sets in, and a teacher who cannot and who does not wish to go on learning will become a hindrance to the progress of knowledge and a danger to the intellectual development of hundreds of children. There must be time to read with freedom in a good library, time to reflect, to assimilate, to apply; time in fact to grow from the schoolgirl into the woman. If time is not given at this stage the years of experience that follow may bring no wisdom with them, and the young assistant who appeared so competent and so confident may develop into an uninspiring and uninspired head.

The staffing of a training college must always be a difficult matter. Teachers of real ability are needed, teachers equally capable of teaching young children and students. Specialists they must be, in order that they may develop their own subject in the college and have a wide experience of its possibilities ; but specialists in no narrow sense, for they must be able to train the students in an all-round competence as class teachers. Interchange of staff for periods of work between the schools and the colleges is desired, but it is difficult in practice. Interchange between college staffs and inspecting staffs might be as helpful, and more practicable from an administrative point of view.

" A typical training college for elementary teachers does not exist." [1] There are at present in England and Wales forty-seven colleges for women, and six for women and for men. Of the total number eighteen are maintained by local education authorities, one by a university and a local authority. Twenty-seven are governed by religious societies and are denominational in character.[2] Five are undenominational, but four of these are old foundations on a religious basis. There are in addition three colleges at which courses leading to the internal examination of the National Froebel Union are recognised for the Board of Education certificate. They have much in common with the other women's training colleges in aim and outlook, but differ in their tradition and in their history. Although three of the forty-seven colleges are non-residential, and many admit day students in varying numbers, yet residence is one of the features most characteristic of the system, if system it can be called. A great deal has been said in disparagement

---

[1] Board of Education *Annual Report*, 1912–1913.
[2] Nineteen colleges are Church of England, seven are Roman Catholic, and one is Wesleyan.

of institutions which exist for intending teachers only, but candidates for the teaching profession outnumber other women students at the universities so far that a certain measure of so-called segregation is inevitable. Within the colleges it is felt that the exhilaration of spirit which can visit a community, when all are bound together by their vocation for a calling which claims the best that men and women can give, is a part of their inheritance few would forego. Two years is a short time, and in youth not only must breadth of view be cultivated, but also depth of feeling and conviction. England is rich in local variety, and the older colleges especially have always prided themselves on attracting students from all parts of the country. It is arguable that more intellectual stimulation arises from the clash of Lancashire, Somerset, Cumberland, and the Midlands than may be found in a society drawn almost entirely from one local area, however diverse the careers to which its members look forward. The national principle in education is one which needs safeguarding, side by side with the growth of local pride and interests. Had the early training colleges been day institutions, it is difficult to believe that they would have survived, but in spite of conventions and restrictions, both pitiable and ludicrous, the delights of comradeship could be enjoyed from the first, bringing with them an education more formative, if less frequently subjected to examination, than that of the class-room. The common life of a college where students live, and are taught by a staff who are also resident, has a quality different in kind and in degree from that of a hostel maintained for the residence of those who attend a larger institution outside. The colleges of Oxford and Cambridge created this fine flower of education, and have cherished it through the centuries, and something of its secret seems to have been known early in the women's training colleges, even when the life was bleak and narrow. Now the life is rich and humane. There are dramatic and literary societies, debating clubs, intercollegiate events, open lectures, concerts, and enterprises of all kinds. Games are played in all colleges, and numbers of students excel in country dancing and swimming. Many of the colleges maintained by local education authorities have beautiful grounds. Music and the arts and crafts are not only studied in the classrooms, but become new ways of living a common life. Yet old students of the seventies who visit the modern colleges know that, although the opportunities for expression are fuller, yet the comradeship which lies behind them is essentially the same as that which delighted their own college days.

The history of the women's training colleges is an essentially English tale. Voluntary effort finds the way, state aid, and the more systematic action of local education authorities follow. Variety in type and in tradition results, at the expense of a uniform plan and a consistent development. No sooner were training colleges established than their efficacy was questioned, and it has been questioned ever since. In spite of criticism, however, they have steadily strengthened and proved their worth. Now they need security of tenure, and in many cases more adequate resources. In growth and in nature alike they are essentially English institutions, and their friends may hope the period of probation is at last over, and that they may be quietly accepted as fulfilling a necessary function in our educational system.

REFERENCES

Smith, F. Life and Work of Sir James Kay-Shuttleworth. Murray, 1923.

Board of Education. Report of the Departmental Committee on the Training of Teachers for Public Elementary Schools, 1925.

Board of Education *Annual Report*, 1925.

UNIVERSITY AND ADULT
EDUCATION

CHAPTER XII

OXFORD AND CAMBRIDGE

By W. R. HALLIDAY

THE Universities of Oxford and Cambridge profoundly differ from the universities and colleges which have mainly been discussed in the chapter that follows this. In England the provincial universities are a growth of yesterday. Of the two incorporated colleges of the University of London the one has but recently celebrated its centenary and the hundredth birthday of the other falls in 1929 ; the University of Liverpool this year commemorates the twenty-fifth anniversary of its independent existence as a degree-giving body ; the University College of the South-West at Exeter has but lately achieved recognition ; at Hull the beginnings of the University College are now being made. The Scottish universities, it is true, have a more comparable antiquity, but these again are wholly different in character from Oxford and Cambridge. They are non-residential universities organised in faculties and to a curious extent maintain certain mediæval traditions, among the more admirable of which is a pass degree of high standard founded upon a broad basis of essential subjects and—which is possibly less admirable—upon courses of lectures to " ordinary classes " of enormous size, a necessity in the Middle Ages, when books were relatively inaccessible, but of more questionable value when textbooks are not beyond the purses even of recipients of Carnegie grants. Oxford and Cambridge, on the other hand, consist of associations of self-governing

residential colleges, societies ecclesiastical in origin or constructed upon the model of ecclesiastical foundations, to
the structure of which the most nearly comparable, though
not exact, analogy is provided by the bishop, dean, and
chapter of a cathedral. These corporations co-opt their
own members, own and manage their own considerable
properties, and may be relatively more wealthy than the
university of which they are a part.

Unique, however, as their history and circumstances
have made them, it would be a great mistake to think of
Oxford and Cambridge as immutable and static. Actually
within living memory the changes have been rapid indeed.
The abolition of religious tests and the throwing open of
scholarships to general competition was not so very long
ago. How incredible to-day seem the earlier recollections
of the senior common room of Lincoln College, Oxford, as
recorded by Warde Fowler, and how different, though there
is possibly still scope for improvement, is the modern
attitude towards the responsibilities of the university to
learning from that of the Oxford in which Mark Pattison
figured as a lonely Athanasius ! Again, to take examples
of far-reaching changes in social conditions, it is sometimes
forgotten how recently the ban of celibacy was lifted from
fellows of a college, though we do not need to be very old
to have known survivals from the time when dons were
perforce cryptogamous. More recent still is the admission
of women to full participation in the University of Oxford,
a change in which Cambridge has not yet completely
acquiesced, though that she will be forced to follow suit
at no distant date must be anticipated even by those who
may regret the introduction of co-education into these two
particular universities.

It cannot then be maintained that Oxford and Cambridge
are insensitive to a changing world or that they are not
subject to rapid processes of mutability. In what way then,
it may be asked, is it probable or proper that they will or

should be modified by the new educational conditions which are being produced in the country as a whole by the modern developments of the secondary school and the new university ? Is it likely, or is it desirable that they should lose their essential differences of character and become approximated to a uniform type ? That they will be profoundly affected is certain, but that they will maintain their peculiar and unique characteristics and position there is good reason to believe and every reason to hope.

Their essential peculiarities of character and function, indeed, are deeply rooted. In the first place, Oxford and Cambridge, unlike the other English and the Scottish universities, are national. They represent neither a single locality nor a restricted social class. They draw their members from all parts of the United Kingdom, and their societies also provide a representative cross-section of the social structure of the country. The other universities of the British Isles, and, if the overseas and foreign element be excluded, this is true even of London, draw their students mainly from a definite local area to which it would not be difficult in each case to assign roughly accurate geographical boundaries. While the broad distinction which is evident in the history of the Great Rebellion or in that of the Tractarian Movement still holds good, that upon the whole Oxford represents the temper of the south and west of England, and Cambridge that of East Anglia and the north, both draw their undergraduates from every part of England and from every social rank.

Amongst other things, this means in practice that Oxford and Cambridge upon the whole attract to themselves the best intellectual material in the kingdom. It is indubitable that, at least as regards the subjects which belong to the Faculty of Arts, the very richest of the cream is skimmed from the area which it serves before the turn of the local university comes round. For the best boys in the best public secondary schools in each district tend to

R

proceed by the aid of scholarships to the older universities. From the selfish point of view of the provincial universities this process may be regretted. That it does make standards more difficult to set and to maintain cannot be denied. But, on the other hand, not only from the point of view of the fortunate scholars, but also from that of the nation, there are advantages which more than compensate for this in itself unfortunate consequence. The scholars gain particular opportunities of intellectual and social self-development which the conditions and resources of local universities are not able to provide : the nation gains by a concentration of the best intellectual abilities of the coming generation under conditions which are peculiarly favourable to mutual stimulation.

To the other national feature of Oxford and Cambridge, the fact that they represent cross-sections of our social order, it would be a mistake to attach too little importance. The older universities are sometimes derided for the social prestige which they rightly enjoy. But of this it is a result that their society contains an element which is sparsely represented, if at all, in the other universities. In fact, each of the older universities and each of their colleges is a microcosm of the nation. All social ranks, thanks to the scholarship system, are represented, except perhaps that of the manual labourer, though it is not impossible to find his son among the members of a college. Now, while it is undoubtedly true that undergraduates with larger means can indulge in some activities which their friends with smaller means must inevitably eschew, there is probably no society in the world in which wealth or social position count for so little in the placing of a man among his fellows. And if neither money nor hereditary social advantages will win an undeserved respect in a society in which merit and social adaptability are the qualifications that mainly order the relations of the constituent individual members, the sentimental fallacy of inverted snobbery which supposes that the poor are universally clever, virtuous, and industrious, and the more fortunate in material opportunity are dull-witted, wicked, and idle, is equally disproved by the experience of every day. For in fact neither industry nor ability are monopolies of the municipal secondary schoolboy or of the sons of the less wealthy members of the community.

It must, of course, be admitted that the privilege of membership of Oxford or Cambridge is necessarily restricted, and that if their essential character is to be maintained, a privilege it must remain. In practice the privileged class may be defined as consisting of those whose parents have sufficient means to afford it for their sons and those whose intellectual promise is of the necessary quality to win them the necessary means by way of scholarships. The proportion of the two classes may possibly vary in the future, but that a proportion between the two should be maintained is wholly to be desired. Actually the system achieves one of those effective compromises which are characteristic of our practical and illogical country, a blending of what may be called the aristocracy of circumstance with the aristocracy of brains. Their interaction is surely from the national point of view to be welcomed without reserve.

This interaction takes place through the peculiarly intimate common social life of the Oxford or Cambridge college, the virtues of which can never wholly be emulated under the conditions of a non-residential university, however strong and active the Union Society or the Guild of Undergraduates may become. Among those who have experienced its so delightful benefits, there will not be two opinions as to the value of this peculiar system in developing and enriching intellectual interests and abilities and in forming character. It has but one disadvantage, which, however, cannot be evaded. It is and must be relatively expensive. On this it is well to be clear, particularly as from time to time there recur agitations in favour of the reduction of the expensiveness of the older universities towards the level of that of the newer. But without destroying what is perhaps the most valuable advantage which Oxford and Cambridge have to offer, this cannot be achieved. If the view be held that a disproportionate number of those who are fortunately placed by material circumstance now enjoy a privilege which is denied to those who lack their means, the proper solution is an increase in the provision of opportunities by means of scholarships for the able poor, not such a dilution of the quality of its benefits as will enable all to share in what will no longer be a privilege, but will also be no longer worth sharing.

Oxford and Cambridge, then, may be thought to hold an unique position which the newer universities cannot attempt to rival. But if what the latter have to offer is not quite what the former can give, it is free to all. The peculiar opportunities offered by the older universities are necessarily conditioned by a limitation of their enjoyment to those who are exceptionally qualified, either by material or mental endowments. On the other hand, since the newer universities exist to provide for the deserving but less fortunate, there is the less need to wish to rob the privileged of what cannot be extended to others but if destroyed would simply be enjoyed by none.

Our discussion has hitherto proceeded upon the assumption that it is the business of a university to provide a general education which will enlarge and enrich the possibilities of the individual's experience through awakening intellectual, æsthetic, and social interests, and will discipline and strengthen his imaginative and critical faculties in such a way as to equip him with a forcible and adaptable mind which may be subsequently applied with the maximum effect in whatever particular vocation he may be called upon to practice. That this view, that it is the function of a university to supply a general education which is a practical preparation for life, has been overstated by Cardinal

Newman, we are reminded by Principal Morgan in the next chapter, and its over-emphasis bred at once the merits and defects of the Oxford which was dominated by Jowett. But because the responsibilities of the university towards learning and research may not properly be thus ignored, it would be a mistake to underestimate the real practical importance of this aspect of the proper functions of a university, an aspect which Jowett unduly stressed only by making it appear to be the *sole* end of a university existence. Here Oxford and Cambridge by maintaining the high standard of their honours schools as instruments for a general preparation for life will set a standard and preserve an educational ideal which is emphatically not superfluous. For, partly owing to the pressure of financial circumstance upon their students, for many of whom it is essential that wage-earning should be as little postponed as possible, partly owing to the indiscreet admiration of the German university system which was prevalent at the time when many of the new universities were being formed, and partly as a result of the increasing specialisation of studies at a yet earlier stage in the secondary schools, which is itself largely an unfortunate consequence of the application of the machinery of advanced courses and higher school certificates, the peculiar danger of the newer universities has lain in the opposite direction. With students less well equipped in matters of general education than those who enter the older universities, some at least of the newer have given a highly specialised character to the curricula of their honours schools, and in all there has been a tendency to encourage premature research. The results, which are what might have been anticipated, have now begun to arouse uneasiness and to attract attention. Luckily we have a warning example in America, where similar causes and results have occurred in an aggravated form. Against this tendency to neglect general education and to attempt to superimpose a technical training upon a defective cultural foundation, a proceeding which in fact produces, not the scholarly habit of mind, but the conceited and arrogant futility of the ignorant pedant, the peculiar predominance of Oxford and Cambridge and the high standards of general education which their schools have maintained serve, and will serve, as an invaluable counterpoise.

On the other hand, it is perhaps a fair criticism of Oxford, though probably less true of Cambridge, that the idea of the proper functions of a university have been unduly restricted. In the past I believe it to be true that too little attention has been paid to the training of graduate students who wished to learn the technique of scholarship. But in this matter a change is taking place and, if there is yet room for improvement, reform is already under way. Here Oxford has in some respects been the victim of her own excellence. A real practical obstacle has lain in the exigencies of the tutorial system, which from the point of view of giving undergraduates a general education is undeniably an instrument of unrivalled merit. It is an interesting testimony to its virtues that Harvard is now experimenting with a modification of the Oxford tutorial system, in the hope of alleviating those evils which result, as we have already had occasion to notice, from the under-emphasis of the importance of general education. But the defect of the tutorial system is the burden of exhausting work which it places upon the individual teacher ; it sacrifices, in fact, the teacher to the student.

An Oxford man may perhaps be allowed to express the opinion that in respect of learning and research the recent record of Cambridge perhaps stands higher than that of his own university : on the other hand, he believes the Oxford " Greats " School to provide an educational preparation for life which is of unrivalled excellence. In other respects, too, there are not unimportant differences both in character and in structure between the two older universities, but both are comparable with each other and incomparable with the new provincial universities. If prophecy be permitted, I am inclined to predict that Oxford and Cambridge will tend towards developing a closer unity within themselves and will also become more assimilated to each other. The modern development of communications has abolished their relative seclusion from the world and from each other. Within both universities old exclusivenesses are breaking down. The increased importance of scientific laboratories, the introduction of new " schools " organised upon a university basis, and the increased attention which is likely to be paid in the near future to graduate research all tend to emphasise the importance of the university as opposed to the college aspect of their organisation. Difficulties of detail in the adjustment of the respective claims of college and university may arise in the process, but that a greater coherence can be achieved by careful and judicious goodwill, without the sacrifice of the peculiar virtues of the college system, without in fact a sacrifice more serious than that of prejudice, I, for one, believe. For this belief there is some ground in experience. It is not so long ago in Oxford that college lectures were restricted to members of the college ; in Cambridge, I am told, that unregretted past is still less distant. Colleges, again, when appointing fellows, do not to-day limit their choice to their own members, and such elections sometimes exceed the bounds not merely of the college but of the university. As regards university appointments, Oxford men to-day hold chairs in Cambridge, and Cambridge men in Oxford. Both within the two universities and in their relations with each other the spirit of exclusiveness which once prevailed has in practice already broken down. Nor has the dreaded catastrophe to college solidarity and college loyalties as yet in fact occurred.

The contact between the two older universities is therefore likely to increase, rather than to diminish ; what can be forecast as to the nature and extent of their contact with the newer ?   Here, too, I believe that contact, though not quite of the same kind, will become closer and more frequent.   In pure science and in arts the newer universities will, I fancy, continue to look to Oxford and Cambridge for their standards.   Here I do not think it probable that they can ever hope to become rivals.   Speaking generally and ignoring individual exceptions, the older universities are, on the whole, likely to attract and keep the foremost teachers and scholars in their subjects, and their organisation allows for a greater variety and range of teaching in the various aspects of particular branches of study than is possible under the departmental organisation or with the more restricted staffs of most modern universities.   And, as we have already had occasion to emphasise, in the older seats of learning, the taught represent the result of a process of selection in which individual accidents may occur, but which on the whole provides the best intellectual material of the country.   One very important field, however, may be thought likely to remain the peculiar preserve of the new universities, that of science in its application to industry. The significance of this side of scientific teaching and research is growing and is likely to grow, and its reactions upon the study of pure science will be far-reaching.[1]   But, important as is this field, it may be thought probable that for practical reasons the older universities will largely leave it to the newer, which to an increasing degree are likely each to form a special centre for the study of the particular applied sciences which are most concerned with the chief industrial needs and activities of its own particular locality.

As regards both staff and students, I look forward to an increasing circulation between the newer universities and the older.   In their early days of necessity the newer universities were largely staffed as regards the higher posts

[1] The reader's notice may perhaps be directed to the too little known collection of addresses by Professor Smithells, *From a Modern University : Some Aims and Aspirations of Science*; Clarendon Press, 1921, in which this topic is handled with a rare combination of vision and common sense.

from Oxford and Cambridge. But they have now been long enough in existence to have brought up their own candidates for chairs, with claims enforced by years of devoted local service. Here lies a real danger of inbreeding, which is aggravated by the local character which we have noticed the modern universities to possess. It will be disastrous, in my view, if the chairs at the newer universities come to be mainly held by men who, however able and devoted they have proved themselves to be as scholars and teachers, have passed directly from being local students to junior positions on the staff of the local university, outside the local boundaries of which they have had no subsequent opportunity of adventuring. Inbreeding of a similar kind is not unknown at the older universities, it is true. Some colleges have been known to appoint young men immediately after graduation or, in some notorious instances, even before the publication of the results of the degree examination, to official teaching fellowships. For obvious reasons that tendency is frankly to be deplored. But, though to be regretted, the resultant evils are not quite so acute in the older universities as they are bound to prove in the new, precisely because of the national as opposed to the local character of the older learned societies. The cage is not actually so narrow. Quite apart from this particular point, however, a greater interchange of teachers at all stages between the older and the new universities is to be desired. Both are likely to profit from contact with different points of view. I am quite sure that a professor or lecturer of a provincial university would find much to learn, as well as to enjoy, in a period of teaching Oxford or Cambridge undergraduates, and I also believe that a college tutor might derive refreshment and profit from the change to the different but very interesting work of a provincial university. Such interchange perhaps is not likely soon to be practicable, but one quite serious obstacle to its realisation has been recently removed by the adoption at the older universities of the Federated Superannuation Scheme, with the result that interchange is no longer penalised by loss of pension rights.

As regards students, I hope to see increasing numbers of the best of those who have taken their degrees at the local universities then proceed to Oxford or Cambridge. This happens now, but the opportunities are not yet sufficient, nor indeed have the English yet acquired that belief in the delayed returns of a more prolonged education, which notoriously has given those Scotsmen who have supplemented a degree in a Scottish university by a subsequent period at Oxford or Cambridge such enviable prominence in practical affairs. The chief difficulties are financial. Some colleges at both universities already open some exhibitions to candidates over nineteen years of age, and more, I hope, will follow suit. At the other end the local benefactors of provincial universities need educating into providing funds which can be applied to such a purpose. At present it is probably true that generosity has amply supplied the needs of entrance scholarships in most modern universities. It is for the best students at the other end of their career that increased endowment is now most needed, not in order to keep them in their own local surroundings, but to send them out to the wider experience of opportunities which a local university can never in equal measure supply.

The topic which I have been called upon to treat is not one to which justice can be done in a few short pages. That the older universities represent something unique in quality as well as in the circumstances of their history, one whose teaching life has been spent in a Scottish and in an English provincial university is prepared gladly to admit. For obvious reasons I should be the last to undervalue the services which the new universities can give and are giving to the nation, but that they can ever attempt to rival just the particular excellences of the older universities I do not believe. Nor is it desirable that they should attempt the task. Whatever local disadvantages may attend the centralisation of the best intellectual material of the country, from the broader aspect of national welfare the maintenance of the unique position of Oxford and Cambridge seems to me wholly to be desired. Modification in their internal structure they will undoubtedly undergo, their contacts with each other and with the newer universities will probably become more intimate and mutually beneficial, but such changes of the future are not likely radically to alter the essential virtues of the older universities nor their peculiar predominence in the educational system of the British Isles. To some of us at least that is matter for satisfaction and not for regret.

REFERENCES

AYDELOTTE, F. The Oxford Stamp and other Essays. Oxford, 1917.

CURZON OF KEDLESTON. Principles and Methods of University Reform. Oxford, 1909.

MALLET, C. E. A History of the University of Oxford. 3 vols. Methuen, 1924–27.

NEWMAN, J. H. The Idea of a University. Longmans, 1852.

PATTISON, M. Suggestions on Academical Organisation. 1868.

SEELEY, JOHN. Liberal Education in the Universities (in Essays on a Liberal Education, ed. F. W. Farrar. Macmillan, 1867).

SMITH, GOLDWIN. Oxford and her Colleges. 1894.

SMITHELLS, A. From a Modern University : Some Aims and Aspirations of Science. Oxford, 1921.

TILLYARD, A. History of University Reform from 1800. Cambridge, 1913.

Reports of Royal Commissions on Oxford and Cambridge, 1852–3.

Report of Royal Commission on the Property and Income of Oxford and Cambridge, 1873.

Report of the Royal Commission on Oxford and Cambridge, 1922.

CHAPTER XIII

THE MODERN UNIVERSITY AND UNIVERSITY COLLEGE

By A. E. Morgan

The first necessity of a university is freedom. On the whole we have attained in this country a high degree of academic liberty, more than Germany enjoyed before the War, certainly more than is to be found in Italy to-day, Russia or America. The intellectual worker needs scope for the free play of his speculative powers. No preconceived conventions, whether they be political, social or religious, should deter him from following what he believes to be the path leading to truth.

The universities of the nineteenth century have called to their assistance a new type of ruler. Whereas the older universities are governed by men of learning and of science, the newer university institutions are controlled chiefly by business men. A very real danger of this radical change in control was the possible loss of academic liberty. In America there have been deplorable examples of limiting freedom of thought and expression; but fortunately such cases, fewer in America than some critics imagine, have been so rare in this country that we hardly realise that there is a similar danger for us.

The nineteenth century was signalised by the triumph of the bourgeois democracy which had been struggling against decaying feudalism since the middle ages. Gradually enlightenment brought a deeper humanitarian spirit; and a growing sense of social responsibility in the middle class, meeting the new self-consciousness of the labouring man, operated favourably to secure many social reforms, amongst which one of the most fundamental was the establishment of a far-reaching system of popular education. The churches played a notable part in the educational revival, but in every respect it was characterised by the new idea of popular control.

Elementary, secondary and technical education all made rapid strides as England became at once freer politically and richer economically. The disinterested motive of social well-being was undoubtedly an important stimulus to the modern educational movement ; but it must also be recognised that an argument, if not a motive, for education was the belief that it contributed to the equipment of more efficient workers to serve that great machine of production which is one of the most stupendous features of our civilisation.

Early in the last century a genuine desire to enlarge the means of university culture beyond the limits of Oxford and Cambridge resulted in the establishment first of University College, London and soon afterwards of King's College. In due course the University of London emerged and has steadily developed into the vast institution, or coalescence of institutions, which it is to-day. In the north of England the University of Durham was established in 1831 under Church auspices on the model of the older English universities.

It was not till the latter part of the century that the newer provincial universities sprang up. Partly through the private benevolence of great citizens like Owens, Mason, Hartley, and in our own day Mr. T. R. Ferens, colleges have come to birth. In many cases these colleges have absorbed or joined forces with existing educational organisations— a working men's college as in Sheffield, a technical institute as in Leeds, or a university extension centre as in Exeter. Assistance by the public, through direct donations or in the form of local or national grants, has promoted the further development of these university colleges as they have been called. Not invested with the power of granting degrees they have been staffed and equipped with the object of preparing students for the external degree of the University of London.

Victoria University was the first institution of the kind in the provinces to acquire the power of granting degrees. Now there are universities in most of the big cities of England ; and in other towns there are a number of university colleges developing towards university status through the preliminary stages which have characterised the growth of the newer English universities. In a century there has been a marvellous growth. Oxford and Cambridge held undisputed sway in England a hundred years ago. To-day there are eleven universities and five non-degree-granting university colleges. In Wales there is the university with its four colleges and the degree-granting college at Lampeter, which is mainly theological in character. The four ancient universities of Scotland have been much enlarged. In Ireland the University of Dublin, with its one College of the Trinity, now has been reinforced by the National University, with three constituent colleges, and by the Queen's University of Belfast.

It was on the occasion of the inauguration of the National University of Ireland that Cardinal Newman, just three quarters of a century ago, stated his belief that universities existed not to carry on research but to teach. We take a very different view to-day. It is true beyond doubt that whatever be the immediate purpose of a university its ultimate aim is the spread of light. In our modern view this can be done in various ways. Orally and by writing the teacher may give his ideas and his learning to those who want it. We interpret this function widely. The professor is fulfilling the end of his calling not only by teaching a class of students how best to outwit the wily examiner, but also by spreading his knowledge through the medium of print, of the public lecture, or even by wireless broadcasting. Yet beyond this we recognise the important duty laid on the members of a university staff of carrying war into the realms of ignorance. By study and experiment they will pursue knowledge along untrodden paths. By research they will strive to extend still further the boundaries of the known. Who are better equipped than they with the spirit, the capacity, and the means for this work ? Further, we see the value to a student of daily contact with men whose lives are dedicated to the search for truth, since in no other way will love of the light be inculcated or encouraged in the pupil. It is certainly possible to over-emphasise, and easier still to emphasise disproportionately, the obligation on university teachers to carry out research ; but we are surely right in denying the dictum of Newman that the function of a university is the diffusion and extension of knowledge rather than its advancement.

With the widening of the function of the universities there arises the question, What are the limits of their scope ? The problem divides itself into two parts. First, for what people does the university cater as a teaching body ? Secondly, what are the proper subjects of inquiry ; what are the fields of knowledge within its purview ?

Let us examine these two sides of the question in order. The introductory chapter of this volume lays stress on the fact that in the middle ages the English system of education existed largely to train an intellectual aristocracy or bureaucracy—call it as you will—which was the real agent of government. The schools and universities and Inns of Court were the training ground for the clerics, the teachers, the doctors, the lawyers, the civil servants who filled the posts requiring minds stored and trained for the service of the community at the highest intellectual level. Even in the sixteenth century, when the education of highborn young gentlemen was the subject of so much discussion, there was an underlying sense of *noblesse oblige*. If a nobleman was educated in manners and deportment, if he was polished as a courtier and trained as a soldier, there was a real perception of his responsibility as a member of the governing class.

There is historical precedent for regarding the universities as the nurseries of those whose calling it is to manage the higher affairs of the nation. As recently as a hundred years ago the number of such men was relatively limited. The age of machinery has produced a community far more complex than anything the world has ever known. With the extension of knowledge life has become far more elaborate. More and more, positions of responsibility call for men with specialist knowledge. Compare the modern doctor, the lawyer, the architect, the banker, the teacher with his counterpart of a century ago ; compare the processes to-day of building, of manufacture, of commerce with those before the era of the scientist and the engineer. At every turn we are faced by the masses of knowledge which have been piled up during the last few generations ; in every sense the needs of the skilled worker are more intricate and extensive than formerly. Our school system has grown and goes some way to meet this new need, but for many vocations it is impossible to give the necessary technical training by the age when boys leave school.

True, this is not altogether a new need ; and in the past there grew up a system of apprenticeship for the professions similar in principle to the method of training for handicrafts. This system achieved much and it is far from obsolete to-day. The entrance to the law, to accountancy, to architecture, to commerce, to banking, is mainly by the avenue of apprenticeship. But the system is perishing rapidly, and the responsibility of training entrants to every profession, and in a lesser degree to the higher positions in industry, is being laid more and more on the universities. Virtually the sole avenue to medicine is through a university leading on to a hospital. The hospitals are becoming university laboratories in which practical training and research are carried on. Some university medical schools have built their own hospitals and, whilst these serve the beneficent end of tending the sick, they are also the practical training ground for the medical profession. Dentistry is following suit. The universities together with the Inns of Court have for long been the schools of the Bar ; and now solicitors must receive approved teaching in law, which is mainly provided by the universities and university colleges. The engineer is usually a university product and to a lesser degree architecture is coming to seek the university as a training ground.

The process of evolution is similar in the different professions. First a system of apprenticeship or articles is established. Next the profession organises itself and imposes a test for ensuring the efficiency of entrants. Examinations call for teaching. At first this is obtained by haphazard means—coaching, correspondence, part-time courses in whatever educational institution will organise them. At length the universities take up the problem in earnest. If they are to teach they must test. Degrees are instituted and virtually the power to license for practice in the profession passes from the professional body to the university.

This process has gone far but it will go further. Probably the next professions to see rapid development on these lines are banking and accountancy. The biggest developments, however, will be in relation to commerce. This is one of the most important problems awaiting the attention of the universities, so important that it must be dwelt on for a moment.

It is not by any means a new problem, and the universities have recognised it for many years. Thought, effort and money have been expended lavishly in an attempt to solve it, and valuable results have been achieved. Nevertheless, a great deal still remains to be done before the universities give the service which industry and commerce need.

We have seen that the question of modern university development depends partly on the problem of deciding for what people it caters, and partly on determining the subjects that come properly within its scope. As Newman put it tersely, " A university may be considered with reference either to its students or to its studies." The relation of the universities to industry is less debatable on the score of students than on that of studies. Industry wants able and trained men and women. Its complaint is that the university does not give them. What is the cause of this criticism, and is it a valid criticism ? To answer these questions we must look at the nature of the studies as well as at the students.

It is not sufficient to reply, as the universities sometimes do, that the industrial and commercial employer does not know what is good for him. It may be admitted that often he is narrow-minded, and that his demands on the universities are unreasonable. But I am inclined to think that the universities are far from blameless, and that they are apt to take too narrow a view of their obligations.

A university school of medicine no longer shrinks from teaching a student the technique of his profession to the last practical detail. Dentists are taught to make sets of artificial teeth ; engineers are practised in the technical details of machinery ; teachers are drilled in the technique of giving lessons. Why then should the industrial employer not expect entrants to the higher walks of his calling to be equipped with similar efficiency ? Even if a man is to carry out higher clerical or secretarial duties, shorthand, minuting, or a knowledge of accounts are just as necessary as the ability in an engineer to run a lathe or to oil an engine, in a lawyer to make out a bill of costs or to draw a conveyance, and in a doctor to bandage an arm. Engineers and lawyers and doctors quite properly learn to do these things, although the time comes when they cease to practise them. The university schools recognise their necessity and lose no prestige in teaching them. But what would be the howl of indignation if it were suggested that a university should teach shorthand and filing! Yet why not ?

We are all familiar with the old contention that the function of the university is to train a man soundly in the liberal arts, and that by giving him breadth of outlook, and developing his critical faculty you are going the best way to make him an adaptable man of affairs. There is a great amount of truth in this contention. If only employers would give a trial to such men there is no doubt that in the long run the experiment would prove successful. Many are doing so and the number is increasing yearly.

On the other hand there are a far greater number of employers who say that they cannot afford the time which is necessary for the training of such men in the details of business. They can find plenty of boys and girls who certainly are less well educated, but who can step on to the first rung of the ladder, equipped with enough technical knowledge of shorthand and typewriting and book-keeping to make a useful contribution to the work of an office. They cost a mere fraction of the university trained man and woman, and they can work their way up to responsible positions, and all the time be unceasingly useful. Does the employer deserve only a scolding as a prejudiced, narrow-minded philistine for preferring the youth who will be immediately useful at a pound a week to the young man who whilst costing him £250 a year will be unable to do a simple job and will quite likely be unwilling to learn it ?

There is a great deal of pig-headedness on both sides ; and, until the universities and industry can establish a closer relation of outlook, this urgent problem will remain unsolved. Industry must learn to realise the great value of a liberal education, and the universities must fight to the uttermost for a retention of a due proportion of those subjects of study which are genuinely cultural. Nothing would be more deplorable than the complete technicalisation of commercial education. It is lamentable to see to what lengths the process has gone in many professional schools, notably in medicine, dentistry, engineering, and the various branches of technology. In these schools there is crying need for a greater infusion of cultural education. And even in schools of pure science the same criticism is well merited. But if industry is to be served, and it has every right to expect to be served, by the universities, the technical demands of industry must have far more generous consideration than they have received heretofore. The universities of this country can, and as soon as they face the problem will, make an immense contribution to the well-being of the nation by supplying a regular flow of trained intelligence to industry and commerce.

To those who believe in the value of university education, it must be a matter of satisfaction to mark the increasing output of university trained men. To-day there are about 42,000 students in the universities and university colleges. But the other side of the picture is darker. There are numbers of university graduates vainly striving to get the humblest posts, fitted for positions that do not exist, unfitted for those that less educated men can fill. That raises another very serious problem—the correlation of demand and supply. Take two facts that ought to be better known. Graduates in chemistry are walking the streets, whilst the demand for properly trained biologists cannot be met. It may be contended that this is the concern of parents or of the students entering the universities. But very often neither have the necessary knowledge on which to plan a wise course of action. It is a question which ought to be faced by the schools and the universities, in conjunction probably with the local and central education authorities.

It is a very difficult problem to tackle, and no system can adjust supply and demand perfectly. Yet the margin of inevitable waste might be reduced. A contributory cause is the tendency of goods in an overstocked market to increase, in an understocked market to diminish. Owing to the popularity of chemistry and physics a generation ago these subjects gained a strong foothold in the schools. Boys having studied chemistry and physics proceeded to read for a degree in science and naturally took the subjects they knew best. Consequently the main scientific output at the universities was of graduates in chemistry and physics. Therefore vacant science masterships were filled mostly by chemists or physicists, who in their turn tended to produce more boys trained especially in chemistry and physics. This vicious spiral has now resulted in a state of affairs that neither the universities nor the schools alone can alter. The institution of Higher School Certificate examinations and the present system of university scholarships by encouraging early specialisation are aggravating a situation which to-day is extremely serious.

Unfortunately the curricula in school and university make for inbreeding through excessive specialisation. It is lamentable that in these days a university graduate may be totally ignorant of all natural science. It is practically impossible for an honours student in arts to take a university course in any of those branches of knowledge which deal with the greatest discoveries achieved by the modern age. Similarly a science student is virtually debarred from continuing his studies of the liberal arts which he may have dropped on taking his matriculation, perhaps at the age of fifteen. There is a little more flexibility in the pass degrees, but even there the differentiation between the faculties of arts and science sets up a substantial barrier.

In this matter we might do well to consider the principles underlying mediæval curricula. The university curriculum, based on a broad foundation, was an attempt to construct a framework of knowledge in general. The mediæval course consisted of the seven liberal arts—grammar, logic, rhetoric, music, arithmetic, geometry, and astronomy. To these were added the three philosophies—natural, moral, and metaphysical. It is true that students entering universities to-day have received a better education than mediæval matriculants ; but we need to fashion our university courses, and especially those for pass degrees, on a broader principle of liberal culture. The time-honoured term " Arts " should never have been displaced. Natural science in these days must have a place in any course of liberal education. It is as much one of the arts as grammar, mathematics, or philosophy. The idea that a man is educated without some understanding of the great scientific principles which are the very foundation, and the practical applications which are the substance, of modern society is absurd. Nevertheless our educational system appears to deny the fact.

The time is probably coming when the present distinction of pass and honours degrees will be replaced by a differentiation of general and special degrees, with the possibility of taking pass or honours in either. There are signs already of this development. But it will prevail only when the value of a general degree is recognised. One of the scandals of the university system to-day is the virtual neglect of the pass student ; and unfortunately the Burnham salary scale has intensified the stigma on the man who takes a general degree.

It might further be contended that, if scientific subjects were included in a general cultural course, it would be necessary to alter methods of teaching radically. That is a question on which any but a scientist must speak with diffidence. It is for the scientists to approach this question in a liberal frame of mind, and to see if they can devise courses and methods which would reduce the more mechanical, experimental side of the work in order to give wider scope to the cultural and philosophical. The experience of certain teachers of adult tutorial classes would indicate the possibility of a more vital system of experimental teaching which might win the interest and stimulate the intellect even of those students to whom we attribute the " arts mind."

This question brings us back to the value of a university training for entrants into industry ; though it really concerns all the professions which the universities serve. The professional schools need humanising and broadening ; the pass degree, which ought to be a training in general culture rather than in specialised learning, needs widening, so that no one taking it can ignore totally either science or arts, to use the bad terms to which we are accustomed. A general degree of this kind, reinforced by some vocational training, both theoretical and practical, would be the best preparation for entrants to the higher walks of industry and commerce.

Nor let us be moved unduly by the argument that we should run a risk by making university degrees more vocational. As we have seen, this is no new thing. In the middle ages the universities were in the highest sense vocational. In many respects they are vocational to-day, not only in the recognised professional faculties, but also in the faculties of liberal knowledge. The most famous avenue to the highest places of service to the state is the Oxford school of *Literæ Humaniores*. Bacon, commenting on the colleges of Europe in his day, complained, " I find strange that they are all dedicated to professions, and none left free to arts and sciences at large." It is interesting to hear this cry against vocational bias three centuries ago. But mark that he proceeds to lay stress on the applicability of general learning to the practical affairs of life. It is the narrow means and not the broad vocational aim which he criticises : " if any man think philosophy and universality to be idle studies, he doth not consider that all professions are from thence served and supplied." [1]

[1] *Advancement of Learning*, Bk. II.

Earlier we posed the question : what are the limits to the scope of the universities ? We have examined the problem from two points of view : for whom do they cater and what are the fields of knowledge properly within their purview ? Can we now answer the question more explicitly ?

An answer is called for in view of the widespread warnings against the multiplication of universities. Certainly there are arguments against increase. It is urged that the existing universities are not full and that they are in dire need of any money available. The first argument is not as sound as the latter. It is true that in the universities there are many departments in which the overhead charges are grossly high in relation to the number of students. But in the majority of universities there are departments of the commoner subjects which are full enough, and in a few cases they are overflowing. This is true of other universities than Oxford, Cambridge, Glasgow, and Edinburgh, which are notoriously crowded in certain departments. The problem is really one of adjustment, and it would appear as if the easiest method of solution will be a careful limitation of the less crowded departments by some central body of control which will ration the universities in the same kind of way as the University of Wales controls the establishment of new departments by its constituent colleges. There is clearly no call for new departments in many specialised subjects so long as the existing provision is not being exploited fully. The difficulty will be to effect control without serious loss of autonomy ; and to the universities autonomy is a priceless heritage of the ages.

On the other hand it may well be that there is room for an increase of university provision in more popular subjects. This suggests the development in the future of institutions, similar to certain American colleges, as distinct from universities, which will provide faculties of arts and pure science.

A far more serious argument against the multiplication

of universities is the real difficulty of securing men and women to staff them. This problem is already with us, and in America it is still more pressing. The only reply is that the increasing demand cannot be denied, and therefore must be met as best it may. Probably this will lead to a decline in the average quality of university teachers ; but we may hope that this will be only temporary, and that the increased supply of graduates will in the end overtake the demand for teachers. In any case it is fair to discount the pessimists. There are and always will be those who think our institutions are going to the dogs. In the actual state of affairs there is no real cause for alarm.

The assertion that the demand for university education will increase is not lightly made. It is true that the number of university students is at present stationary at about 42,000 in England, Scotland and Wales. Actually in 1924 the number dropped by over one thousand, but, as the University Grants Committee stated, this fact is not serious and is to be explained easily in the light of the peculiar circumstances prevailing after the War. A wider survey of the field lends support to the opinion of the Grants Committee in their report published in 1926 that " the decline . . . will now come to an end, and will be succeeded by a small but steady increase." The latest figures show a substantially reduced decline of the total number of students, and a marked increase of entries.[1]

The important factor is the state of the secondary schools —the reservoir on which the universities draw. Secondary education has increased very considerably since 1914. At the moment the numbers of secondary pupils are virtually stationary. The total admissions have declined on the whole since 1919, though they have increased slightly in the last two years. The latest figures show that the number of pupils in secondary schools bears a ratio to the total popula-

[1] *Returns from Universities and University Colleges in Receipt of Treasury Grant*, 1925–1926, H.M. Stationery Office, p. 3.

tion of 9·1 per 1,000. In a public pronouncement in 1926
the President of the Board of Education is reported as saying
that he was working to a proportion of twenty. He estimated
the increase in the secondary school attendants as between
7,000 and 8,000 in a year. It is true that the policy with
regard to post-primary education is undergoing a profound
change, and it seems likely that increased attention will be
paid to higher schools different from the orthodox secondary
school. One result may be a delay in the growth of that type
of secondary school from which university students are
drawn, but a large increase of university students is bound
to result eventually even from this line of policy. Only the
other day, the President is stated to have said that whereas
Bradford, which is probably most advanced in this respect,
was offering secondary education to rather more than a
quarter of the children in its elementary schools, one must
face the necessity of providing for all. Long before that
point is reached the walls of the universities will be full to
bursting.

The basic fact is that life has become so complex that
the world's workers must be more elaborately equipped than
was necessary in a simpler age. It is well worth remembering that the longevity of civilised man has been materially
increased in the last few generations by improvements in
housing, food, sanitation, and health services. How could
that increase of years, or part of it, be better invested than
in extended education ? Society depends more and more
on skilled work. Technical schools and colleges will make
their valuable contribution, but the universities must play
their part. Not only the learned professions and the higher
services of the state call for the best preliminary training.
As we have tried to show, other professions are now calling
for the help of the universities ; and local government, trade
unions, and above all manufacture and commerce will
utilise the university trained mind to an increasing extent.
The universities have an immense responsibility laid upon

them. It is scarcely too much to say that the commonweal is theirs to make or mar.

It is a reasonable presumption that the next half-century will see an appreciable increase not only in the number of men and women seeking a university training, but in the number of university institutions. On the universities as a whole lies the task of meeting the demand. They cannot meet it without a great increase in expenditure, but it rests with them to see that the funds, which will surely come, are properly expended.

The future bristles with problems. Though they are too many and too complex to be discussed fully, we may point to a few. The first is to see that curricula are suited to the needs of the community. There must be no lowering of standard or denial of the eternal worth of a liberal education. But we must be sure that liberalism is properly understood, and we must not scorn the vocational demands of a society needing trained men and women to do its highest work.

Another problem is the size of universities. Signs are not wanting that certain universities have reached a point where numbers are a burden rather than a source of strength. In America excellent results are being obtained in small colleges, and this is not altogether untrue of this country. If, as seems probable, we shall be obliged to found more places of university education it may be well worth considering the advisability of experimenting with small colleges. The main difficulty in the path of the university college to-day is the question of academic autonomy. So long as it is dependent on an external authority for the conduct of its examinations, and still more for the framing of its courses, it labours under a very serious disadvantage. The American method is worth study and perhaps imitation. There certain smaller colleges have only the faculties of arts and pure science and give only initial degrees. Within these limits they have complete self-government. In this country we are, most fortunately, very jealous of standards, and in order to ensure these it might be well to put new colleges through a probationary period during which they should have the guiding supervision of an established university. This suggestion has been made, and even worked out, though it has never been put in practice.

Yet another problem is the location of new institutions. The great majority of modern universities and university colleges have been established in large centres of population. The result has been that a relatively small proportion of students are in residence. Social and athletic activities have suffered, which means that there has been a serious loss of the effective value of a university education. The recent signs of an attempt to recapture an older ideal are encouraging. Universities in big cities are either moving nearer the country or are strenuously increasing their residential accommodation. It still remains to realise completely in a modern English university the American plan of a campus lay-out, though something has already been done in that direction.

The nineteenth century university was generally an imposing institution planted on an urban site to the great good of the city which it came to illuminate. The ancient universities were academic retreats from the worry and hum of men, where teachers and learners cultivated a dignified and placid life of intellectual endeavour and splendid comradeship. Will the universities, or the limited colleges, of the future attempt to combine these ideals ? A university should be something more than an institution. It should be a home, albeit only temporary. With simpler buildings, spread on a spacious campus, where young and old, teachers and taught, can cultivate a more intimate society, in which teaching, enquiry, recreation, athletics, and to some degree at any rate residence have a part, we may add yet another storey to the already noble edifice of our university system.

Yet we must not lose sight of the great value which has

accrued to the modern urban university from contact with
the business of life. The benefit has been mutual. It is
good for teachers and students that they should keep closely
in touch with the stream of life. The backwaters are allur-
ing, but it is the main tide which carries us on. Reciprocally
the university of to-day recognises, and in the future will
recognise still more, that it has a range of action beyond its
academic walls. It is not for me to trench on the ground of
another chapter which will deal fully with the important
question of adult and extra-mural education ; nor to dilate
on the strengthening of the bonds between the universities
and the schools. Through examination, inspection, and the
forging of intellectual and social links between the teaching
staffs in universities, training colleges, and schools the whole
educational system stands to gain. The influence on
secondary education of the university scholarship system is
deeper than is sometimes recognised ; and it behoves the
universities to guard against the temptation to regard only
their own interests. The perilous increase of specialisation in
secondary school curricula is to a great extent attributable
to the nature of the university scholarship syllabus ; and it
lies largely, if not primarily, with the universities to check
this dangerous tendency. This also is a question, a full
treatment of which lies beyond the limits of this chapter.
Suffice it to record a profound belief that no university is
true to its high calling unless it recognises the duty of shedding
light beyond its own purlieus. Every university and college
should be, and increasingly is, a local centre of light and
culture, irradiating the surrounding community and the
educational system within the scope of its influence.

The universities, beset by problems, will be faced with
many difficult decisions. Perhaps the hardest, which will
occur and recur, will be the choice between freedom and the
material means of progress. So far the banner of freedom
has been kept flying honourably, largely because those who
have financed the universities have had the wisdom to see

that by using their generosity as a lever to gain control they would defeat their own object. Benevolent donors in this country have on the whole shown an exemplary spirit. The state, making to-day a contribution to the universities ten times as great as before the War, has recognised to the full the necessity of leaving the universities free. But the possibility of danger is there, and any encroachment on the liberty of the universities must be watched and opposed to the uttermost.

To prophesy is the pastime of fools, but to hope is splendid. I have traversed a wide territory, yet the survey has been far from complete. I have striven, I hope with a due sense of humility, to expose various problems and difficulties which beset those who are concerned in university education, and to suggest certain lines along which it may be worth while seeking for a solution. I realise that there is no royal road, and that many of these problems have exercised the wisest minds for generations. The main thing is to recognise that these difficulties and responsibilities do exist. I have enough faith in the soundness of English tradition and English brains to hope that the universities will not cease to play, indeed that they will play increasingly, their part in serving the commonwealth. We whose lives are dedicate to the universities have in our keeping the Solomon's house of this England, and, to borrow the words of Bacon, it is " the noblest foundation (as we think) that ever was upon the earth." May it continue to be in the future, as it was in the past, " the lantern of this Kingdom."

REFERENCES

CURZON OF KEDLESTON, LORD. Principles and Methods of University Reform. Oxford, 1909.

FIDDES, E. The Development of Manchester University (Chap. I of Education at Work, ed. H. Bompas Smith). Univ. of Manchester Press, 1927.

HARTOG, P. J. Owens College, Manchester. Cornish, Manchester, 1900.

HUXLEY, T. H. Science and Education. Macmillan, 1893.

LINDSAY, K. Social Progress and Educational Waste. Routledge, 1926.

NEWMAN, J. H. The Idea of a University. Longmans, 1852.

SEELEY, JOHN. Liberal Education in the Universities (Essay III in Essays on a Liberal Education, ed. F. W. Farrar). Macmillan, 1867.

SMITH, G. C. MOORE. The Story of the People's College, Sheffield, 1842–1878. Northend, Sheffield, 1912.

SMITHELLS, A. From a Modern University. Oxford, 1921.

From Nursery School to University : a Labour Policy. Labour Party.

Reports of the Royal Commission on University Education in London, 1913.

Reports of the Royal Commission on University Education in Wales, 1918.

Reports of Royal Commissions on Oxford and Cambridge Universities and Appendices, 1922.

University Grants Committee. Returns from Universities and University Colleges in receipt of Treasury Grant (full returns issued annually up to 1921, since then only comparative summaries printed).

Reports of the University Grants Committee, 1921, 1925.

Report of Committee on Industry and Trade. Factors in Industrial and Commercial Efficiency, 1927.

CHAPTER XIV

ADULT EDUCATION

By Robert Peers

THE branch of education which is the subject of this chapter may be regarded either as a criticism of our national system of education, or as its greatest achievement. Indeed, it is both. For it is possible to look at modern adult education, from one point of view, as a makeshift substitute for a better education at earlier stages ; or, from another point of view as a high training for the greater opportunities and greater responsibilities of modern citizenship, made possible through what has already been accomplished by the individual in the earlier years of life. Both views would be right, even to-day ; but it is becoming increasingly easy to adopt the second ; and I hope to show that adult education does not exist merely to make good deficiencies, but that it also has its own place in a national system of education and in the life of the nation. My task is perhaps more difficult than that of most of the other contributors to this volume, in that I have to describe not an institution or institutions, but a great and complicated movement, with nearly a century and a half of history behind it.

Because of the peculiar circumstances of its origin and development, adult education in this country has sometimes suffered from an unduly narrow interpretation of its scope and functions. The modern movement can only be understood in its historical setting ; and this must be the excuse for the brief survey which follows.

A. The Background

Little more than a century ago adult education meant reading, sometimes writing—when that was not barred as a dangerous accomplishment in the hands of the poor—and rarely arithmetic. The poor scholars who attended the adult schools of the early nineteenth century, denied almost every blessing but that of religion, went on Sundays to gather up some of the educational crumbs which fell or were gently dropped from the tables of the more fortunate. I do not wish to minimise the value of these early efforts. They at least demonstrated the possibilities of adult learning at a time when it was seriously argued that children who entered the factories after the age of seven were too old to learn. The following passage from Hudson's *History of Adult Education*, written in 1851, suggests that this was something of a new discovery :

" In the success which attended the establishment of adult schools, the strongest evidence is adduced of the general and rapid improvement which adults are capable of making in sound knowledge. They enter their schools with different feelings from children, who have little conception of the advantages which they are subsequently to derive from what they regard as a task, and have frequently no ideas associated with what they are taught. The adult attends the school from his own desire to learn, and he understands the value of the work in which he is engaged, keeping its end in view, and therefore assiduously applying the means for its attainment."

In the growing social ferment of the first two decades of the nineteenth century the knowledge of reading gained in the adult schools was often used for other purposes than those intended by the benevolent promoters of these institutions. The writings of Tom Paine and even of Godwin competed with the publications of the Society

T

for the Diffusion of Useful Knowledge, and politics and religion were often intermingled in the discussions which were carried on by groups of artisans in London and in the industrial towns of the north. Godwin and his followers had deduced the significant connection between poverty and ignorance ; and they insisted upon the diffusion of knowledge, not as a kind of fire insurance or as the gift of charity, but as a right and as a necessary condition of human advancement. They saw no end to the possible progress of humanity, given a better distribution of human toil, and a better use of wealth and leisure :

" How rapid and sublime would be the advances of intellect if all men were admitted into the field of knowledge ! At present ninety-nine persons in an hundred are no more excited to any regular exertions of general and curious thought than the brutes themselves. What would be the state of public mind in a nation where all were wise, all had laid aside the shackles of prejudice and implicit faith, all adopted with fearless confidence the suggestions of truth, and the lethargy of the soul was dismissed for ever ? "

Godwin contrasts with this picture the existing system, and asks :

" What is the fruit of this disproportioned and unceasing toil ? At evening they return to a family famished with hunger, exposed half-naked to the inclemencies of the sky, hardly sheltered, and denied the slenderest instruction, unless in a few instances where it is dispensed by the hands of ostentatious charity and the first lesson communicated is unprincipled servility." [1]

This was the spirit which animated much of the later growth of organised adult education during the nineteenth century. It was infused by Robert Owen into every social movement of his day. Numerous examples could be cited

[1] Godwin, *Political Justice*, Bk. VIII, ch. 1 (1st edit.).

of the insistence upon the need for education in all those popular movements which came under his influence—the early co-operative societies, the trade unions, and above all the Chartist movement; but that would carry me far beyond the limits of a single chapter, and I must confine myself to one or two illustrations. William Lovett, one of the earliest of the Chartist leaders, tells of his association with a group of Owenite working men who called themselves the Liberals, and met for discussions in London in 1825. The first discussion he attended " was a metaphysical one respecting the soul." He gives, in his autobiography, a moving account of his own struggles to educate himself.[1] In 1831 he joined the National Union of the Working Classes, a body which, in an age of political turmoil and economic distress, could set down the following as one of its aims :

" To concentrate into one focus a knowledge of moral and political economy, that all classes of society may be enlightened by its radiation, the National Union feeling assured that the submission of the people to misrule and oppression arises from the absence of sound moral and political knowledge amongst the mass of the community."

Lovett was responsible for drawing up a remarkable *Address to the working classes on the subject of national education*, issued by the London Working Men's Association in 1837.[2] The address contained a complete scheme of national education, embracing national and local school boards elected by popular vote, primary schools, secondary schools, state training colleges for teachers, and colleges which were to be open in the evenings for adults. This last proposal was to have important results in the later history of adult education.

Let me quote the remarkable words of another self-

[1] *Life and Struggles of William Lovett*, ch. ii.
[2] *Ibid.* ch. vi.

educated Chartist leader, Thomas Cooper, written in the
Plain Speaker, a periodical which he edited and published
after his release from prison. They are taken from letters
addressed to " The Young Men of the Working Classes "
in 1849 :

" If I could use words of fire—syllables of lightning—
they should be employed, if by such means I could arouse
you to the noblest of all aspirations—that of becoming truly
intelligent men.

" If you must ask the tradesman's question, ' What use
is it ? ' which really always means ' What can I gain by it ? '
and that too often in a sordid sense—I answer : It will give
you the key to unlock a grand treasury of thought—the most
valuable riches to every man who does not pride himself
on being merely an animal."

So vital was the impulse given to the demand for knowledge by the leaders of the popular movements of that day,
that it survived the general apathy which succeeded the
revolt against the evils of early industrialism, and was the
living seed from which was to spring a great renaissance in
our own generation.

In the meantime, another movement of a somewhat
different character had sprung from the work of Dr. George
Birkbeck, the founder of the Mechanics' Institutes. This
movement started with all the enthusiasm which characterised the general popular demand for education at that time,
and the number of institutes increased rapidly, especially
in the years 1824–25. At the meeting held to start the
London Institute in 1823, " Cobbett . . . said a few words
at the end," and others associated with the project were
Francis Place, Hodgskin and Brougham, while the authorities,
we are told, looked coldly upon it. Birkbeck himself was
inspired by the loftiest motives, " nothing short, indeed, of
the moral and intellectual amelioration and aggrandisement
of the human race." Speaking at the foundation-stone
laying of the London Institute, he said :

" Now have we founded an edifice for the diffusion and advancement of human knowledge. Now have we begun to erect a temple, wherein man shall extend his acquaintance with the universe of mind, and shall acquire the means of enlarging his dominion over the universe of matter. In this spot hereafter the charms of literature shall be displayed, and the powers of science shall be unfolded to the most humble enquirers." [1]

In view of the high hopes with which it started, the mechanics' institute movement was a curious misfire. The institutes became purely utilitarian in character and so lost touch with the working classes, who, in any case, were insufficiently prepared to benefit by the scientific instruction offered. Some few survived and became great educational institutions serving a different purpose, like Birkbeck College and the Manchester College of Technology. Most of them, however, degenerated into middle-class reading rooms and clubs with no serious educational purpose.

It remains now to trace briefly the genesis of the modern adult education movement and its connection with the past. The Owenite influence survived, of course, in the new co-operative movement started by the Rochdale pioneers in 1844 and inspired many of the more recent movements which I shall describe later. But it bore fruit also in other directions. The People's College at Sheffield, established by a group of impoverished working men in 1842, was the direct outcome of the scheme proposed by William Lovett.[2] Upon the model of the Sheffield experiment, the London Working Men's College was founded under the leadership of Frederick Denison Maurice, with whom were associated Charles Kingsley and J. M. Ludlow, both influenced by the social ideals of Robert Owen, and

---

[1] The quotations are taken from *George Birkbeck*, by J. G. Godard (1884).

[2] Lovett also, at the request of Mr. George Gill the founder, drew up a constitution for the People's College, Nottingham, in 1856 (*Life and Struggles*, ch. xvii).

E. Vansittart Neale, an ardent co-operator. The London Working Men's College brought together a remarkable body of men—lawyers, doctors, writers, and leaders of thought—and their influence prepared the way for the next great development of adult education in co-operation with the universities, just then awakening from a long lethargy.[1]

The new phase began with the foundation of the university extension movement through the influence of Professor Stuart of Cambridge. The first university extension courses were established by that university in 1873, and it is significant that this work had its greatest success in the early days in the industrial Midlands and in the North. Rochdale was one of the most vigorous centres ; and one of the first three courses started in 1873 was given at Nottingham at the request of the local trades council. The example of Cambridge was shortly followed by London and Oxford, and the work grew rapidly.[2]

The awakening of the older universities to a sense of wider responsibilities coincided with the assumption by the state of the duty of providing for the elementary education of all its citizens. It needed then but the time for a new generation to grow up, and the moment was ripe for another great step forward. In 1903, the body which was after-wards to be called the Workers' Educational Association came into being. It owed its birth to Albert Mansbridge, who, through his connection with the Co-operative Union, had inherited the long tradition of faith in the power of education to raise the mass of the people. The new association was formed because of " the absolute necessity for the successful working of a strong and powerfully organised association, so constructed as to be in distinct and immediate

[1] See F. D. Maurice, *Learning and Working*.
[2] For an account of this movement, see Draper, *University Extension*, 1873–1923.

ADULT EDUCATION 279

relationship, equally with the universities as with working-class movements."[1]

The groups of working men who came together through the Workers' Educational Association found university lectures stimulating but unsatisfying. They asked for something more, and the University of Oxford responded by setting up in 1907 a Joint Committee with representatives of labour to provide university tutorial classes for working-class students.[2] The first two classes were established at Longton and again at Rochdale, and so began one of the greatest educational experiments ever attempted. Every other university in this country has now followed the example set by Oxford, and the movement has spread also to the Dominions. The number of tutorial classes has grown rapidly year by year. In the year before the War they numbered 110 ; last session the number had grown to 559, and they contained approximately 9,000 students.

I have sketched very briefly the main line of development in the history of adult education, culminating in the present century in the growth of a voluntary educational movement which has attracted the attention of the whole world. If that were the whole story, it would be remarkable enough ; but it is not. University extension gave us not merely the tutorial class movement, but also many of our modern universities. The mechanics' institutes, as we have seen, also contributed to this same development, and in addition they prepared the way for the great modern growth of technical education in this country. But even that is not all. I have no desire to leave the impression that adult education, whether in the past or in our own day, has been confined to any one class of society or even that it must be narrowly identified with university extra-mural teaching. If interest in social betterment has provided one powerful

[1] Mansbridge, *An Adventure in Working-Class Education*, p. 13. See also Price, *The Story of the W. E. A.*
[2] *Oxford and Working-Class Education* (1908) ; Mansbridge, *University Tutorial Classes* (1913).

motive to the pursuit of knowledge, the religious interest has also contributed to the same end, as witness the striking revival of the Adult School Movement at the end of the last century.[1] Hardly less potent was the widespread curiosity aroused by the great discoveries of modern science and the work of Huxley and others in popularising scientific knowledge in the last quarter of the nineteenth century.

B. The Modern Movement

The scope and the variety of adult education have been increasing rapidly in recent years, and I have next to describe, as far as the limits of my space allow, these more recent developments. Any detailed analysis of the modern adult education movement would, of course, be impossible in a single chapter, and I can only deal with some of the principal types of work, and with some general considerations applying to this branch of education as a whole.

Non-vocational classes and courses for adults are conducted in the main by university extra-mural bodies, and by certain voluntary associations, with the aid of grants from public funds. As far as the more regular types of courses are concerned, I cannot do better than follow the divisions of the Regulations of the Board of Education under which these courses are recognised. Separate Regulations for Adult Education were issued for the first time in 1924.[2]

Chapter II of the Regulations deals with courses " conducted under the control and direction of a University or University College as Responsible Body." These are Classes Preparatory to Three-year Tutorial Classes, Three-

[1] Cf. also the powerful influence of the Methodist " class " system in the first half of the nineteenth century.

[2] Grant Regulations, No. 33. The Regulations for non-vocational adult classes were formerly included in the Regulations for Technical Schools.

year Tutorial Classes, Advanced Tutorial Classes, Tutorial Class vacation courses and University Extension courses. The university tutorial class has become the core of university extra-mural teaching. Each class consists of a group of students, normally not exceeding twenty-four in number, and starting as a rule with at least eighteen students. A tutorial course lasts for three years, meeting for twenty-four periods of two hours each during each winter session. " Where the subject of the course is such as to make the standard of university work in honours a possible aim, the course must be planned to reach, within the limits of the subject, that standard." Preparatory tutorial classes meet for the same periods, but last for one year only, and as their name suggests are designed to meet the needs of students who require some preparation before embarking upon a three-year course. Advanced tutorial classes, which are exceedingly few in number, must be planned to provide work of a distinctly more advanced standard than that of an ordinary three-year course in the same subject, and the majority of the students must have passed through a three-year course in the same or a related subject.

All of these courses are designed for serious students who are capable of concentrated study and who have in view, not examinations or professional qualifications, but the attainment of knowledge.

University extension courses meet a somewhat different need. Some subjects are less suited than others for the intensive method of the tutorial class, whether because of the character of the subject itself, or because of the limitations of the students in relation to particular subjects. " Musical appreciation " and certain branches of science are obvious examples. Each meeting of a university extension course falls into two parts, the lecture and the class. Any number may attend the lecture ; but the class is confined to a limited number of students who are prepared to attend the whole course and do written work. The chief difference between this type of course and the ordinary class is that while, in the former, the emphasis is placed upon the lecture and the presentation of the subject by the lecturer, in the tutorial class and other similar classes the lecture method falls more and more into the background, and stress is laid rather upon class discussion and the work of the students. Each method, of course, has its place. If the aim is to turn out students and to carry them on to a more advanced stage, the tutorial method is clearly the best ; and the university tutorial class is the distinctive achievement of English adult education. If, however, the aim is merely to stimulate interest and to increase the fund of general knowledge, the lecture course has its value, even apart from the class with which it is now generally associated. The tendency on the part of some people to condemn the lecture method as educationally unsound suggests a somewhat rigid and narrow conception of what is involved in adult education. Not everybody is capable of intensive study ; and nobody can possibly attain to an expert knowledge of every subject in which he happens to be interested. There is room for general courses which are frankly informational in character, not merely for the dilettante, but also for those who will go much farther once their interest is aroused, and for those too who are already students of other subjects. The ideal arrangement for most adult students, given the necessary leisure, would probably be an intensive tutorial course in the subject of special interest, combined with a series of lecture courses on important background subjects, and subjects which naturally link on to the special interest. The student of economics, for instance, should certainly be familiar with the main conclusions of biology and psychology, and also with the broad outlines of world history ; and he cannot always obtain what he needs in this way by reading. It is possible that the emphasis placed in modern adult education on the three-year tutorial class may have encouraged a certain narrowness of study, which is indeed paralleled in much of the internal work of the universities themselves.

University extension courses were recognised for grant purposes for the first time in 1924. In order to be eligible for grant, they must be of not less than eighteen hours' duration, and a minimum of twelve students must satisfy the requirements as to attendance and written work. University extension courses aided by the Board increased from 10 in 1923–24 to 179 in 1926–27. Other non-recognised university extension courses, usually of shorter duration, numbered 215 last session.

Chapter III of the Regulations lays down the conditions under which courses arranged by certain " Approved Associations " are eligible for recognition by the Board. The associations recognised for this purpose at present are the Workers' Educational Association, the Educational Settlements Association, the National Industrial Alliance, the National Council of Y.M.C.A.'s and the Welsh National Executive of the same body, and the Welsh National Council of Music. Until 1924, the Workers' Educational Association was the only voluntary body receiving grant aid for adult classes, and the other bodies mentioned, which were admitted for the first time under the new Regulations, have not yet been able to develop a large number of recognised courses. In the session 1926–27, 441 one-year classes and 478 terminal courses were organised by the Workers' Educational Association.[1]

One-year classes meet for not less than twenty weeks in the session, each meeting lasting for not less than one and a half hours. Terminal courses consist of not less than twelve meetings of not less than one and a half hours each.

There is, of course, a great deal of similarity between the

---

[1] One-year classes may also be conducted by local education authorities, but in that case they are administered under the Regulations for Further Education. Some authorities, notably that of Warwickshire, employ full-time tutors to conduct one-year classes.

work carried out in one-year classes and terminal courses and that arranged by the universities under Chapter II of the Regulations. In fact there is often a greater difference between extension courses and tutorial classes than there is between the latter and one-year classes. These classes are all organised in the same way through the voluntary efforts of those who are to benefit by them. The scheme of study is devised as far as possible in consultation with the students, and the tutor is appointed with their approval and sanction. There is, however, great variety in the standard and quality of the work carried out in one-year classes. In some cases they may almost be regarded as one-year tutorial classes ; at the other extreme are classes of a very elementary type, in some cases frankly of poor quality. The confusion of standards and aims in one-year classes is increased by the fact that in some areas, notably the East Midlands, the university joint committee takes responsibility for these classes, although this is exceptional ; in others, notably Kent, the West Riding of Yorkshire and Durham, the local education authority accepts full financial responsibility for many one-year classes arranged by the voluntary association, approves the tutor and determines the rates of pay, although it may in these matters seek the advice of the organising body or of a tutors' panel. This great diversity suggests that the function of the one-year class needs to be more clearly defined, especially now that university extension courses and terminal courses are recognised for grant purposes.

Terminal courses were recognised for the first time for grant purposes in 1924. They serve definitely as " pioneer " courses and do not usually involve written work on the part of students, although according to the Regulations such work should be encouraged. The rapid increase of these courses since the new Regulations came into operation suggests that, in the attempt to meet a growing demand for a more elementary approach to adult education, the voluntary associations, and in particular the Workers' Educational Association, have found for themselves a distinctive piece of work which needed to be done and which no other agency was attempting.[1]

The growth of pioneer adult education in recent years has not been confined to any one organisation or to any particular class of the community. Nor has it been limited to grant-earning courses. A great and growing amount of educational work amongst adults, mostly at the more elementary stages, is, as we shall see, undertaken directly by some local education authorities. While a great deal of similar work is also going on in connection with other bodies, it is difficult to give any detailed account of it. Most of the organisations mentioned promote other educational activities than those already described, such as week-end schools, study circles, single lectures and short courses of lectures on a great variety of subjects. These do not depend on grants and therefore never appear completely in statistical returns. In connection with the Adult School Movement, some 1,500 schools meet regularly throughout the year with an average weekly attendance of about 30,000 members. Literary and scientific societies exist in considerable numbers in most large towns and in many smaller ones. Radio societies have now swelled the number. Settlements—both the older type of university settlement and the newer type of educational settlement—are providing centres for these less formal activities, as well as for the more formal class work. Many churches now have societies which appeal to intellectual interests, and most co-operative societies, true to their early tradition, have educational guilds supported out of society funds. Moreover, we have got so much into the habit of looking back to pre-war days as to a sort of golden age, that we sometimes

---

[1] One-year classes conducted by the Workers' Educational Association declined from 459 in the session 1925–26 to 441 in 1926–27. In the same period, terminal courses increased from 440 to 478 (W. E. A. Annual Report, 1927).

fail to realise how great has been the awakening of quite new interests since the War. The War brought to light new social needs and stimulated into activity sections of the community previously untouched by educational influences. Adult education before the war was largely an urban development. It is now spreading to the countryside and is bringing fresh life and interest into the villages. Women's Institutes, which have sprung up in over 4,000 villages in England and Wales in the course of twelve years, have led to the growth of a widespread demand amongst country women for lectures and courses on subjects of domestic interest. This is now leading to a further demand for courses on local history, literature, music, and other cultural subjects. In many counties Rural Community Councils have been formed to co-ordinate the various social activities which exist, including adult education, and some of these councils are actually co-operating with the neighbouring university in the appointment of full-time tutors. All are helping to develop facilities for pioneer adult education, largely in association with the local education authority.

Side by side with this extension of the appeal of adult education, there has been a broadening of the range of subjects included. In the early days of the tutorial class movement, the classes were to an overwhelming extent engaged in the study of economic subjects In the year before the War, for instance, there were 74 tutorial classes in economics, out of a total of 145. In the session 1926–27 the number was 151 out of 559. To take another subject for comparison, the number of classes taking literature numbered 17 in 1913–14 ; in the session 1926–27 there were no less than 117 tutorial classes in that subject, and if other types of course were included the growth of liberal studies would be even more striking. The subjects now include, in addition to economics and literature, philosophy, history, psychology, music, geography, and biology, to mention only the more usual. The study of science in tutorial and similar classes has not yet been widely developed.[1]

C. THE WORK OF LOCAL EDUCATION AUTHORITIES

During recent years, local education authorities have shown increasing interest in adult education and a growing tendency to regard it as part of the normal provision which they make in the areas for which they are responsible. Evening classes and courses arranged directly by local authorities, especially in the larger towns, have always attracted some adult students ; but the experience of voluntary organisations and university joint committees pointed to the need for special arrangements to meet their requirements. The London County Council has led the way in the direct provision of classes for adults, and the " literary institutes " which, since the War, have grown out of the earlier experiments of that authority, constitute one of the most important new departures in adult education in recent years. The literary institutes, thirteen in number, provide courses of general culture for men and women over the age of eighteen, and there were some 10,000 students enrolled in the session 1926–27. The success which has attended this remarkable movement has been due to the way in which the London County Council has succeeded in combining the best traditions of the adult education movement as a whole with the advantages arising out of the concentration of this work in special centres devoted entirely to adult education. Classes and courses are provided in response to the demands of the students, who are also encouraged to make suggestions for the improvement of the institutes. Various clubs and societies provide a means of social intercourse outside the

[1] For a full discussion of this question, see the Report of the Adult Education Committee of the Board of Education on " Natural Science in Adult Education " (Paper No. 8).

classes, and the institutes have developed a vigorous life of their own in a way which is impossible for isolated groups. The range of the subjects is wide, but the chief demand appears to have been for courses in literature and music. The keen interest in economics and similar subjects which has been characteristic of the tutorial class movement is not much in evidence in the institutes; and there appears also to be a little call for scientific subjects. So far, the bulk of this work has been less intensive in character than that of tutorial and similar classes, and it is comparable rather with the work done in the older type of university extension courses. There are, of course, exceptions to this, as for instance, the classes in languages, of which there is a considerable number.

There can be no doubt that the literary institutes of the London County Council have met a real and widespread need. They have provided in the main for a class of the community hitherto untouched by the adult education movement, at least in London, and are exercising a cultural influence of the highest character.

The London County Council were not content to confine their efforts to those members of the general public who were attracted by the literary institutes. Beginning in 1920, experiments were made with a new type of work in what are known as "men's institutes," established in great working-class districts like Bethnal Green, Battersea, etc. The men's institutes are necessarily different from the literary institutes. Academic methods are avoided, and an appeal is made to existing interests in hobbies and craftsmanship by the provision of workshop facilities. Musical interests are cultivated through the formation of bands, and popular science is encouraged by linking it to the present interest in "wireless." In these and many other ways the men's institutes have succeeded in attracting people for whom adult education in the more formal sense had no appeal, and the experience gained has for this reason a peculiar value.

Few other local authorities have experimented on a large scale in the direct provision of adult education. The Warwickshire County Authority have for many years maintained full-time tutors for adult education. The Leicestershire Authority have adopted the same plan, but have gone a good deal further in working out an admirable scheme of co-operation between the different interests concerned, in association with the University College, Nottingham, and the Local College at Loughborough. The four full-time tutors who work in the county are members of the staff of Loughborough College, and are at the same time recognised tutors of the University College extra-mural department, which accepts academic responsibility for their work. The whole scheme is administered through a sub-joint committee at Loughborough, under the direction of the senior tutor, and the effect of the arrangement is to secure an adequate financial basis for the work, to maintain academic standards, and at the same time to preserve complete elasticity in association with voluntary bodies. The West Riding Education Committee also have a long record in the direct provision of non-vocational classes for adults. In the sessions 1926–27 their classes of this kind numbered 95—the largest volume of work undertaken by any authority outside London.

Apart from this direct provision by local education authorities, the great majority are assisting classes and courses provided by university extra-mural bodies and voluntary associations, leaving to those bodies the actual organisation and control of the work. This assistance takes the form not only of grant aid, but also of help in the provision of rooms in schools, either free or at a nominal charge for the services of the caretaker.

Another way in which authorities aid adult education is by taking financial responsibility for courses arranged by voluntary associations and sometimes by university joint committees. Direct expenditure on such work is, of

U

course, recognised by the Board for deficiency grant. The most notable examples of this arrangement are in the West Riding of Yorkshire, Kent, and Durham.

When the local education authority accepts full financial responsibility for courses organised by voluntary bodies, there is some danger that standards may suffer, since the courses are recognised under the Regulations for Further Education, not under the Adult Education Regulations. It is sometimes difficult to persuade local authorities to recognise the distinctive character of this work and to pay tutors on the scale which is made possible by the maximum rates of grant payable under the Adult Education Regulations. Moreover, there are not the same requirements concerning written work and attendance. It is very desirable, if the character of the work is to be maintained, that courses for which local authorities assume financial responsibility, but which are otherwise comparable with the one-year classes and terminal courses arranged directly by " approved associations," should be brought under the same set of regulations as the latter, and that some agreement should be reached to prevent such a lowering of standards of remuneration as must ultimately affect injuriously the quality of the work as a whole. Keeping up the standard is not, of course, merely a question of rates of remuneration ; it involves also the setting up of machinery to secure the appointment of tutors who are suitably qualified, not alone in the academic sense, but also in their ability to sympathise with and to understand the special needs of adult students.

D. BOOK SUPPLY

It is obvious that this great volume of educational work, much of it of an advanced character, could not have been carried out without a considerable growth in the facilities for borrowing books. In most of the classes, each student is required to buy a cheap textbook, and many also make great sacrifices to build up libraries of their own. But most students have to rely largely upon borrowed books ; and the problem of providing these books is an exceedingly difficult one.

Almost all university joint committees have built up libraries from which boxes of books can be supplied to the classes under their control. These cannot, however, meet the whole need, and the movement relies to a very considerable extent upon the valuable help of the Central Library for Students in London, which issues boxes to classes through the responsible joint committee or other organising body. The Central Library issued no less than 45,004 volumes in the session 1926–27, and the scope of the service is increasing year by year. So far, the Library has relied mainly for its funds on grants from the Carnegie United Kingdom Trust, and on subscriptions from university joint committees and other bodies which benefit by the service. The recent report of the Departmental Committee on Libraries [1] recommends, however, that the Library should receive a grant of £5,000 per annum from public funds and should be placed under the general control of the trustees of the British Museum.

Municipal libraries in the past few years have shown increasing willingness to help, but the rather rigid rules under which books are issued, and particularly the tendency to store the most valuable books in reference libraries, limits their usefulness to adult classes. Another extremely valuable source of supply has been found in the remarkable growth of county libraries, also under the stimulus of grants from the Carnegie Trustees. These have now been established in all but five counties in England and Wales, and many are building up special " student sections " with the aid of funds provided partly from the higher education rate.

The problem of the book supply for adult classes is by

[1] Cmd. 2868.

no means solved; it is still not possible, for instance, to supply large numbers of copies of the same books to classes studying literary or historical texts; nevertheless, the position, compared with that of a few years ago, is almost incredibly improved, and seems likely to go on improving.

E. FULL-TIME STUDIES

I can do no more than touch upon another important development of adult education, which is at the opposite extreme from pioneer work, but which also belongs mainly to the period since the War. Before the War there had been few opportunities of full-time study for adult students. Ruskin College, Oxford, founded in 1899, provided for a certain number of working-class students, who were able to go into residence with the aid of scholarships from trade unions, co-operative societies, and some local education authorities.[1] Fircroft, at Bournville, formed on the model of the Danish High Schools, was opened in 1909 and provided full-time instruction largely for the " adult school "

---

[1] The present brief account of adult education in England is necessarily confined to the growth and organisation of adult education in its relation to education as a whole. It obviously cannot deal with institutions and movements of a partisan character, in which educational effort is directed to the spread of particular ideas. Their exclusion is not intended to suggest that they are not of importance. A complete survey would have to include, for instance, an account of the Labour College movement, which grew up as the result of a split at Ruskin College in 1909. A section of the students, dissatisfied with the curriculum and with what they regarded as the undue influence of the University, formed themselves into an organisation to secure " the education of the workers in the interests of the workers." The result of the schism was the establishment first at Oxford and afterwards in London of the Central Labour College (now the Labour College). In addition to this residential institution, classes were established in many industrial centres under the auspices of the " Plebs League," and a comprehensive organisation known as the National Council of Labour Colleges came into being in 1921. The movement repudiates the idea of " impartiality " in education and aims frankly at providing instruction which will be of " practical usefulness to the workers in their class struggle " (J. F. and Winifred Horrabin, *Working-Class Education*, *q.v.*).

type of student. Apart from these, there was nothing but a week or two at the annual summer vacation school for the adult student who wanted to carry his studies further than was possible in the tutorial class. Occasionally, a very exceptional student found his way to a university; but that was rare indeed.

Since the War, the number of residential colleges providing for adult students has increased. The principal post-War developments have been the opening of the Catholic Workers' College at Oxford in 1921, the foundation of the Residential College for Working Women immediately after the War, and the inauguration of the scheme for a Co-operative College in 1918. The latest development is the opening of Avoncroft, a college similar to Fircroft, but providing for agricultural workers. The universities also are now making definite provision for the admission of extra-mural students to their internal courses.

There has been no dearth of suitable students for these courses; indeed, the difficulty has been to select from the large number of qualified candidates who have presented themselves whenever an opportunity has been provided. The Cassel Trustees rendered a very great service to adult education when, a few years ago, they decided to place an annual sum at the disposal of the tutorial class movement to provide scholarships for adult students tenable at the universities and at Ruskin College. The scholarships were limited at first to one term's residence only—much too short a period to give satisfactory results; but the scheme has since been modified in the direction of awarding fewer scholarships, each providing for a year's residence. The enterprise of the trustees made possible a valuable experiment which is now bearing fruit, and which enabled both the universities and the bodies charged with the selection of students to gain the experience necessary to make further experiment possible.

Oxford and Cambridge through their extra-mural

departments both offer a number of scholarships annually to adult students, and there is also a scheme in operation at University College, Nottingham. Recently, the Central Miners' Welfare Committee has instituted a scholarship scheme for adult students employed in the industry, which provides ten scholarships annually, tenable at a university or a constituent college of a university. A recent report of the Adult Education Committee of the Board of Education recommends the provision of state scholarships for adult students.[1]

The chief difficulty in the way of a large increase in facilities of this character is a financial one. Adult scholarships are costly, and machinery for co-operation between universities, adult education bodies, public authorities and educational trusts in the provision of the necessary funds does not exist. But apart from that problem, satisfactory methods of selecting students need to be worked out, and much more will have to be done in the way of adapting arrangements at the universities to the needs of extra-mural students who are capable of benefiting by a period of full-time study. There is as yet little agreement as to the best type of course to offer, or even as to the ideal length of course.

Another difficulty is the relation of the residential colleges to the universities—the question, for instance, whether adult students should pass normally from one to the other, or whether the two types of institution should aim at satisfying different needs.

The whole problem is less simple than it appears. Some students of extra-mural classes need a full-time course because their class work has discovered in them a bent for scholarship which has never had a chance before. For them, the university should never be closed ; for it needs them and

[1] Paper No. 7 : " Full-Time Studies : A Report on the Opportunities given to Adult Students to pursue their Studies on a full-time basis at Universities and other Institutions."

their ripe experience as much as they need what the university has to offer. Others need training for more effective service in the organisations to which they belong. Possibly a shorter period of full-time study will meet their need, and they may find what they require in one or other of the residential colleges. Finally, there is the problem of training tutors drawn from the ranks of the students themselves—a problem which is at present occupying the attention of a strong committee of enquiry, set up under the joint auspices of the British Institute of Adult Education and the Tutors' Association. The solution of this problem is an urgent one, if an adequate supply of qualified tutors is to be maintained ; and it will depend upon careful experiment and upon the closest co-operation between the universities and the other bodies concerned.

The most urgent need, if experiment in this field is to continue, is that increased funds should be made available for the provision of scholarships. The remaining problems can be worked out by co-operation between all the bodies concerned, and all have already shown themselves willing to work together to this end.

F. Finance and Administration

This brings us to the wider question of the finance and machinery of adult eduation in general. Neither, in this branch of education, has kept pace with the need.

The question of finance may be lightly passed over. We all want more money ; and adult education is not peculiar in this respect. But apart from that, it suffers from a much too rigid system of finance. In the first place, grants are based upon classes, and the maximum grants payable by the Board of Education vary from £60 (or even £75 in some cases) per session of twenty-four meetings for tutorial classes, to £8 for the ordinary terminal course of twelve meetings. Maximum grants for one-year classes are paid at the rate of £36 for forty-eight hours. The rate for preparatory tutorial Classes and university extension courses is £45 for forty-eight hours. In all cases the grants are payable, of course, subject to the carrying out of certain conditions as to attendance and written work. The grant actually paid in each case is either the maximum or three fourths of the tutor's salary, whichever is less. Local education authorities also as a rule aid classes in their areas, the rates varying according to the type of class.

This system of grants has certain undesirable consequences. In the first place, the great disparity in the grants paid for different types of courses encourages the formation of tutorial classes when other types of classes or courses might be more suitable in the particular circumstances ; and, in the second place, it leads to the employment of less highly qualified tutors and lecturers for what is often the most difficult work, viz., that of breaking new ground. What is wanted is not only an increase in the resources available, but also greater freedom for responsible bodies to use those resources in the most effective way possible, subject, of course, to approval by the Board of a general programme. This greater freedom might be given at least in connection with the employment of staff tutors. At present they have to be used almost exclusively in conducting three-year tutorial classes, since that is usually the only way to obtain sufficient funds to pay their salaries.

Another difficulty arising out of the present system of basing grants on teachers' salaries, is that the funds at the disposal of responsible bodies for administration are hopelessly inadequate, and it is therefore becoming increasingly difficult to cope with the growing burden of work. Not only that, but expenditure on books and other equipment is unduly restricted, to the great hindrance of the work of teaching. This could only be remedied by the payment of over-riding block grants in addition to grants paid on a class basis ; or possibly, in the case of universities, by an addition to the ordinary Treasury grant earmarked specially for extra-mural work, the precedent for which is already established by the finding of the recent Royal Commission on the Universities of Oxford and Cambridge.

The actual administration of adult education in the country presents many difficult problems which can only be touched upon here. As the work increases in amount and variety, the need for devising satisfactory machinery of administration becomes more urgent, and the task of devising such machinery becomes more difficult. The bodies chiefly concerned are the universities, local education authorities, and the voluntary associations already mentioned.

The difficulty is to give stability and permanence to the work and to preserve its high standard and quality without at the same time destroying its spontaneity. Adults cannot be treated like children. They must be allowed to initiate and control their own activities, if the work is to succeed. Any attempt to dictate to them what they shall study or how they are to study it must lead to ultimate failure, and insistence upon irksome conditions and formalities will have the same result. Great care and discrimination has to be exercised in the appointment of tutors to adult classes. The tutor who is to guide their studies must not only be a man of wide knowledge and attainments, but must also be able to enter into the experience of his students and to understand something of their point of view.

All this means that the voluntary basis of the work must be maintained. Nevertheless, if an increasing amount of public money is to be devoted to it, there must be some guarantee of standards and of efficient administration. The voluntary associations, however admirably fitted they may be to stir up enthusiasm for adult education, and so to promote and maintain the demand, may not be equally fitted to provide this necessary guarantee of quality. Local education authorities, on the other hand, may be quite well able to ensure efficiency of administration, but they may not always be able to preserve the personal enthusiasms upon which so much of the success of this work depends, or the high standards which have been set up in the past. Not all authorities approach the problems of adult education in their areas even with sympathy, much less understanding, although in some districts adult education owes more to the wise guidance and help of the authority than to any other agency. So long as these differences remain, it would be fatal to force all the more formal activities of bodies like the Workers' Educational Association, as suggested in the preface to the Regulations of 1924, into the hands of the local authority. Experience has proved that, where local education authorities have been successful in the promotion of this work, that success has been made possible only by the closest co-operation with voluntary agencies and with the universities.

The universities in the early days solved the problem of administration by setting up joint committees composed, as to half their membership, of academic representatives, the other half consisting of working-class representatives nominated by the appropriate district organisation of the Workers' Educational Association. In view of the wider scope of modern adult education, this somewhat rigid type of organisation is no longer adequate by itself. It may serve for the promotion of three-year tutorial classes for working-class students, although even here it seems desirable that local education authorities should be represented. It cannot possibly serve to develop all the many-sided activities for all sections of the community which now fall properly within the scope of university extra-mural work. The Report of the Adult Education Committee of the Ministry of Reconstruction, presided over by the late Master of Balliol,[1] recommended the establishment in each university of a Department of Extra-mural Studies, with an academic

[1] Published by H.M. Stationery Office in 1919, but now, unfortunately, out of print.

head. This recommendation was first adopted by the University College, Nottingham, in 1920 ; and this college also led the way by creating the first professorship of Adult Education. Some other universities have now set up similar departments, and the striking developments which have followed in all these cases have amply proved the wisdom of the original recommendation.

It is difficult to say what the future of the administration of adult education will be in this country. One thing is certain : the work in every district in all its variety must be envisaged as a whole and in relation to other branches of education. It may, in the future, become mainly a part of the normal work of local education authorities. There are some, on the other hand, who look rather to the growth of the extra-mural university, with its classrooms spread over a wide area, and building up a high standard of humane teaching under professors no less distinguished than those whose work lies mainly within the walls of the university. There is room for both developments ; they are not incompatible but complementary ; and the voluntary organisation of students must find an important place in either.

The greatest difficulty in the future will be to maintain an adequate supply of suitably qualified tutors, and for this reason if for no other it is important that other universities should create Departments of Adult Education, which will provide a reasonable status and reasonable prospects for those who are attracted to this work, and will also be able to make arrangements for the training of tutors both for university extra-mural classes and also for other types of adult education not under the control of the universities. When all has been said and done about the machinery of adult education, the preservation of standards and the further growth of the work will depend ultimately upon the quality of teaching and leadership, and to provide and maintain this is the great task of the universities, whatever the particular machinery of control.

G. THE SIGNIFICANCE OF ADULT EDUCATION

It is difficult, standing in the midst of a development of this kind, to appraise its significance. In spite of the difficulties of the post-war period, it is still going on and is gathering force. We are, I believe, at the beginning of a great educational revival which may be of tremendous import for the whole future of civilisation. There were very definite signs of such a revival in other branches of education in the last quarter of the nineteenth century. In adult education, it is unmistakable in the present century.

The evidence for this optimistic interpretation of the facts is not confined to the adult education movement alone. It is also seen in the world of printed books and in the daily and periodical press. Most of us can still remember the earliest of the cheap reprints of the " classics " which we greeted with so much joy. Some of these series have now grown to amazing proportions, and they have been supplemented by the appearance of other series of cheap monographs, written for the general reader by the greatest authorities on all the important subjects of knowledge. This kind of publishing has become good business. Further, in the cheap daily and weekly press, there is an increasing tendency to print articles of definitely educational interest, and there is no end to the number of " self-educators " and other monumental works of wisdom which appear from time to time in fortnightly parts. Even cigarette cards are now educational !

Perhaps the most striking indication of all, however, is the modern development of broadcasting. Is it possible to imagine the present programmes in any age but this ? When all the unpleasant things have been said about jazz music and " variety turns," remembering the universal appeal of broadcasting, we cannot but be struck by the high level of general taste and culture which the programmes represent. If there is any doubt about it, we have only to compare the present tendencies in broadcasting with the earlier development of the cinema. The educational talks in the B.B.C. programmes have always maintained a very high level, and an important committee appointed jointly by the Corporation and the British Institute of Adult Education, under the chairmanship of Sir Henry Hadow, is at present considering the future of educational broadcasting as part of the general scheme of adult education.

In view of this great revival of popular interest in education, it becomes important that we should ask ourselves what is to be the relation of adult education to other branches of education and what part it has to play in the life of the nation.

Let us be clear about one thing. Adult education cannot be considered apart from education as a whole. Its aims are the aims of education in general, and these are not sectarian but universal. Education, as I conceive it, must have a twofold aim : it must be concerned with the development of the character and personality of the individual ; and it must provide for the handing on from generation to generation of the great and growing body of knowledge without which the continuance of civilisation itself would be impossible.

As to the first, I can only say that experience in adult education is calling into question all those generalisations of the educational psychologists which suggest a limited period of " plasticity " in the mental life of the individual. There is no shred of scientific evidence for the theory, advanced by James and blindly accepted by others, that most people cease to be " educable " after the age of twenty-five. The little evidence that exists contradicts it, and this is confirmed by the experience of all who have been engaged in the work of adult education. Apart, however, from this question, can there be any real doubt that the use of leisure for the pursuit of knowledge, at whatever age it begins in the life of the individual, must make for a more harmonious and a more effective personality ? The creative or even recreative use of leisure through adult education must be an important part of the experience of every intelligent member of the community. This view of adult education becomes doubly important in view of the monotonous and uneducative character of many occupations to-day, and in view also of the shorter hours of labour which are beginning to be characteristic of modern industry.

We are on even surer ground when we consider adult education in relation to the second aim, the transmission of knowledge. All that knowledge which enables us to live in communities on a higher plane than that of the ant or the bee has to be learned afresh by each new generation ; and as knowledge increases and civilisation is raised to higher levels, the task becomes at once more difficult and more important. Custom and oral tradition are no longer sufficient in modern communities. Elementary education for everybody will not enable us to carry the burden. Even an extension of school education for all would not meet the need, for much of this later education, not least in the universities, must be specialised. Adult education has its own place in the educational system and in the life of the nation. The elementary school, even when followed by the secondary school, can do no more than lay the necessary foundations of knowledge. Even that is impossible so long as school life ends for the vast majority at the age of fourteen, and adult education can only become really effective as part of our national system of education when the great gap which at present exists between the elementary school and higher stages of education is effectively bridged. Adult education cannot take the place of secondary education ; its business is to help the mature student to weave the isolated bits of knowledge into the web of his experience, to find for himself a philosophy of life and a harmonious way of living, and to make the best contribution of which he is capable to the common life.

If all this is true, the appeal of adult education must not be a limited one. It may in fact serve sectional interests, but that cannot be its aim. The business man and the university graduate need it as much as the trade unionist. In every sphere the wider diffusion of a broad and humane culture is necessary to counteract the narrowing effects of modern specialisation. It is necessary, too, if contact is to be maintained between succeeding generations ; for one serious disharmony of our common life is due to the lack of understanding which separates one generation from another with the more rapid growth of knowledge. Adult education must help the older generation to keep pace in knowledge with the new.

Beginning as a makeshift substitute for elementary education, adult education now bases itself upon the claim that education must be a life-long process ; that no one is ever too old to learn ; that there are phases in the educational process suited to different stages in the growth of the individual ; and that adult education is just as essential a part of the whole as school education. Finally, the growing dependence of civilised life upon the wide diffusion of knowledge as knowledge itself grows, makes adult education no longer a makeshift or a luxury, but a necessity.

REFERENCES

DOBBS, A. E. Education and Social Movements, 1700–1850. Longmans, Green, 1919.

DRAPER, W. H. University Extension, 1873–1923. Cambridge, 1923.

GODARD, J. G. George Birkbeck. Derby, 1884.

HOLE, JAMES. History and Management of Literary, Scientific, and Mechanics Institutes. 1849.

HUDSON, J. W. A History of Adult Education. London, 1851.

MANSBRIDGE, A. An Adventure in Working-Class Education. Longmans, Green, 1920.

MANSBRIDGE, A.   University Tutorial Classes.   Longmans, Green, 1913.

MARTIN, G. CURRIE.   The Adult School Movement.   National Adult School Union, 1924.

MAURICE, F. D.   Learning and Working.   Cambridge : Macmillan, 1885.

PRICE, T. W.   The Story of the W.E.A.   Labour Publishing Co., 1924.

SADLER, M. E.   Continuation Schools in England and elsewhere, 1780–1907.   Manchester Univ. Press, 1907.

STANLEY, O. [editor].   The Way Out.   Essays on the Meaning and Purpose of Adult Education.   Humphrey Milford, 1923.

YEAXLEE, B. A.   Spiritual Values in Adult Education, 2 vols.   Oxford, 1925.

Cambridge Essays on Adult Education.   Ed. R. St. J. Parry.   Cambridge, 1920.

Final Report of the Adult Education Committee of the Ministry of Reconstruction, 1919.   H.M. Stationery Office, but out of print.

The publications of the Adult Education Committee (H.M. Stationery Office), Papers 1–9, especially " Full-Time Studies " (No. 7), and " Pioneer Work and other Developments in Adult Education " (No. 9).

The Handbook and Directory of Adult Education, 1926–7.   Compiled under the auspices of the British Institute of Adult Education.   H. F. W. Deane & Sons, 1926.

The Journal of Adult Education, ed. by J. Dover Wilson and A. E. Heath.   First issue, Sept. 1926.

EDUCATION IN THE FIGHTING SERVICES

CHAPTER XV

THE EDUCATION OF THE NAVAL CADET

By Sir Cyril Ashford

EDUCATION in the Navy covers so vast a field and comprises so miscellaneous an assortment of institutions and activities that it is impossible to cope with it as a whole within the limits of one chapter. The Admiralty has its " university " at the Royal Naval College, Greenwich, its technological institute at the Royal Naval Engineering College, Keyham, and its " public school " at Dartmouth. Its " lower-deck " and dockyard education comprises schools of every grade and in every part of the globe, while it has recently (since 1918) blossomed out with a new scheme for adult education, which provides continuous educational facilities for all, and last year produced over 2,000 voluntary candidates for the Higher Educational Test, the examination which tests educational fitness for promotion to warrant and commissioned rank.

A book might be written on any one of these topics. It has therefore been thought best, for the purpose of the present volume, to concentrate upon that area which is at once one of the most interesting from the educational point of view, and one of the most important from the national point of view, viz. the education of the naval cadet. Most of what follows will be concerned with a single school, the junior division of which formed the separate establishment at Osborne until 1921, when it was added to the senior division at Dartmouth ; but the reader will not perhaps regard the treatment as disproportionate when he remembers that in the future, under existing regulations, most officers of superior rank in H.M. Navy will receive their education first of all in this same school.

Before 1903 officers of the executive branch of the Navy were for the most part prepared for their career by a preliminary shore course almost entirely technical in character and given in H.M.S. *Britannia*, the course lasting for fifteen months and beginning at about the age of fifteen. But at Christmas, 1902, Lord Selborne announced a profound modification in the functions of the great majority of commissioned officers ; it was decided to amalgamate the executive and engineering and marine branches, in the belief that, as the modern fighting ship was becoming a " box of engines," all officers of the military branch must be engineers, whatever else they might be. The normal training of an engineer has always been a very lengthy one, and to provide adequate time for it without undue postponement of the time of joining a sea-going ship it was found necessary that the shore course should start before the age of thirteen, and should last some four years.

This early age of starting involved the provision of a concurrent general education, in the widest sense of the term ; so the Admiralty boldly (and Sir John Fisher, the real begetter of the scheme, was nothing if not bold) launched out on a pioneering policy. In broad outline it embraced, so far as concerned instruction, a combination of the methods of a public school and a technical college, suited to the tender age of the pupils. This meant an interesting innovation in the educational practice current at that time. About one-third of the boy's working hours were devoted to engineering or subjects directly akin to engineering. At this time, Sanderson was experimenting along similar lines at Oundle, and in both cases the daily admixture of bookish and rather abstract studies with concrete practical subjects was found to work admirably, even (or perhaps especially) with these quite young boys. It was, of course, necessary, at Osborne and Dartmouth as at Oundle, to redesign the traditional methods of approach to physical science and engineering, based on a fairly comprehensive body of theoretical knowledge, which the student would test and verify in particular cases in the laboratory or workshop.

As for character formation, it was hoped to combine a definitely naval atmosphere with the traditions and experience of public schools. Hence there was introduced the " dual control," which was at first regarded as a highly delicate experiment; pessimists declared that it was so delicate that it spelt failure. A complete naval staff was appointed, responsible for all out-of-school activities, with a post-captain in general command; while provision was made for an equally complete staff of civilian masters, with headmaster, heads of departments, tutors, and so on, to be recruited in the same way and from the same sources as at a public school. No written constitution was laid down by the Admiralty; it was left to work itself out in practice, and this eminently English plan proved its wisdom. For every one was keen on its success and full of enthusiasm, especially in the first and most critical years; mere *amour propre*, if it existed in such circumstances, was subordinated to the desire to further the welfare of the scheme.

Although the Admiralty gave a very free hand to those to whom it entrusted the task of inaugurating the new routine, few experiments have been watched more closely by all the parties concerned, and the watchers were accustomed to praise sparingly and blame unhesitatingly. This was the more valuable, in that the Admiralty is accountable to no one; parents surrender all right of determination of the upbringing of their sons when once they have been accepted as cadets, and the Admiralty trains them as it wills. Doubtless the parents reserve their right of criticism, and freely exercise it, whether over their tea-cups or through their representatives in Parliament. Such criticism is by no means ineffective ; for instance, an impression gradually became widespread, though I believe it was baseless, that Osborne was unhealthy, and so, partly owing to this criticism and partly for reasons of economy, Osborne was closed and the cadets transferred to Dartmouth. With the war-time additions to its magnificent buildings, the College provides a commodious hive for the 560 cadets now housed there.

The governing body, then, could prescribe any curriculum it chose, and vary it as often as it pleased. As a matter of fact, very considerable changes have gradually been made during the quarter of a century since the scheme was launched, partly as the fruit of experience and partly through changes of Admiralty policy. Looking back now, it is easy to see that Sir John Fisher was over-ambitious and too optimistic. He intended that practically all formal instruction should cease when a cadet became a midshipman and went to sea. The theory was that a naval officer goes on learning all his life ; if he does not, he is very soon relegated to the beach. He learns best by performing his duties and by the private study necessary to fit himself for their performance, under the immediate stimulus of making that performance efficient enough to satisfy the exacting standard of his commanding officer, who is in turn responsible to the admiral in charge of his fleet, and so on ; there are few weak links in that naval chain.

So it was proposed to abolish the naval instructor (borne in each ship carrying midshipmen, whose duty it was to teach them the science and practice of navigation), to do away with the short courses on shore in gunnery, seamanship, and torpedo, that used to precede the qualifying examinations in those subjects, and to substitute for those examinations severely practical tests in the ships themselves by the specialist officers serving in the fleet. All these proposals have gone by the board since the war.

It is by no means easy to determine the actual cause of the abandonment of proposals so full of common sense, which in many respects follow the most approved lines of modern educational thought. Probably a multitude of causes contributed. But above all there was an under-estimation of the range of technical knowledge involved in modern conditions, which require increasing intensity of specialisation afloat as well as on shore. It has always been the wise tradition of the service that an officer ceases to be a specialist on taking command, and that a captain of a ship should trust to his expert advisers in all branches, while assuming full responsibility for the advice he accepts and acts on. There is a close parallel in the ministers of the Crown, who seldom begin as specialists in the work of their departments or stay long enough in them to become experts. But in the grades below the rank of captain (and all officers pass through these grades) the specialist must be expert, and this demands in some cases restriction to one branch for a substantial period or even for the whole of a man's service.

But whatever be the cause, the amalgamation of branches that led to the foundation of Osborne and Dartmouth has now been, except to a negligible extent, altogether abandoned, and the function of Dartmouth consists in training future executive officers alone. Nevertheless the experience gained has by no means been wasted, from an educational point of view, whatever discomforts and dissatisfactions have resulted from the changes in Admiralty plans to individual officers who have good reason to feel that they have been the victims of an unsettled policy. The education of a present-day Dartmouth cadet is immeasurably wider, more humanistic, fuller of interest, more stimulating and better suited to his needs, than that of his predecessor in H.M.S. *Britannia*.

The attempt to give both a general education and a specialist training in engineering meant a seriously overcrowded curriculum. Its abandonment has made it possible to retain only as much of the latter as is judged to be desirable in a liberal education for those who will spend their lives in highly "mechanised" surroundings, but whose main function will be to deal with human beings under those conditions. The amount of engineering thus retained is, however, substantial. The majority of the officers would never pretend to compete with their subordinates in manual dexterity, or even in the detailed knowledge acquired during long years spent in a narrow groove, but they must be able to command the respect of such men by the possession of wider powers. In these days birth alone provides no such sanction, helpful though it is ; breeding is far more potent, for men thrown into the close contact with their officers, which even the vast modern fighting ship enforces, instantly recognise the character and ideals which are the hall-mark of a well-bred man, and almost instinctively accept his leadership. The officer must have a broad knowledge of all those subjects in the details of which each subordinate is a master, a knowledge broad enough to enable him to accept readily and intelligently the fresh applications of modern science which are continually being introduced into the everyday life of the fleets.

Hence their scientific training should not aim at the acquisition of a large body of facts or detailed knowledge in a small range of subjects ; such a training may be suitable for a subordinate, but the officer's should be directed rather to the acquisition and development of a habit of mind, which will enable him to face novel problems or machines and bring to bear all the varied knowledge he may possess. This particular faculty can be developed by practical and theoretical engineering and physical and chemical science, suitably treated, and there is no doubt whatever that these subjects, so used, form an essential part of a truly liberal education for modern civilised life. The proportions in which the available time should be divided between them and the humanities differ, of course, according to the future career of the student, but neither can safely have its proportion so reduced as to be negligible. In particular, the future executive officer is probably best suited by a roughly equal division between them, which is now carried out at Dartmouth.

As a cadet progresses in his course at the college he spends a gradually increasing amount of time in acquiring definitely professional knowledge, such as boat-sailing, signalling, rifle-drill, the rudiments of seamanship, the elements of fleet tactics, the organisation of a ship's company, and so on, culminating in three cruises of a week each in a minesweeper attached to the college. Although of little or no intellectual value, this knowledge is perhaps useful enough in itself to justify the time spent in its acquirement before he goes to sea. Further, the inclusion of such professional subjects in the curriculum undoubtedly tends to make a cadet feel that his training is not divorced from the life he will lead after he leaves the college. Few boys of past generations can have escaped a sense of unreality in the normal curricula, since it needs a very mature mind to realise the value of an exclusively classical education as a preparation for the conduct of life in a workaday world. But the real justification is probably that such direct professional training gives many excellent opportunities for practice in " taking charge "—a vital part of education that can hardly be supplied in class-teaching, except by rather artificial devices.

If it were not for the games in all schools and for house duties in boarding-schools, there would be a lamentable lack of opportunities of this kind in the training of the ordinary schoolboy, and even with games, etc., the amount is probably seriously deficient. It is, I believe, safe to say that one of the greatest benefits that has accrued from withdrawing a large number of officers from the active life of their profession, to spend a couple of years of co-operation with schoolmasters in the training of those who will follow in their footsteps, is that in matters of this kind they have a truer perspective than those who devote their whole lives to the profession of teaching.

The isolation of schoolmasters is to a certain extent imposed on them by the circumstances of their calling, but it is inevitably a handicap. They have learnt to protect themselves against the amateur suggestions of the anxious mother, and the habit has perhaps made them reluctant to give full consideration to the advice of men of the world, who have of late become increasingly ready to give it. But the experience of Dartmouth may well encourage them to do so ; it would be idle to pretend that the close co-operation of naval officers and civilian schoolmasters always makes for an easy life for either body, but the gain to the cadet has fully repaid any inconvenience to the authorities, and I believe that all who have had the privilege of serving the common cause would readily admit that they had themselves incidentally learnt a vast deal of real value during their service.

REFERENCES

Beyond what is to be found in " The King's Regulations and Admiralty Instructions," there appears to be no literature of any importance upon naval education.

CHAPTER XVI

EDUCATIONAL TRAINING IN THE ARMY

By Major Simpson

When sufficient time has elapsed to enable the events of the War to be seen in their true perspective, the development of the educational movement among the armed forces will stand out as one of the most striking and unpredictable. As the President of the Board of Education, speaking at the Cambridge School for Army Education Instructors, said, " Nothing in the shape of adult education has ever before been attempted on the same scale in the whole history of the world." [1]

Educational Training has been carried on in the Army for over 150 years. The Royal Military Academy (" The Shop ") was founded in 1741, and a general scheme of education was in existence by 1750. It was not, however, until the opening years of the nineteenth century, when H.R.H. The Duke of York was Commander-in-Chief, that education became a recognised part of the soldier's training. In 1802 the Royal Military College (" Sandhurst ") was founded, and in the following year the Duke of York's Royal Military School was constituted by Royal Warrant. In 1811 Circular 79 was issued authorising the establishment of a regimental school in each battalion or corps—the schoolmaster being appointed by the colonel—and laying down a detailed scheme of education for the soldier and for the soldier's children. This scheme was finally approved

[1] Final Report of the Adult Education Committee, p. 349 (Cmd. 321), 1919.

by the Royal Warrant of July 24, 1812, and educational training was given a definite place in the soldier's life.

The need for teachers to cope with the work arising from this expansion of educational training became evident, and in 1846 a Royal Warrant created the special rank of " Schoolmaster Sergeant." In the same year a department for the training of schoolmasters was opened at the Duke of York's Royal Military School. In the early years attendance of recruits was voluntary, but in 1849 the Commander-in-Chief issued an order requiring recruits to attend school for two hours daily. About the same time an impetus was given to the general education of the ordinary soldier, and there is record of the men attending classes, during the winter season, for four hours a day. In 1857 an educational standard for promotion to the non-commissioned ranks was laid down. The instruction of the soldier and of the soldier's children, both at home and abroad, called for an increasing number of teachers, and in order to improve their status the instructors were formed into the Corps of Army Schoolmasters, which included officers and warrant officers in addition to the schoolmaster sergeants. The members of this corps were responsible, down to the end of the War, for educational training in all its branches, and for the teaching in the children's schools.

The Armistice of November, 1918, produced two new and urgent educational problems. In the first place, there were thousands of men, awaiting demobilisation, for whom it was imperative to provide some interest and training during the time they necessarily remained in the army ; in the second place, the late War had conclusively proved that an educated man is much more easily trained than an uneducated one, and, other things being equal, makes the better, because the more adaptable, soldier.

The outcome of these two problems was the creation, in 1920, of a new corps, the Army Educational Corps, consisting of officers, warrant officers, and sergeants.

The duties of the Army Educational Corps at present comprise :

(*a*) The general education of the soldier with a view to making him a better subject for military training and a better citizen on return to civil life.

(*b*) The organisation, supervision, and testing of this system of education.

(*c*) Lecturing on the principles and methods of education at the Army Schools of Education at Shorncliffe and Belgaum (India). These two schools are training centres for the officers and men who will become organisers of and instructors in educational training in their own units ; and for those men anxious to transfer to the Army Educational Corps.

(*d*) The general education of the cadets at the Royal Military College, as much on the lines of a university as is possible in the limited time available.

(*e*) The staffing of the Duke of York's Royal Military School, and Queen Victoria's School, at which the boys are given a secondary education up to matriculation standard.

(*f*) The general education of the boys at the Boys' Technical Schools.

(*g*) The elementary education of soldiers' children in places where civilian schools are not available.

The scheme of educational training in the Army provides a continuous course of instruction throughout the man's service. In this course four stages are marked by examinations :

(*a*) The Army Third Class Certificate of Education.

(*b*) The Army Second Class Certificate of Education.

(*c*) The Army First Class Certificate of Education.

(*d*) The Army Special Class Certificate of Education.

Each recruit is tested, on joining, as to his mental standard, and is classified for the purposes of further educational training. He is then put into a class suitable to his attainments and prepared for the third or second class certificate examination. The preparation for the third class certificate consists in revising and bringing back to the candidate's mind the knowledge he acquired at the elementary school. Regimental history has its place in the syllabus in order that the recruit may learn the history of his regiment, and be imbued with *esprit de corps*. The second class takes him on a stage further, and a soldier must pass this examination before he can receive proficiency pay. Up to this point attendance is compulsory. The first class certificate approximates to the standard of a school leaving certificate. The possession of a " First " is necessary for promotion to warrant rank, and all those men who aim at promotion to the higher ranks continue their studies and work for this examination. The special certificate is equivalent in standard to the matriculation, and is accepted by many universities in lieu of their preliminary examination.

The principle which has been adopted throughout is that army education, particularly in its earlier stages, should be linked up as far as possible with military training and interests. For instance, the teaching of mathematics largely relies on examples and experiments of military value ; the teaching of English starts with the assumption that the soldier must be " articulate," in order to frame a clear report or message, orally or in writing ; whilst history and geography begin with the story of the soldier's own regiment, and work up through the part played by the Army in the development of the Empire to the more general syllabus of the special certificate.

But there is a further very important purpose in all this educational effort which may not be generally recognised. Not only is it desirable to quicken the soldier's wits and broaden his outlook on life generally, but it is essential to teach him initiative. The days when the soldier could be the passive instrument of the commander have now definitely passed. Modern war with its changing weapons, its vast distances, and the impossibility of close control during battle, demands co-operation by, and decentralisation to, the humblest private ; the strength of an army depends more and more on its individual components. Accordingly the modern soldier must be trained, not only in discipline and skill at arms, but also to think and act for himself in times of crisis. To this end general education can make a definite contribution. Once a man has been brought by the orthodox methods of the class-room to a certain standard in reading, writing, and calculation, he must more and more be encouraged to work by himself without the direct supervision of an instructor, with a view to developing his personal initiative and sense of responsibility. A beginning has already been made with these methods, and once the principle has been firmly established in the army a great advance in the development of the individual can be looked for.

All the early educational training aims at improving the soldier as a subject for military training, but when the soldier has passed his " First " and is getting towards the end of his service, it is realised that he is beginning to be alive to the economic demands of his future life as a civil citizen of the Empire. The educational training, therefore, takes rather a different form, and the needs of the individual student are studied so as to create in him an aptitude and liking for the labour by which he will live. With this end in view special courses are organised at the Vocational Training Centres for soldiers during their last six months of military service.

The results of the seven or eight years' education since the War show the keenness with which the opportunities for education are appreciated by the soldier. More than 13,000 men have obtained their first class or special certificates, and at the last examination, in October, 1927, 2,202 candidates sat for the " First " and 328 for the " Special " certificate of education. In addition to these statistics, reports have been received of the very noticeable increase of interest and intelligence shown by the soldier at manœuvres and other forms of large-scale collective training, a type of military activity which, in pre-war days, was apt to leave him intellectually unmoved. Finally it must not be forgotten how much a sound system of mental and moral training, whilst he is in the army, enhances the prospects of the soldier's employment on his return to civil life, while an annual contribution of 30,000 men from the army who have benefited by from three to seven years' adult education cannot but have a beneficial effect, even though on a small scale, on the life of the nation.

The work of education in the services holds a very distinct place in the general scheme of the education of the nation, in that it fills the gap between the elementary school and adult education as carried on by the civil institutions.

The number of British troops at home and in India is approximately 200,000 men, so the Army is, numerically, the greatest of adult institutions, and the problems which arise in connection with educational training are many and varied. The experiments now being made to adapt educational methods to special conditions must add considerably to the general body of educational knowledge and experience.

The fruits of the scheme must be judged, not by examination results, but by whether the training has made the recruit a better soldier, and by whether the present-day soldier on returning to civil life can reflect, weigh evidence, draw conclusions, form judgments, and has the power to translate thought into effective and controlled action—in short, by whether the educational training he has received has made him a better, more useful, and complete citizen of the Commonwealth of Nations.

REFERENCES

Educational Training.   H.M. Stationery Office.   3*d*.

The following may be consulted at the War Office Library :—
Education in the Army, by Capt. A. E. Watts, A.E.C.
Reports by the Council of Military Education on Army Schools.
General Reports by the Council of Military Education.
Reports by the Director-General of Military Education.

CHAPTER XVII

THE EDUCATIONAL SCHEME OF THE AIR FORCE

By Colonel Curtis

THE educational system of the Air Force has one feature which differentiates it from those of the older services. Like the Air Force itself it is new and has had to be designed and built from the foundations upwards for its particular purpose.

The Navy and the Army have grown slowly through the ages. The origins of their history, their traditions, and their way of thought are lost in the mists of the past. The Air Force alone of all the fighting services sprang to life in a day, at the call of a great emergency, armed cap-à-pie for war. Now, with the coming of peace and reduced to a tithe of its war strength, it is faced with the task not only of building up a permanent organisation, but of creating for itself, in a period measured by months rather than centuries, a tradition and an outlook of its own. It has to solve for itself the problem of what air-power means, for that is a question to which the Great War gave no answer, the Air Force in those days acting only as an auxiliary service to the Navy and the Army. The science of aeronautics also is still in its infancy, and from every movement forward there come changes in the *matériel* and in the practice of the service. To deal with problems such as these, a highly trained personnel is needed, and the education of this personnel must be commensurate not only in standard but in range with the task which faces it.

322

This question of newness affects the educational system at every point. When reconstruction started after the War, education in the Air Force found itself, in the latter part of 1919, without staff, without schools, and without equipment. What is more, there were no precedents, no recognised system of school attendance, and no examinations, but only the remnants of three separate traditions—of the Navy, Army, and civil life—in many essential respects mutually incompatible. Further, when the educational staff turned to the technical side of its work, it found that many of the subjects of instruction were so new that neither accepted textbooks nor laboratory equipment and methods existed.

The Air Force has also a special characteristic which provides the educational staff with yet another problem. No other service makes so great a call on the individual initiative and resource of its personnel. What is there quite to compare for instance with the loneliness of the pilot on patrol 10,000 feet above the earth ? Or, when is a young officer thrown more completely on his own resources than in starting alone to intercept raiding aircraft at night ? The airman not only shares these experiences in the air as pilot, mechanic, or wireless operator, but on the ground is for the most part a specialist in some particular trade or occupation, and on his personal resource and ability may turn the question of whether an aeroplane can be ready in time for some essential service, and of whether the pilot returns safely or is reported missing.

It is considerations such as these which have made it essential for the Air Force to recruit so large a proportion of its numbers from boys and young men who have had the benefit of a secondary or technical education, and the presence of this type of man, not merely as a leaven but as constituting nearly one-half of the service, has in turn affected the whole character of the educational scheme.

It is not practicable in the space available to deal fully

with a scheme, the activities of which extend from the kindergarten for children in overseas commands at one end of the scale to university courses for specialist officers at the other, but it may perhaps be possible by taking some particular and characteristic parts of it in greater detail to indicate something of the method and of the spirit in which the problem is being attacked.

In the first place, however, it will be well to summarise briefly its main features. The Air Force has at Cranwell in Lincolnshire its Cadet College, which corresponds to the Royal Military Academy at Woolwich for the Army. Here education is represented by a Professor of Aeronautical Science, and a Professor of English and History, with three Education Officers as lecturers. Then there are the schools for officers specialising in such subjects as engineering, wireless, and armament, each course of which has an educational section. No college for more advanced training in these subjects has been set up such as the Navy possesses at Greenwich, and the Army at Woolwich ; arrangements having been made instead, with the help of the respective university authorities, for selected officers to become resident undergraduates at Cambridge or students at the Imperial College, South Kensington. Officers specialising in engineering, for instance, who are selected as of sufficient promise at the end of the regular Air Force course, go first to Cambridge for two years to take the honours course in the engineering laboratory (or, for the present, in certain cases the corresponding course for the ordinary degree), and if they do well enough, pass on for a further year to the Aeronautical Department of the Imperial College, South Kensington. From among those who give proof of the requisite capacity for research work and are recommended, one or two each year may be chosen for a further course of aeronautical research. The aim of this latter course is not so much to produce qualified research workers, as to make available in time a number of officers, with sufficient understanding of what is involved in such work, to act as really effective liaison officers between the service on the one hand and the scientific and industrial world on the other.

As regards airmen, the Air Force recruits its personnel partly as apprentices at about sixteen years of age and partly as men over eighteen years of age. There is no entry of boys, except as apprentices. The apprentice class is likely in due course to form more than one-third of the service. About 1,000 aircraft apprentices and 120 apprentice clerks are required each year. The majority of the aircraft apprentices to the number of nearly 3,000 are trained at a special school at Halton Camp, Bucks. There is also a smaller school for about 300 apprentices to the electrical trades at Flowerdown, near Winchester. The apprentice clerks to the number of about 250 are trained at the Royal Air Force Record Office, Ruislip. The aircraft apprentice scheme has a particular educational interest : first, because it represents a considered attempt to take advantage, on a large scale, for service purposes, of the qualities of initiative, responsibility, and *esprit de corps* associated with schools of higher education; and secondly, because underlying it there is the definite theory that the standard of a boy's education affords a measure of the rate at which he can absorb technical training—the better his education, the shorter the time in which a given course of such training can be completed. The attempt in fact is being made, and not unsuccessfully, by confining the entries to boys whose education is up to a fair secondary or technical school standard, to complete in three years a course of instruction normally expected to take five.

The aircraft apprentices undergo a three years' course, of which twenty hours a week are spent in the workshops, eight hours in the school, and nine in organised games, physical training, and drill. The boys are entered twice a year by competitive examinations, one of which, conducted by the Civil Service Commissioners, is open, and the other, conducted by the Air Ministry, is limited to candidates nominated by education authorities. The aim of the latter system is two-fold—first, to obtain the co-operation of the education authorities and the benefit of local knowledge in the selection of suitable boys ; and secondly, to bring the examination to the boy instead of the boy to the examination. About 75 per cent. of these boys come from the secondary and technical schools ; they are capable, therefore, of comparatively advanced work in the school, and the standard of the course is very much that of a good day technical school. Special attention has been given to the development of a course of general studies and of English, to which one-quarter of the whole school time is given. The educational staff consists wholly of university graduates or men of corresponding qualifications, each of whom is a specialist in his own particular subject. At the end of each course a few outstanding boys, considered for selection in the order of their place on the combined result list in all subjects—service, workshops, and school—are granted cadetships, and join the next entry at the Cadet College. They join on a full equality with the cadets entered by open competition, and take the same course. Experience shows that they are almost always to be found among the first few cadets in the order of merit list on passing out as pilot officers.

The apprentice clerks have a two-year course, of which six hours a week are spent in the school, the work comprising such subjects as English and " general studies," mathematics, industrial history, book-keeping, and the elements of accountancy.

For airmen who enter as men recruits there is a school at the Royal Air Force Depot which all attend for five hours a week during the preliminary course of training. Here the course is very elastic to meet the wide range of educational qualifications to be found among the recruits. There is also a school at each of the training centres for the mechanical and the electrical trades, where those entered as skilled or semi-skilled men learn the Air Force applications of their trade, the work in which corresponds very much to that of the evening technical schools for men of similar trades in civil life.

What is perhaps the most characteristic feature of the Air Force educational system is the scheme under which educational facilities are provided for officers and men on all stations at home and abroad during their period of service. This scheme is known as the Area Education Scheme. It will be remembered that in the months immediately following the Armistice an endeavour was made by the provision of educational facilities to assist soldiers and airmen, more particularly the younger men, to begin to fit themselves for a career in civil life, or to help them through that difficult period of transition between war service and re-employment. This is a side of education which the services in pre-war days ignored. Clearly, however, it is one of the first importance, whether as making for a more intelligent and more contented personnel, or as helping to reduce the unemployment of discharged service men, and thus generally to assist in raising the standard of national efficiency. This has now been recognised, and the work forms an integral part of the Air Force educational system. The Area Education Scheme, therefore, has to provide facilities as far as possible to meet not merely service requirements, but also the individual and personal needs of officers and men. The provision it endeavours to make includes :

(a) Assistance to officers reading such subjects as history and imperial geography for their promotion examinations or for entrance to the Staff College, or technical subjects such as mathematics and engineering science with a view to specialisation or to qualifying for a university course.

(b) Guidance and help to officers in general reading and study, more particularly to those holding short service commissions, in preparation for some opening in civil life on the completion of their engagement.

(c) The preparation of airmen for their service educational tests. Of these tests two, for reclassification as leading aircraftman and for the rank of sergeant, are compulsory and strictly utilitarian tests in such subjects as are considered essential for fully efficient work in the posts in question. The Higher Education Certificate, on the other hand, is not essential for promotion to any rank, though its possession constitutes a recommendation for advancement. The standard of their test is comparatively high and its range wide.

(d) Assistance to airmen in the study of the principles underlying their several trades and occupations, either in preparation for the various trade tests or more generally with a view to improving their understanding of the methods and processes of their trade and the principles on which these are based.

(e) Guidance and help to airmen in general reading and study, with a view to some career in civil life on discharge or to personal interests and self-development.

(f) General oversight of the arrangements for the education of airmen's children in local schools at home and in Air Force schools overseas.

Having thus given in rather bare outline a general description of the educational system, it remains to deal briefly with the question of the staff and its organisation, and also with certain fundamental principles on which the scheme is based. The more outstanding points are, perhaps, first, that the educational work, apart from the regular courses in the schools, is organised on a voluntary basis ; and secondly, that the staff is wholly civilian in character. When it is said that the work is on a voluntary basis it is not suggested, of course, that class attendance is optional on the part of any registered student. The position is that no airman need enter his name for a course, but having done so, and having received permission to attend, he then attends as a duty. The same principle of voluntary work applies also in the schools so far as evening work, outside the regular school hours, is concerned. No aircraft apprentice, for instance, is obliged to prepare educational work in the evenings, though in fact the majority do a great deal voluntarily. This adoption of the voluntary principle has undoubtedly affected both the character of the scheme and the relation in which it stands to the service. The load of the teacher is greater, as it rests with him to overcome the inherent inertia of human nature ; but for this the atmosphere of keenness and life in the classroom provides ample compensation The freedom which comes from the absence of uniform and rank on the part of the staff also contributes definitely to the creation of a really educational atmosphere.

The institution of a purely civilian staff within a combatant service was, of course, a considerable departure from precedent, and was approved only after much heart-searching. Now that it has been tried for a few years, however, it seems very doubtful whether, if the question arose, any officer, airman, or education officer would vote for a reversion to the older practice of a uniformed staff. While civilian status throws a greater load on all grades of the educational staff, making a special call on the qualities of tact, *savoir-faire*, initiative, and responsibility, it has a number of outstanding advantages. It removes the bar of uniform between teacher and student on the one hand, and between education officer and commanding officer on the other. It makes possible a closer liaison between the staff and the educational world in general. It makes for unity, because the whole staff can be of officer status and all of a kind. Men of years and standing can and do serve in the lower grades who could not possibly do so in a service where these grades are of non-commissioned or of warrant rank. So far no serious difficulty, either as regards discipline or the general conduct of the scheme, has arisen owing to the absence of rank and uniform, in spite of the fact that education officers serve not only at home but overseas, in Malta, Egypt, Palestine, Iraq, and India. Experience, indeed, seems to show that discipline of the kind required for effective educational work is more easily maintained.

The general organisation and control of the educational staff and its work rests with an Educational Adviser, also a civilian, in the department of the Air Member for Personnel at the Air Ministry. It is laid down, however, as a fundamental principle that the responsibility for the education of Air Force personnel rests with the officer commanding, and that the senior education officer of the command, unit, or school, as the case may be, will be directly responsible to him, and will act as his adviser on all educational matters. The chain of communication from the Air Ministry to the various schools and individual members of the staff is a double one. One line runs in official channels through the principal and subordinate commands to the school or station concerned; the other, which is confined to matters of a purely educational character, is direct, the Educational Adviser communicating as requisite with any education officer. The same principle holds good within the commands, each command education officer being free to maintain direct touch with all the education officers under him, although all official communications must proceed through the ordinary service channels. This dual arrangement has been found very effective, and while no doubt it might be abused and must always call for judgment and discretion on the part of senior education officers, it does not seem in practice to possess any disadvantages such as might outweigh its very real merits.

Among its other activities, the education branch at the Air Ministry is responsible for the general oversight of the university courses at Cambridge and at the Imperial College, for advising and assisting short-service officers with a view to obtaining suitable employment on discharge at the end of their five years' service, and for liaison with the educational authorities throughout the country in connection with the entry of aircraft apprentices and of apprentice clerks.

To sum up, the Air Force Educational Scheme is new in a new service; it has had to be designed and built complete from the foundations for its particular purpose; its problems, too, are in many respects new, whether regarded from the standpoint of the subjects of instruction or of the abnormally large proportion of the personnel whose educational training both before and after joining the service approximates closely to what has hitherto been considered necessary only for officers. For a service scheme its organisation is on somewhat new lines, the voluntary principle underlying all its work and the staff being constituted on a wholly civilian basis without division as between commissioned and non-commissioned rank, or between officer and civilian. A single system deals alike with officers and men, with service requirements and with personal needs. The range of the work is wide, extending from the kindergarten class to the university course.

It remains, as proposed at the outset, to consider some particular part of the scheme rather more in detail with a view to giving in this way if possible some indication of the spirit and of the circumstances in which the work is carried on.

The part of the scheme chosen for this purpose is the Area Education Scheme, under which provision of educational facilities is made on all Air Force stations at home and overseas. Such facilities are necessary, partly for purposes of service training, and partly to ensure that officers and airmen are not penalised too severely by the absence of the facilities which would be available to them in civil life. Air Force stations, it must be remembered, are situated mainly in out-of-the-way places, and, even where local schools are within reach, service duties and routine make regular attendance at normal hours almost impossible.

The needs which this part of the scheme endeavours to meet have already been enumerated, and it will be clear that no one education officer could in general cover effectively the very wide range of instruction involved. It has been necessary, therefore, to make provision by which the personal efforts of the education officer at each station may be supplemented. Arrangements have accordingly been made, first, for the provision at every station of a reading-room, with a reference library of professional and technical books and of good general literature; secondly, for a sum of money to be placed annually at the disposal of the Air Officer Commanding each independent command, out of which payment may be made for the services of part-time teachers, occasional lecturers, and, where practicable, attendance at classes under the local education authority. The part-time work may be undertaken either by civilian teachers, paid at the normal rates for similar classes under the local education authority, or by airmen with the requisite qualifications. The latter receive extra-duty pay, depending on the standard of the instruction to be given. They are paid not by the hour but by the course of ten to twelve lessons, with the corresponding setting of test-papers and the correction of written work, for in the Air Force there is no general school, such as has been customary in the older services, open regularly at specified times, but, instead, short intensive courses are held in particular subjects or for some specific purpose, such as preparation for a promotion test. Payments out of this fund may also be made for miscellaneous expenditure, such as the supply of lantern slides or the purchase of gramophone records for foreign language instruction, and, in overseas commands, the salaries of women teachers for the local children's schools.

Furthermore, arrangements have been made for the preparation of a series of " tutorial courses," very similar in purpose and character to the much advertised courses of various correspondence colleges, but with the administration decentralised, each station education officer being responsible for the working of the system on his own station and for the supervision of the students' work. These courses extend from quite elementary subjects, such as reading and writing or elementary calculations to more advanced work in such subjects as the calculus, the theory of the internal combustion engine, or the history of the modern world. They are intended to serve a number of purposes. The more advanced courses are available for the assistance and guidance of officers and airmen able to work independently, with some help from the station education officer ; other courses help to meet the needs of airmen, particularly the N.C.O.'s, whose service duties will not permit of their attending for regular class instruction. The lessons are also valuable to the station education officer in other ways, as when, for instance, two separate classes must attend at the same time, or, as is normally the case, some member of a class has missed the last meeting and needs to catch up the work.

Finally, the staff as a whole is organised as a " pool " for various miscellaneous duties, such as examination work, the preparation of the tutorial courses, or the conduct of such a course by correspondence when the subject is beyond the powers of the station education officer concerned ; and generally for mutual assistance. It is the business of each command education officer to see that all the various qualifications of the station education officers are used to the best advantage for the work of the command as a whole, and of the Educational Adviser to do the same for the service generally. All the examination work which falls to the Education Branch, with the exception of that connected with the entry of aircraft apprentices, is carried out by the " pool " as part of the regular work.

The educational work on a station falls naturally under two heads, that with officers, which is mainly of a tutorial character, and that with airmen. As regards both officers and airmen the work may be sub-divided into that required for service purposes and that of a more personal character, directed towards general self-development or to preparation for a career in civil life. In the case of officers, service subjects include those of a technical character such as mathematics and engineering science preparatory to specialisation or perhaps to a university course, and those of a more general character, such as imperial geography, history, and essay writing, required for the promotion examination or for entry to the Staff College. An education officer does not, of course, undertake any instruction of a definitely professional character, though he may act as a sort of organising secretary to a course in such subjects arranged for a station or command.

As regards airmen, service work includes preparation for the two compulsory educational tests for reclassification as leading aircraftman and for promotion to sergeant respectively. In the Air Force these tests have been limited deliberately to subjects a knowledge of which is considered necessary for the duties involved. Thus the test for leading aircraftman asks only for a knowledge of service and technical terms, for ability to write a simple letter or report, and to make elementary calculations, while that for sergeant extends these to include the writing of a report in proper service form, ability to précis an order or regulation, to tabulate data, to keep simple accounts, and to have a practical knowledge of maps and of map-reading. All subjects of a more advanced or more general character are reserved for a purely voluntary test, which will not serve as a stumbling-block to promotion. In addition to the educational tests, airmen seeking advancement have to qualify in trade and service subjects, and in this connection look to the education officer for assistance, first in the matter of self-expression in technical subjects, and secondly in the principles underlying the work of their trade or occupation.

On the more personal side, airmen can, and do, study a wide variety of subjects, partly from the standpoint of general interest, but more often with an eye to their future careers within or without the service. The policy is to give them all the assistance available within the limits of the educational scheme, so that they may be penalised as little as possible by the lack of the facilities which would have been open to them had they remained in civil life. Intermediate between the service and the personal sides of the work comes preparation for the Air Force Educational Certificate. This is given on the results of a purely voluntary examination, and is not a necessary qualification for any position ; but its possession will count as a definite recommendation for advancement in the service. The examination is wide in its scope and the standard is fairly high. It has to be taken in three parts at intervals of not less than a year. Part I., which must be taken by all candidates, consists of two papers, " English and General Studies " and " The Elements of Practical Mathematics and of the Properties of Matter." In Part II. the papers are divided into four groups each of two subjects, and a candidate has his choice of any one group. Similarly in Part III. there is a rather more extended choice of one group out of eight. The subjects of these groups are arranged on the one hand to fit in with the work of the various trades and occupations for the benefit of those who want a technical qualification, and on the other to cover a number of subjects of more general interest, such as " English Language and Literature " or " The British Commonwealth (its origin, growth, geography and government)." Any airman who has obtained the certificate may sit for examination subsequently in other groups with a view to having it endorsed with further subjects. The standard of the examination is being kept fairly high, partly with a view to making it something really worth working for and, it is hoped, of direct value to the airman on discharge, and partly because of the higher standard of education of so many of the men and apprentices now entering the service. Thus in practical mathematics the syllabus includes the elements of the calculus, and other subjects are taken to a corresponding level. Having regard to this standard and to the demand for three years' work involved, the reception of the test and the results so far obtained have been most encouraging.

In addition to his instructional duties, the station education officer finds much work of a very varied character ready to his hand. He has to act as adviser on educational matters to the officer commanding, to whom also he is directly responsible for the general conduct of the scheme on the station ; he has to look after the arrangements for the education of the airmen's children ; he is responsible for the station reference library and reading-room ; and he must be prepared to undertake external work assigned to him from time to time in connection with examinations, the preparation of tutorial courses, or perhaps the guidance by correspondence in his own particular subject of some individual student. He must be available regularly for consultation in his office at certain fixed times, and experience shows that his civilian status encourages airmen to bring to him personal problems on which his help and advice can be of real value. If his work is to be effective he must also take part in all station activities, and in this and other ways become personally acquainted with officers and airmen.

The system under which the work is organised and controlled has already been indicated. The scheme, as will no doubt have been appreciated, contemplates a considerable measure of decentralisation. General control is exercised by the Education Adviser in two ways, officially through the usual service channels in regard to all matters of policy and general administration, and semi-officially direct or through the command education officers in the case of purely technical matters or in regard to the work of the educational " pool." It is fundamental that the officer commanding, whether a command school or station, remains responsible for the education of the officers and men of his command, the education officer acting as his adviser. So far as the educational staff is concerned, the general principle is that each member must be prepared to shoulder his personal responsibilities, looking for support and guidance to his immediate superior, while touch all along the line is maintained by personal correspondence, visits, and periodical conferences of a somewhat informal character.

To any combatant service its moral is more important even than its science, and education if ill-directed can be as harmful to moral as it can be helpful under other circumstances. A little learning also still remains a dangerous thing. It is the subconscious appreciation of this danger which is largely responsible for the rather cold welcome given education by the services in the past. To-day, however, education is with us whether we will or not ; it can no longer either be excluded or ignored. The question how it can be directed and controlled for the highest good of the service is therefore becoming one of the first importance. To this the quiet and unnoticed work of the station education officer, day in day out, in his office, in the mess, and about the camp, not only at home but overseas also, in India, Palestine, Egypt, Iraq, and Malta, is helping to provide the answer and is by no means a negligible quantity among the forces moulding the form and soul of the youngest of the fighting services.

REFERENCES

The educational work of the Air Force is so new that no literature upon it of any importance yet exists.   Students may, however, be referred to the " Final Report of the Adult Education Committee," 1919, which contains an account of the work of the demobilisation period.

APPENDICES
By B. C. L. James

CONTENTS

APPENDIX A

Some Statistical Information, with Explanatory Notes

APPENDIX B

Chronological Tables

APPENDIX A

Some Statistical Information, with Explanatory Notes

PREFATORY NOTE

THE aim of these summaries is not to give an exhaustive quantitive survey of English education, but merely to illumine certain of its salient features. There are in effect two separate systems of education in England : the greater, the still embryonic public system ; the lesser, the still vigorous private system ; and it is hoped that the accompanying figures and comments will help to an understanding of the few, but increasing, points of contact between the two systems as well as between the separate stages within each system.

In Section I there is given an outline of the way in which the country is divided for the purpose of administering the public system. The section enumerates the types of local authority which work in conjunction with the central authority, the Board of Education, and shows how varied are the size and nature, and, by inference, the problems of these bodies.

Broadly speaking, this system consists of the state-supported elementary and secondary schools and the modern universities, while the private system consists of the preparatory and " public " schools together with Oxford and Cambridge. The universities, which are dealt with in Section V, all benefit from the extensive state grants shown in Table C of the financial section, and it is at the university stage that there is the greatest contact between individuals in the two systems. So far as men are concerned, the proportion from secondary schools on the Grant List at the older universities is probably much higher than the proportion from the more exclusive " public " schools at the modern universities. Accurate information as to these proportions cannot be given, but certain relevant figures may be quoted from the Board's *Statistics* for 1925–26. In that year 242 boys and 86 girls left secondary schools on the Grant List for Oxford, and 376 boys and 71 girls for Cambridge. Of these, 111 boys and 27 girls, and 188 boys and 24 girls respectively were ex-public elementary school pupils. The total of pupils leaving secondary schools on the Grant List for all universities was 3,556.

The aim of Section II is to clear up some of the confusion which exists about the pre-university stage of the two systems. It will be seen that there is much overlapping in the classification of secondary schools, and it will be inferred that the distinctions between the schools rest on more fundamental considerations than correct nomenclature. The tables show that a big proportion of the schools popularly classed with the private system are in reality integral parts of the public system, and a further distinction may be made here between the two systems. It may be said that, whereas a prominent characteristic of the private system is that almost all pupils proceed automatically to the secondary stage, and a big proportion to the university stage, an equally prominent characteristic of the public system is that only a small minority of pupils proceed from the primary to the secondary stage, and a still smaller proportion to the university stage.

It is with the proportions in the public system that Section III is concerned. Table A, Note 3, shows that in 1925 only 8·85 per cent., or 1 in 11·3, of the suitable age group passed from elementary schools to secondary schools on the Grant List, and it should be noted here that of the 3,556 mentioned above as going on to universities, 2,190 were ex-public elementary school pupils. The unequal distribution of educational opportunity is further illustrated in Tables B and C, while the rate of the movement to lessen this inequality is shown in Tables E and F. Unfortunately circumstances did not allow of a comprehensive treatment of two important factors in this tendency, the scholarship and the maintenance grant, but the extent to which free places operate is shown and certain figures under the other two heads may be given here. The number of State Scholarships held by boys at English universities in 1925–26 was 211, and by girls 173. The number of maintenance grants taken up during the year at universities, secondary schools, and technical schools was 31,039.

Table A also lessens slightly a further defect in the tables as a whole, namely the lack of comparative information about other countries. This defect is due to the impossibility of making satisfactory comparisons in short tabular form owing to the differences in the classification of schools adopted by the respective authorities. The Table compares the figures for English primary and secondary education with those of Wales and Scotland, but even in this, so far as Scotland is concerned, the comparison is not complete. With regard to university education in these countries such inferences as can be drawn from the available information are clearly set out in *The Poor Student and the University*, by Mr. G. S. M. Ellis, and two relevant conclusions may be quoted. He estimates the number of university students per 10,000 of the population in England as 7·8 ; in Wales, 12 ; and in Scotland, 21·1 ; and calculates the number of ex-elementary school pupils in universities in relation to the same unit as respectively 3·4, 11·2, and 8·7. While admittedly only rough estimates, these figures may be taken as a sufficiently definite indication of the general proportions.

Another factor which does not emerge clearly from the tables, is the variation in educational opportunity between different districts in any one area. Table B in Section III gives some indication of the wide variation in opportunity prevailing in different areas, but only very scattered information exists in regard to the other aspects of the problem. Valuable tables and a suggestive commentary in this connection are contained in Mr. Kenneth Lindsay's *Social Progress and Educational Waste*. Mr. Lindsay takes five areas and examines them in detail, with results that cannot be ignored in any discussion on this subject.

The whole question of the equal distribution of educational opportunity is so intricate and so bound up with apparently irrelevant considerations that one aspect of it can alone be touched on here, and that only in part. Some of the outstanding tendencies in this direction are, however, indicated, and a study of the tables and notes in the light of these remarks, together with the working out of further comparisons from the information given, should at least show where more rapid development is needed.

Apart from the two broad systems which have been dealt with, there is a mass of education, supplementary and complementary to the various stages, which it is difficult to classify. This has been dealt with to some extent in Section IV, on " Technical and Other Instruction," while in Section VI some financial aspects of the general situation have been briefly summarised.

Except where otherwise stated, the figures in the tables relate to England alone, excluding Monmouthshire, for the school year 1921–22. This year is taken for convenience of comparison with the census of 1921 and for the opportunity it gives of showing development since that date. This has been done mainly in footnotes, but Section III, Tables F, covers the period 1921–26 in some detail. Monmouthshire is excluded in accordance with official custom, which groups it with Wales. In the main the tables are based upon, and in some cases taken bodily from, the Board of Education's *Statistics of Public Education* for the year 1921–22, published in 1925. The Board's *Statistics* for Wales, published separately, for the same year have been used as a means, by subtraction, of arriving at the figure for England where that is not given separately in the joint publication. The *Statistics* for 1925–26 have also been used.

The figures relating to " public " schools are mainly based upon the *Public Schools' Year Book* for 1926, and the Board's list of secondary schools, known as " List 60," for 1925–26, published in 1927, while the university tables are abstracted from the " Returns for Universities and University Colleges in Receipt of Treasury Grant," issued by the University Grants' Committee in 1927, for the year 1925–26.

ABBREVIATIONS

B.	Borough.
C.B.	County Borough.
C.C.	County Council.
U.D.	Urban District.
Board.	Board of Education.
L.E.A.	Local Education Authority.
P.E.S.	Public Elementary School.
†	Approximate.
(1)	Numbers in parenthesis refer to explanatory notes. Asterisks, and other unclassified signs, serve for notes on minor points which require comment.

SECTION I

TABLE A

A Summary of the Number and Population of each Type of Area under Local Education Authorities.

Type of Area.*	No. of Areas.	Population on 19th June, 1921.
1. Administrative counties (other than London)	48	18,654,371
Areas for elementary education within administrative counties :		
(*a*) Areas under county councils	48	13,165,815
(*b*) Boroughs	119	3,612,076
(*c*) Urban districts	40	1,876,480
2. County boroughs	78	12,090,210
3. London	1	4,483,249
Total for areas under urban authorities (1 (*b*) and (*c*), 2 and 3)	238	22,062,015
4. Total for England	286	35,227,830

* The council of every administrative county and of every county borough is the local education authority for that county or county borough for both elementary and higher education ; except that the council of every borough with a population of over 10,000, and of every urban district with a population of over 20,000 (calculated, in either case, according to the census of 1901), is the local education authority for that borough or urban district for elementary education. This gives rise to the necessity of the three sub-divisions for elementary education under the first main heading. See the Education Act, 1921, sect. 3.

London is, of course, an administrative county, but is here classified separately for purposes of comparison.

The total for England is reached by adding the figures under 1 (*a*) to the total for areas under urban authorities.

TABLE B

Table to Illustrate the Wide Variation in the Size and Nature of P.E.S. Areas.

Area.				No. of Schools.	Total No. on Registers.
Birmingham C.B.	..	..	..	193	148,095
Cannock U.D.	..	..	..	17	6,376
Chesterfield B.	..	..	..	21	10,769
Chiswick U.D.	..	..	..	6	4,565
Darlington C.B.	..	..	..	22	11,061
Durham B. ..	..	..	..	10	2,583
Durham C.C. ..	..	..	..	406	149,078
Lincoln C.B. ..	..	..	..	24	9,780
London C.C. ..	..	..	..	946	696,159
Middlesex C.C.	..	..	..	123	41,475
Penzance B. ..	..	..	..	5	1,507
Tottenham U.D.	..	..	..	30	25,734
West Ham C.B.	..	..	..	64	60,042
Westmorland C.C.	..	..	..	108	6,282
West Riding C.C.	..	..	..	857	188,237

Cf. especially—

Cannock	..	..	6,376 children in	17	schools, *and*
Westmorland		..	6,282 ,,	108	,,
Also London	..	..	696,159 ,,	946	,, *and*
West Riding		..	188,237 ,,	857	,,

SECTION II

A Comparison between Schools of Different Types.

TABLE A.—*General.*

	(1) ¶ Nursery Schools. Boys and Girls.	(2) Public Elementary Schools. Boys and Girls.	(3) Preparatory Schools recognised as Efficient. Boys and Girls.	(4) Preparatory Schools in the Public Schools Year Book, 1926. Boys.	(5) Secondary Schools on the Grant List (see Table B). Boys and Girls.	(6) Secondary Schools in the Public Schools Year Book, 1926 (see Table C). Boys.*	(7) Secondary Schools recognised as Efficient but not on the Grant List. Boys and Girls.
No. of schools	24	19,036	72	449	1,115	130	220
No. of teachers	49	161,492	—	—	17,352	3,320 †	—
No. of scholars	993	5,409,701	6,463	—	324,572	53,845 †	44,539

* Except in one case, a co-education school with 107 boys and 99 girls.

TABLE B.—*Secondary Schools on the Grant List* (5).

	Boys' Schools.	Girls' Schools.	Mixed Schools.	Total of Schools.	Total of Pupils.
Council schools (8)	147	230	192	569	170,240
Roman Catholic schools (9)	14	52	—	66	17,622
Foundation and other schools (10) ..	271	137	72	480	136,710
Total	432	419	264	1,115	324,572 *

* Of these 166,584 were boys and 157,988 were girls.   For 1925–26 figures, see p. 350.
¶ For notes on these tables, see pp. 349–352.

TABLE C.—*Public Schools* (6), 1926.

	Schools.	Masters.‡	Boys.
Schools represented on the Headmasters' Conference, which are also secondary schools on the Grant List	58	1,350 †	25,971
Schools represented on the Headmasters' Conference, which are also secondary schools recognised by the Board of Education as efficient, but are not on the Grant List	55	1,430 †	20,593
Other schools represented on the headmasters' conference *	17 ¶	540 †	7,241 †
Total	130	3,320 †	53,805 †

* See note 7, second paragraph.

¶ One of these schools claims to be recognised by the Board, but no trace of it could be found on the Efficient List.

‡ All the figures in this column are rough approximations, owing to there being no standard classification in the lists of staff. In large part music and drawing masters, physical training and manual instructors, masters of commercial subjects and others indicated as supernumerary have been omitted, whereas, for the purpose of comparison with other schools, they should probably have been included. Where it could be inferred that they were full-time members of the regular staff they have been included.

NOTES

(1) Nursery schools are schools for children over two and under five years of age provided under section 21 of the Education Act, 1921.

(2) An elementary school is defined by section 170 (1) of the Education Act, 1921, as a school " at which elementary education is the principal part of the education there given." But it is provided in section 20 of that Act that courses of advanced instruction shall be provided for older children.

A public elementary school is a school which satisfies certain further requirements imposed by section 27 (1) of the 1921 Act, namely, that certain conditions as to attendance at religious observance and instruction shall be observed, that the school shall be open to inspection, and that it shall be conducted in accordance with the condition laid down in the Code of Regulations for public elementary schools in force for the time being.

APPENDIX A

(3) The Board of Education defines a preparatory school as one which provides a general education, suited to an age range of not less than three years between the ages of 8 and 13, and from which the pupils normally proceed to continue their education at a secondary school or an institution of similar type. In order to be recognised as efficient such schools have to be inspected by the Board.

(4) This list of preparatory schools is confined to schools preparing boys for the " public " schools. Schools for boys of all ages are not included unless the preparatory department is kept absolutely distinct from the senior department. Some of the schools in this list are also on the Board's list of efficient preparatory schools.

(5) A secondary school, as defined by the Board, is a school which offers to all its pupils a progressive course of general education, with the requisite organisation, curriculum, teaching staff, and equipment suitable in kind and amount for boys or girls of an age-range at least as wide as from 12 to 17, and which also makes similarly suitable and correlated provision for any pupils below the age of 12. An adequate proportion of the pupils must normally remain at least four years at school, and the school life of the pupils must normally extend at least to the age of 16.

When, as a result of inspection, the Board is satisfied that these conditions, and others relating to management, religious tests, financial position, scale of fees, etc., are fulfilled, it may, on the application of the responsible body, place the school on the Grant List. In that event the said school is required, under Article 15 of the Regulations for Secondary Schools, to offer free places to the number of not less than 25 per cent. of the total number of admissions in the previous school year to pupils from Public Elementary Schools. The total number of free places awarded in a school year must not exceed 40 per cent. In certain circumstances a lower percentage than 25 is approved and 97 of the schools in these columns take as few as 10 per cent., 28 taking 12½ per cent., 13 taking 15 per cent., and 8 taking 20 per cent. Table F in Section III shows the number of free places held expressed as a percentage of the total number in the schools.

By 1925–26 there had been an increase of 46 secondary schools on the Grant List, the total of schools being 1,161. This number represents an increase of 55 council schools and 6 Roman Catholic schools, and a decrease of 15 Foundation schools. The pupils increased by 3,502. (See also Section III, Table A, note 3.)

6. The schools in this column are those represented on the Headmasters' Conference, and known popularly as "Public Schools." It will be seen from Table C that a big proportion are also on the Grant List, and a further big proportion on the Efficient List.

The conditions, as stated in the *Public Schools' Year Book*, under which a school may be represented at the Headmasters' Conference, are briefly these : that the school shall be controlled in the public interest by a governing body created by some statute, scheme, or other trust deed, and that in considering what schools shall be included in the List of Members or removed from it, the committee will have regard to the scheme or other instrument under which the school is administered, the numbers in the school, and, in the case of schools in Great Britain and Ireland, the number of resident undergraduates at Oxford and Cambridge educated at the school. The committee may also take into account the proportion of boys in the school, who, having passed the school certificate or other equivalent examination, are continuing their studies beyond that stage.

It will be gathered that membership is not restricted to schools in the British Isles, and members to the number of 24 are, in fact, to be found in various parts of the Empire, in addition to two in the Channel Isles.

(7) When the provisions outlined in the first paragraph of Note 5 are judged, on inspection by the Board, to be adequate, a school may be placed on " The Efficient List." The schools in this column are schools of this type which for various reasons are without grant. These reasons may be summed up broadly as lack of need and objection to complying with the further conditions required.

It should be noted that it rests with each school to initiate the inspection which is preliminary to " recognition," and that as a certain number of secondary schools, as well as a large proportion of preparatory schools, of known and high efficiency have never applied to the Board for inspection, no inference as to a school's efficiency or inefficiency can be drawn from the fact of its not being included in the Efficient List.

It should be further noted here that there is also a large number of schools which do not appear in any of these figures. The 1928 edition of *Schools*, by Messrs. Truman and Knightley, has a list over 100 pages long of schools in England of various types other than P.E.S., a big proportion of which do not come under any of the heads in these tables, and are for the most part popularly known as " Private " schools. There must be in addition a very big number of small private schools which do not appear even in this list. Such schools, usually run single-handed, for young children, are to be found in almost every district where half a dozen, or so, people can afford them.

8. The classification of the schools in Table B is based on the type of body responsible for the school. Council schools are schools for which local authorities are responsible, including not only schools provided by local authorities, but also endowed schools of which the government and finance were under municipal or county control, the council being the responsible body.

(9) Roman Catholic schools are classed separately in the Board's statistics as forming a specially homogeneous group.

(10) This group includes all schools subject to educational trusts, which are not included under the other heads in the table, together with some other unclassified schools.

SECTION III

TABLE A

A comparison for England and Wales between the number of pupils in Secondary Schools, and the number of pupils in Public Elementary Schools considered in relation to the total population ; together with a note on Scotland.

	England.	Wales.
(a) Population, 1921	35,227,830	2,657,412
(b) Total of pupils in secondary schools on the Grant List	324,572	30,384
(c) No. of above (b) per 1,000 of the population	9·2	11·4
(d) No. of pupils in P.E.S. aged 10 and under 11	601,084	52,081
(e) No. of ex-P.E.S. pupils admitted to secondary schools on the Grant List	53,093	8,679
(f) Percentage of P.E.S. pupils aged 10-11 entering secondary schools	8·8	16·7

NOTES

1. *Scotland—*

Population, 1921	4,882,497
Number in secondary schools, excluding primary and preparatory departments..	65,769
Number of above per 1,000 of the population	13·5

2. The numbers in secondary schools per 1,000 of the 1921 population in 1925 had risen to—

England	9·3
Wales	12·2
Scotland	15·6

3. The figures for England in 1925–26 under the respective heads of the table were :

(b)	328,074
(c)	9·3
(d)	600,087
(e)	53,087
(f)	8·85

TABLE B

An illustration of the wide variation in the numbers proceeding from Public Elementary Schools to Secondary Schools on the Grant List in different areas, showing the way in which accident of birth affects educational opportunity.

Area.	Number in Secondary Schools per 1,000 of the population.	Percentage of P.E.S. pupils aged 10–11 entering Secondary Schools.
Bradford C.B.	.. 20·9 ..	.. 26·7
Leeds C.B.	.. 13·0 ..	.. 10·9
Sheffield C.B.	.. 7·0 ..	.. 6·5
Chester C.B.	.. 14·6 ..	.. 8·4
Wallasey C.B.	.. 20·4 ..	.. 18·9
Liverpool C.B.	.. 9·2 ..	.. 8·8
Sunderland C.B. ..	5·3 ..	.. 2·9
West Hartlepool C.B.	11·0 ..	.. 10·6

Area.	Number in Secondary Schools per 1,000 of the population.		Percentage of P.E.S. pupils aged 10-11 entering Secondary Schools.
Gloucester C.C.	11·6	..	12·8
Bristol C.B.	11·1	..	9·8
Wiltshire C.C.	11·6	..	12·9
Berkshire C.C.	8·4	..	6·2
Reading C.B.	7·6	..	4·1
London C.C.	7·8	..	6·4
Middlesex C.C.	12·8	..	15·3
Essex C.C.	10·8	..	8·6
West Ham C.B.	4·7	..	3·5
Southend C.B.	11·7	..	18·4
Croydon C.B.	13·7	..	9·0
Eastbourne C.B.	10·6	..	14·9
England	9·2	..	8·8

TABLE C

The relation between the total numbers in each age-group and those of each group who are in state-maintained, or state-aided, schools in England and Wales.

Age.	Elementary Schools.	(1) Junior Technical Schools.	Secondary Schools.	(2) Pupil Teachers in Centres.	(3) Rural Pupil Teachers.	Total.	Population.
Under 3	38	—	—	—	—	38	2,174,018
3–4	35,933	—	4	—	—	35,937	536,703
4–5	122,653	—	69	—	—	122,722	610,982
5–6	495,024	—	1,134	—	—	496,158	655,122
6–7	594,445	—	2,574	—	—	597,019	707,334
7–8	665,167	—	3,838	—	—	669,005	724,753
8–9	661,398	—	5,883	—	—	667,281	721,087
9–10	656,269	—	9,167	—	—	665,436	710,630
10–11	651,339	—	14,828	—	—	666,167	716,074
11–12	644,456	100	28,137	19	—	672,712	729,133
12–13	625,943	1,220	52,980	55	—	680,198	742,026
13–14	547,708	4,043	67,427	133	—	619,311	744,768
14–15	146,256	4,739	65,661	405	274	217,335	727,895
15–16	12,637	1,944	51,500	278	517	66,876	718,798
16–17	1,368	188	31,225	539	467	33,787	715,729
17 and over	110	22	20,529	2,865	611	24,137	* 2,718,534
Total	5,860,744	12,256	354,956	¶4,294	‡1,869	6,234,119	14,653,486

* Over 17 and under 21.   ¶ 1925–26: 2,643.   ‡ 1925–26: 901.

NOTES

(1) Junior technical schools are day schools providing courses for boys and girls during two or three years after leaving public elementary schools, in which a continued general education is combined with a definite preparation for some industrial or domestic employment.

(2) The Regulations for the Training of Teachers, 1922, provided that boys and girls who were receiving (*a*) training in teaching in public elementary schools, together with (*b*) instruction accepted by the Board, might be recognised as " pupil-teachers." Where possible, the instruction of pupil-teachers had to be given in a pupil-teacher centre recognised by the Board. These centres might either form integral parts of secondary schools, or, in certain circumstances, be attached to secondary schools or to public elementary schools, or be separately organised.

(3) In rural districts pupil-teachers for whom instruction in a secondary school or centre is not available might receive such instruction in central classes or otherwise, as the Board approved.

TABLE D

The Numercial Relationship between Council Schools and Voluntary Schools.

I

Type of Area.	No. of Schools (P.E.S.).		Average Attendance.	
	Council (Provided).	Voluntary (Non-provided).	Council Schools.	Voluntary Schools.
1. Areas under C.C.'s				
(*a*) Rural	3,157	7,110	409,844	521,599
(*b*) Urban	1,412	1,551	498,135	329,622
2. B.'s and U.D.'s	841	907	446,651	258,332
3. C.B.'s	1,616	1,444	1,124,001	572,061
4. London	588	358	490,612	124,540
5. Total for England	7,614	11,370	2,969,243	1,806,154

II

1. Urban areas	4,457	4,260	2,559,399	1,284,555
2. Rural areas	3,157	7,110	409,844	521,599
3. Total for England	7,614	11,370	2,969,243	1,806,154

Note.—Under the Act of 1902 (*see* section 17 of the 1921 Act) a P.E.S. must, with certain exceptions, be maintained by the L.E.A. If the buildings are also provided by the L.E.A., the school is termed a council school, or in the phraseology of the Act, a school provided by the L.E.A. Otherwise it is called a voluntary school, *i.e.* a school not provided by the L.E.A. Voluntary schools are usually provided by religious bodies, the Church of England being responsible for the bulk of those here shown, the majority of the remainder being Roman Catholic.

By 1925–26 the number of council schools in England and Wales had increased by 207, and the voluntary schools had decreased by 420.

TABLE E

A Historical Table showing the number on the Registers of Elementary Schools in comparison with the total population between the ages of 3 and 15.

ENGLAND AND WALES

Year.	Pupils.	Year.	Population (3–15).
1870–71	1,795,732	1871	6,315,928
1875–76	2,924,471	—	—
1880–81	4,058,669	1881	7,307,542
1885–86	4,516,734	—	—
1890–91	4,832,586	1891	8,014,536
1895–96	5,421,209	—	—
1900–01	5,767,359	1901	8,277,230
1905–06	6,015,747	—	—
1910–11	6,060,148	1911	8,737,026
1913–14	6,073,058	—	—
1919–20	5,958,839	—	—
1920–21	5,893,242	1921	8,326,437
1925–26	5,621,727	—	—

TABLE F

Secondary Schools on the Grant List—Historical Table.

ENGLAND AND WALES

Year.	No. of Schools.	No. of Pupils.*	Per cent. of Free Places. ¶	No. of Teachers.
1908–9	804	135,671	31·2	8,436
1913–14	1,027	187,207	32·6	10,824
1918–19	1,081	269,887	30·5	14,499
1921–22	1,249	354,956	34·0	18,964
1922–23	1,264	354,165	35·6	18,485
1923–24	1,270	349,141	35·7	18,658
1924–25	1,284	352,605	35·8	19,069
1925–26	1,301	360,503	36·5	19,640

* The totals of pupils given in the Historical Table on p. 69 of the *Statistics* for 1925–26 do not correspond with those given in other tables in that volume or in the earlier volumes. Except for 1918–19 the figures in this column have therefore been taken from these other sources.

¶ See p. 350.

SECTION IV

TABLE A

*Numbers taking Technical Institution Courses and Courses of Advanced Instruction in Arts *—England and Wales.*

	No. of Institutions	BOYS AND MEN.					GIRLS AND WOMEN.				
		Age 15–16.	Age 16–18.	Age 18–21.	Age 21 and over.	Total.	Age 15–16.	Age 16–18.	Age 18–21.	Age 21 and over.	Total.
Administrative counties	6	3	70	192	511	776	—	—	1	4	5
County boroughs	28	112	684	863	969	2,628	1	40	71	42	154
London ..	12	51	407	524	781	1,763	1	25	127	107	260
Total ..	46	166	1,161	1,579	2,261	5,167 ¶	2	65	199	153	419

* The characteristic of this type of provision is full-time advanced instruction in science or arts. The courses must be of at least two years' duration, and only students of suitable age and previous education may be admitted.

There were, in addition to the above, 6,459 boys and men, and 7,003 girls and women in day technical classes which are of a somewhat different character, including part-time students.

There may also be noticed here 1,308 pupils in schools of nautical training, which are day schools providing a continued full-time education for pupils from elementary schools in preparation for employment at sea ; 22,856 boys and men, and 23,422 girls and women in schools of art ; and 1,444 boys and men, and 2,447 girls and women in art classes, distinct from the classes held in schools of art.

¶ This figure had fallen to 3,670 in 1925–26. The biggest drop being in the age-group 21 and over, the number falling to 843.

TABLE B

Part-time Technical and other Instruction.

Type of Area.	Popula-tion.	Ordinary Continuation and Technical Courses.		Day Continuation Courses.		Courses for Teachers.		
		No. of Schools.	No. of Students.	No. of Schools.	No. of Students.	No. of Schools.	No. of Students, Men.	No. of Students, Women.
Administrative counties	18,654,371	2,854	221,252	34	4,619	273	1,417	6,938
County boroughs ..	12,090,210	923	264,468	41	10,578	84	1,026	6,064
London ..	4,483,249	294	161,161	47	80,333	10	3,398	12,923
Total ..	35,227,830	4,071	646,881	122	*95,530	367	5,841	25,925

* The total of this class of student had dropped to 24,308 in the year 1925–26 (*v.* pp. 184–186).

NOTE.—There may also be noted here the numbers in university tutorial classes : 342 classes, 206 tutors, 7,746 students. These classes give part-time courses in subjects of general, as distinct from vocational, education under the supervision of a university college.

SECTION V

A Table of Full-time University Students, 1925–26 [1]

University.	Men.	Women.	Total.	Within 30 miles.	Other parts of British Isles.	British Empire.	Foreign Countries.
				Home Residence.			
Birmingham	904	498	1,402	1,020	265	28	89
Bristol ..	463	309	772	433	313	9	17
(2) Cambridge..	4,728	475	5,203	4,644		352	207
(2) Durham ..	878	452	1,330	989	291	24	26
Leeds ..	1,006	366	1,372	985	295	35	57
Liverpool ..	1,001	573	1,574	1,098	397	50	29
(3) London ..	5,668	3,129	8,797	4,713	2,784	860	440
Manchester	1,108	640	1,748	1,231	455	32	30
(2) Oxford ..	3,533	820	4,353	3,820		272	261
(2) Reading ..	174	384	558	159	384	6	9
Sheffield ..	440	240	680	458	177	24	21
Other institutions of University rank	996	490	1,486	859	493	81	53
Total ..	20,899	8,376	29,275	11,945	14,318	1,773	1,239

(1) This year has been taken because previous figures are complicated by the 26,000 men taking advantage of the government scheme for the higher education of ex-service men. It should be noted that, having made allowance for this factor, the committee, in their report for 1923–24, state that in spite of serious financial distress among the classes from which university students are mainly drawn, in spite of a rise in fees and in personal expenses, there are now 56·9 per cent. more full-time students of both sexes at our universities and colleges than before the war.

(2) Oxford and Cambridge are entirely residential, and Reading is mainly so. The Durham division of Durham University is also residential, but Armstrong College and the College of Medicine, both of which are at Newcastle, and which contain three-fourths of the members of the university, are non-residential.

(3) Some of the colleges and schools of London University—

	Men.	Women.	Total.
University College	912	723	1,635
King's College *	721	407	1,128

* Not including the Theological Department.

	Men.	Women.	Total.
Bedford College	—	565	565
East London College	265	130	395
Imperial College	909	36	945
School of Economics	356	185	541

Medical Colleges and Schools :

King's College Hospital	144	80	224
London Hospital	379	16	395
Middlesex Hospital..	218	—	218
St. Bartholomew's Hospital	623	—	623
St. Mary's Hospital..	176	82	258
St. Thomas's	376	—	376
University College Hospital	200	59	259

SECTION VI

TABLE A

Summary of the Expenditure of the Board of Education out of the Parliamentary Vote for the Financial Year 1921–22—England and Wales.

		£	£
1. *Grants to L.E.A.'s :—*			
(a) Elementary		35,593,217	
(b) Higher		5,511,943	
(c) Total			41,105,160
2. *Grants to Non-L.E.A. Institutions :*			
(a) Elementary		86,972	
(b) Higher		2,181,068	
(c) Total			2,268,040
3. *Miscellaneous :*			
(a) Administration and inspection ..		904,675	
(b) Pensions to teachers		1,550,687	
(c) Museums, etc.		234,465	
(d) Higher education of ex-service officers and men *		1,965,566	
(e) Total			4,655,393
4. *Gross total*			48,028,593
Deduct : Appropriations in aid ¶			175,199
5. *Net total*			47,853,394

* This item no longer occurs.

¶ Appropriations in aid consist of payments made direct to government departments which are not paid into the Consolidated Fund but retained and deducted from the gross sum of the Vote.

NOTE.—The totals of the grants for elementary and higher education respectively, in 1921–22, were as follows :—

				£
Elementary	..	..	..	35,680,189
Higher	..	..	..	7,693,011
				43,373,200

The Board's Estimates for 1927 were :—

Elementary	..	..	..	31,940,630
Higher	..	..	..	7,100,230
				39,040,860

Miscellaneous	..	..	..	5,309,169

These figures should be read in conjunction with the Memorandum on the Board of Education Estimates, 1927 (Stationery Office, 6d.).

TABLE B

Summary of the Expenditure of Local Education Authorities which had to be met by the Rates in the Financial Year 1921–22.

Area.	Elementary Education.		Higher Education.
	Amount.	Per Child.	
	£	s. d.	£
County councils ..	7,146,872	81 1	2,406,692
Boroughs	1,899,119	85 6	—
Urban districts ..	1,295,309	99 4	—
County boroughs ..	7,753,365	91 7	2,086,027
London	5,403,507	175 8	1,369,275
Total	23,498,172	98 5	5,861,994

TABLE C

Income and Expenditure of the Universities, 1925–26.

INCOME :—

Source of Income :   *Amount.*

	£	£
Endowments		477,505
Donations and subscriptions		92,970
Grants from local authorities		413,638
Parliamentary grants :		
Treasury	1,143,762	
Board of Education	77,845	
Other government departments	179,006	
		1,400,613
Tuition fees		811,534
Examination, graduation, matriculation, and registration fees		304,464
Income from other sources		266,106
Total		3,766,830
EXPENDITURE		3,695,015

APPENDIX B

CHRONOLOGICAL TABLES

Note.—*c.*=about ; *f.*=and following period.

Table A

General to 1800.

c. 600–650. King's School, Canterbury ; King's School, Rochester ; and St. Peter's School, York, originate.

878 *f.* Alfred the Great's educational work.

1066 *f.* The stimulus of the Anglo-Norman clergy.

c. 1200. Emergence of Oxford and Cambridge.

1249–1274. University, Balliol, and Merton Colleges founded at Oxford.

c. 1250 *f.* The Craft Gilds.

1284. Peterhouse College founded at Cambridge.

1382. Winchester College founded.

1439. William Byngham erects " God's House " at Cambridge for the training of Grammar School masters.

1476. Caxton introduces printing to England.

c. 1490–1531. The Renaissance begins in England ; Colet, Erasmus, Grocyn, Linacre, More, Warham, Elyot.

1526. Tyndale's New Testament.

1534 *f.* The Reformation in England breaks the clerical monopoly of educational management and draws attention to the need of general education for the poor.

1536–1603. Big increase of Grammar School endowments, mainly by private benevolence.

1547. Chantries Act retards education by dissolving the Chantry Schools.

1559 and 1662. Acts of Uniformity.

1562–1814. Legal apprenticeship.

1604. The Canons of the Church of England codify its policy of uniformity ; followed by a considerable growth of Church primary schools.

1699. The Society for Promoting Christian Knowledge starts the Charity School movement.

c. 1700–1800. Development of private academies.

1779. Protestant Dissenters become legally free to teach.

1782. Robert Raikes establishes his first Sunday School.

TABLE B

Elementary Education from 1800

1796–1804. Lancaster, Bell, and the Monitorial System.

1802. Peel's Act.

1803. Mrs. Trimmer starts the Religious Controversy.

1807. Whitbread's Bill for Parish Schools rejected by the Lords.

1808. A committee of management takes over Lancaster's School.

1811. Marsh's sermon at the annual Charity School service in St. Paul's leads to the establishment of " The National Society."

1814. Lancaster's Committee becomes " The British and Foreign School Society."

1816. Robert Owen's Institution for the Formation of Character, including his Infant School, at New Lanark.
Select Committee appointed to inquire into the " Education of the Lower Orders."

1820. Brougham's Bill for Parish Schools fails to pass the Commons.

1827. The Society for the Diffusion of Useful Knowledge founded.

1832. Reform Bill.

1833. Rejection by the Commons of Roebuck's resolution for the universal and national education of the whole people.
First Treasury Grant in aid of private subscriptions for the erection of school-houses.
Factory Act.

1833–1848. Chartism.

1834. Poor Law Reform Act.

1836. Stamp duty on newspapers reduced to one penny per copy.

1839. The Committee of the Privy Council on Education created by Order in Council.
Minute of the Committee initiating State Inspection.

1844. Factory Act.

1853. The Department of Science and Art.

1855. Stamp duty on newspapers abolished.

1856. The Education Department.

1858. The Duke of Newcastle's Commission appointed to investigate popular education and advise as to the measures requisite for the extension of elementary instruction to all classes ; reports 1861.

1860. The Minutes of the Education Committee digested into " The Code."

1861. The Revised Code initiates " payment by results." Tax on paper abolished.

1867. Second Reform Bill.

1870. First Education Act.

1876. Lord Sandon's Act.

1880. Mundella's Act makes attendance compulsory.

1884. Third Reform Bill.

1886. The Cross Commission.

1888. The Local Government Act.

1891. Free Education Act.

c. 1895. End of the individual examinations upon which " payment by results " was based.

1899. Board of Education Act.

1902. Balfour's Education Act makes possible a national system of education of all grades.

1906. Education (Provision of Meals) Act.

1907. Education (Administrative Provisions) Act makes the provision of medical inspection compulsory.

1911. First Central School.

1918. Fisher's Act.

1919. The Burnham Salary Committee.

1921. Education (Consolidation) Act.

TABLE C

Secondary and Technical Education from 1800

1798. Samuel Butler becomes head master of Shrewsbury.

1803. The first of the Hill family's private boarding schools ; characterized by self-government and a wide curriculum, including modern studies.

1805. Court of Chancery ruling prohibits the application of grammar school funds to modern studies.

1818. Commission to investigate educational charities ; first report 1819 (rept. 32, pt. vi., 1840) ; the reports led to the creation of the Charity Commission, 1853.

1823. The London Mechanics Institute (now Birkbeck College).

1828. Thomas Arnold becomes head master of Rugby.

1829–1853. The foundation of proprietary colleges strengthens the movement to modernize studies ; *e.g.* King's and University College Schools, Cheltenham, Liverpool, Marlborough, Radley, and Wellington Colleges.

1836–8. Kennedy introduces French, German, and Mathematics into the curriculum at Shrewsbury.

1837. School of Design opened, under the Board of Trade.

1840. The Grammar Schools Act gives facilities for the introduction of modern subjects.

1842. The People's College, Sheffield.

1843. The Governesses' Benevolent Institution ; leads to the organization of education for women and girls.

1848. Queen's College, Harley Street.

1849. Bedford College.

1850. North London Collegiate School.

1851. The Great Exhibition.

1853. The Department of Science and Art.
The Ladies' College, Cheltenham.

1856. The Education Department.

1857. Oxford Local Examinations. (Cambridge Locals, 1858.)

1864. Report of the Clarendon Commission on the nine leading Public Schools.

1865. Girls allowed to take Cambridge Locals.

1867. Report of the Taunton Commission on secondary education, including that of girls, in schools other than those examined by the Clarendon Commission.

1868. The Public Schools Act.

1869. The Endowed Schools Act ; Commission appointed to remodel educational endowments ; its function transferred to the Charity Commission, 1874.
Edward Thring starts the Headmasters' Conference.

1872. Girls' Public Day School Trust.

1874. Miss Buss founds the Association of Head Mistresses.

1880. The City and Guilds of London Institute incorporated.

1881. Regent Street Polytechnic opened.

1888. Local Government Act.

1889. Technical Instruction Act empowers local authorities to aid technical instruction from the rates.

1890. "Whisky Money." (Local Taxation — Customs and Excise—Act.)
Head Masters' Association.

1895. Report of the Bryce Commission recommends the creation of a Ministry of Education and Local Education Authorities for secondary education.

1899. The Board of Education Act.
1900. The Cockerton Judgment.
1902. The Education Act constitutes the County Councils and County Borough Councils as local authorities for secondary education with power to raise rates for the purpose.
1907. The Free Place Regulation.
1908. Prevention of Crime (Borstal) Act.
1911. The First Central School.
1918. Fisher's Act. (Clause 10, establishing compulsory Day Continuation schools for boys and girls, 14–18, never enforced.)
1920. Report of the Departmental Committee on Scholarships and Free Places.
1921. Education (Consolidation) Act.
1923. Report of the Consultative Committee on the Differentiation of the Curriculum for Boys and Girls respectively in Secondary Schools.
1926. Report of the Consultative Committee on the Education of the Adolescent.

Table D

The Training of Teachers from 1800

Abbreviations

c. =Council Training College ; undenominational.
d. =Day Training Departments of Universities.
c.e. =Church of England Voluntary Training College.
r.c. =Roman Catholic Voluntary Training College.
u. =Undenominational Voluntary Training College.
w. =Wesleyan Voluntary Training College.

1798–1808. u. Borough Road originates in Lancaster's Monitorial School.
1836. c.e. Home and Colonial, Wood Green.
1839. The Minute of the Committee of Council on Education as to the proposed State Normal School.
c.e. Chester Diocesan ; c.e. Chichester Diocesan ; c.e. Winchester Diocesan.
1840. Kay-Shuttleworth's Training College at Battersea ; the origin of c.e. St. John's, Battersea.
c.e. Exeter Diocesan ; c.e. Norwich Diocesan.
1841. c.e. Brighton Diocesan ; c.e. St. Mark's, Chelsea ; c.e. Whitelands, Chelsea ; c.e. Durham, Bede ; c.e. Salisbury ; c.e. York Diocesan.
1844. c.e. Warrington.

1846. Minutes of the Committee of Council formulate the pupil-teacher system to supersede the monitorial system.
College of Preceptors.
C.E. Ripon Diocesan.

1847. C.E. St. Mary's, Cheltenham ; C.E. St. Paul's, Cheltenham.

1851. C.E. Derby Diocesan ; R.C. St. Mary's, Hammersmith ; W. Westminster.

1852. C.E. Bishop's Stortford, Hockerill ; U. Homerton, Cambridge ; C.E. Saltley, Birmingham.

1853. C.E. Culham ; C.E. Fishponds, Bristol.

1856. R.C. Mount Pleasant, Liverpool.

1857. C.E. Truro Diocesan.

1858. C.E. St. Hild's, Durham.

1859. C.E. Peterborough.

1861. C.E. Lincoln Diocesan ; U. Stockwell.

1872. U. Darlington ; W. Southlands, Battersea.

1874. U. Roehampton, Froebel Educational Institute ; R.C. St. Charles's, Kensington.

1878. U. Maria Grey ; C.E. St. Katharine's, Tottenham.

1882. U. Bedford.

1884. U. Saffron-Walden.

1885. U. Edge Hill, Liverpool.

1890. The Code institutes Day Training Departments at Universities.
D. King's College, London ; D. Manchester ; D. Armstrong Coll., Durham ; D. Birmingham ; D. Nottingham.

1891. D. Cambridge ; D. Leeds ; D. Liverpool ; D. Sheffield.

1892. D. Oxford ; D. Bristol.

1898. C. Shoreditch Technical Institute.

1899. D. Reading ; D. Southampton ; C.E. St. Gabriel's, Kennington.

1901. D. Exeter.

1902. Balfour's Act.
C.E. St. Mary's, Lancaster Gate.

1903. R.C. Salford.

1904. C. Hereford County ; R.C. Southampton.

1905. R.C. Hull ; R.C. St. Mary's, Newcastle-on-Tyne ; D. Goldsmiths' College, London ; C. Graystoke Place, London ; C. Sheffield City.

1906. C. Avery Hill, London.

1907. D. London Day Training College, Southampton Row ; C. Leeds City ; C. Portsmouth.

1908. c. Sunderland ; c. Crewe, Cheshire County.
1909. c. Brighton Municipal ; c. Dudley.
1910. c. Manchester Municipal ; R.C. Selly Park, Birmingham.
1911. c. Bingley, Yorks.
1912. The Teachers' Registration Council.
1913. c. Hull Municipal.
1919. U. Gipsy Hill, Sydenham ; c. Furzedown, London ; c. Manchester Mather.
1921. D. Durham Division of Durham University ; c. Neville's Cross, Durham ; c. Kenton Lodge, Newcastle-on-Tyne.
1925. Report of the Departmental Committee on the Training of Teachers for Public Elementary Schools.
1926. The new Board of Education Regulations for the Training of Teachers.

NOTE.—The dates of the establishment of the Training Colleges here given are based for the most part on those given in Mr. Lance Jones's *The Training of Teachers*. They are not necessarily the same as the date of recognition by the Board.

TABLE E

University and Adult Education from 1800

1800. Public Examination Statute at Oxford.
1823. The London Mechanics' Institute (now Birkbeck College).
1824. Oxford Union Society.
1827. University College, London.
1829. King's College, London.
1832. Durham University.
1836. London University Charter.
1841. William Lovett's complete educational plan published in *Chartism ; A New Organisation of the People.*
1842. The People's College, Sheffield.
1844. The Rochdale Co-operative Society.
1849. Bedford College, London.
1850. Royal Commissions on Oxford and Cambridge appointed.
1851. Owens College, Manchester (Univ. Charters, 1880, 1903).
1854. Working Men's College, London.
1859. Hartley College, Southampton.
1869. Hitchin College for Women (later Girton).

1871. Universities Tests Act.
      The College of Science, Newcastle, affiliated to Durham.
      Newnham College, Cambridge.
1873. University Extension.
      Girton College, Cambridge (moved from Hitchin).
1874. Yorkshire College, Leeds (Univ. Charter, 1904).
1876. University College, Bristol (Univ. Charter, 1909).
1877. Universities of Oxford and Cambridge Act.
1878. London opens its degree examinations to women.
1879. Somerville Hall and Lady Margaret Hall, Oxford.
      Firth College, Sheffield (Univ. Charter, 1905).
1880. Mason College, Birmingham (Univ. Charter, 1900).
1881. University College, Liverpool (Univ. Charter, 1903).
      University College, Nottingham.
      Women admitted to Cambridge Triposes.
1882. Westfield College, London.
1884. Oxford admit women to some Honours Schools.
      Toynbee Hall.
1886. Holloway College, London.
1892. University College, Reading (Univ. Charter, 1926).
1893. University of Wales.
      University College, Exeter.
1899. Ruskin College, Oxford.
1903. The Workers' Educational Association.
1907. University Tutorial Classes.
1913. Report of the Haldane Commission on London.
1919. Final Report of the Adult Education Committee.
      University Grants Committee appointed.
1922. Report of the Royal Commission on Oxford and Cambridge.
1924. Separate Board of Education Regulations for Adult Education.
1927. University College, Hull.

INDEX

Burstall, Miss, 140
Buss, Frances Mary, 139, 140, 143
Butler, Samuel, 125, 365

C

Cadet Corps, 123
Cambridge School for Army Education Instructors, 315
Cambridge University, Ch. XII; other references: Air Force students at, 324, 331; antiquity of, 4, 16, 164; college life at, 235; and connection with "public" schools, 116, 177, 341, 351; crowded departments at, 264; and modern universities, 253, 254; origin of women's colleges at, 139; and "public" school masters, 131; scholarships for adult students at, 293–4; and the School Certificate, 120; statistics of, 342, 359; and university extension, 278; and the University Tests Act, 24
Camp, Duke of York's, 134
Campus, American University, 268
Canford School, 119
Canterbury, 4, 96, 164
Captains, naval, 311
Careers, women's, 150
Carlisle Grammar School, 96
Carnegie, United Kingdom Trust, 291
Cassel Trustees, 293
Catholic Workers' College, Oxford, 293
Central Library for Students, London, 291
Central Miners' Welfare Committee, 294
Certificate, Teachers', 204, 206, 207, 210 f., 222, 227
Chadwick, Edwin, 17
Channel Isles, "public" schools in, 351
Chapel, the school, 125
Charlemagne, 4
Charterhouse, 98, 119
Chartist movement, 275
Cheam, 64
Cheltenham College, 119

Cheltenham Ladies' College, 139
Christ's Hospital, 85
Church of England, 7, 8 n., 95, 253; training colleges, 234, 367–368
Cigarette cards, 300
Cinema, the, 301
Citizenship, 152 f., 165
City and Guilds of London Institute, 174, 177
City of London School, 101
Civil Service Commissioners, 325
Classes, at Borstal, 194
  extra-mural, 294 f.
  nursery, 36 f.
  in "public" schools, 120; size of, 122
  school, 33, 51, 54, 57, 58, 157
  in Scottish universities, 239
  Workers' Educational, 283 f.
  University Tutorial, 189, 263, 279, 280 f., 288, 293, 298, 358
Classification of secondary schools, 342, 348 f.
Class, social (v. also Snobbery), and the Act of 1870, 23
  and adult education, 279, 285, 286, 288, 298, 303
  and Borstal, 198
  and early movements for popular education, 274 f.
  and education in the "forties," 225
  of elementary teachers, 205 f., 215
  and the Free-place system, 104 f., 133 f.
  and the Froebel movement, 31
  and girls' boarding schools, 147
  middle-class, and educational reform, 252 f.; and mediæval schools, 7; and "public" schools, 118
  and the navy, 312
  at Oxford and Cambridge, 10, 241, 242 f.
  and the "Plebs League," 292 n.
  and preparatory schools, 80, 82 f.
  and "public" school foundations, 116 f.
  at Ruskin College, 292
  and secondary education, 113 f.
  universities and, 255 f.
  well-to-do, and elementary schools, 58
  working and lack of education, 25

THE END

PRINTED IN GREAT BRITAIN BY WILLIAM CLOWES AND SONS, LIMITED, LONDON AND BECCLES